"Thanks to the mindset that I was able to develop from Chris's teachings, I attracted Rhonda Byrne of *The Secret* last summer and was chosen to be the PR company behind *The Secret* around the world. That led to a mass media frenzy and to the realization of my dream to take a client (*The Secret*) to the *Oprah Winfrey Show*."

> —*John Stellar*
> **President, Stellar Communications, www.e-pr.com**

"Chris makes the keys to creating a successful life easy to understand. When I read his book, I was unable to put it down, thinking . . . *I can do this*."

> —*Keylee Sanders*
> **TV host and former Miss Teen USA**

"I was a struggling artist with a limited psychology and a personal debt of £30,000. Having studied the same methods you are about to learn in this book, I now have a net worth of over £2 million and own over 25 properties."

> —*Rob Moore*
> **Founder and CEO, Progressive Property**

"With the strategies I learned from Christopher Howard Training, within one year I negotiated a deal that netted me $600,000 in a single day. That was a minor breakthrough compared to how spectacular my life has now become. My net worth has increased by millions, I now own over 20 fitness centers, and I was actually able to retire at the age of 38. This stuff works, if you work it!"

> —*Phil Anderson*
> **Former Mr. Australia;**
> **CEO of Life Corp. Pty Ltd**

"Wow, what an amazing life experience! Thanks to all that I've learned from Chris, I'm finally creating true wealth in my life. I've purchased 25 investment properties in Australia and abroad, I balance my life with yoga and meditation daily, and I fulfilled my dream holiday of skiing in Canada for eight weeks—I plan to do this *every* year now!"

> —*Anthony La Frenais*
> **Real Estate Investor**

"Christopher Howard provides you with the tools for taking you personally into the mindset of total abundance."

—*Renee O'Conner*
Actor—*Gabrielle, Xena Warrior Princess*

"We have built the UK's leading property networking event, the Berkshire Property Meet, which, from a standing start, became the biggest and best in less than six months. Our accelerated success owes a huge thanks to the methods taught by Chris and his team. We pushed ourselves beyond boundaries we never thought would be possible to now having a net worth of over £2 million, including 12 properties—and we're still growing our wealth!"

—Juswant and Sylvia Rai
Founders, Co-Hosts, and Directors
Berkshire Property Meet, UK

"If you really want to create enormous wealth and an extraordinary lifestyle, you've come to the right place! After adopting the psychology and tools in *Instant Wealth*, I closed a $2 million deal in a single month and made a net profit of over half a million dollars in the same amount of time. I wish I had learned these things years ago!"

—*Lisa Garr*
Media personality/CEO, *The Aware Show*

INSTANT WEALTH
WAKE UP RICH!

INSTANT WEALTH
WAKE UP RICH!

DISCOVER THE SECRET OF THE NEW ENTREPRENEURIAL MIND

CHRISTOPHER HOWARD

John Wiley & Sons, Inc.

For general information on our other products and services or for technical support, please contact our Customer Care Department within the United States at (800) 762-2974, outside the United States at (317) 572-3993 or fax (317) 572-4002.

Wiley also publishes its books in a variety of electronic formats. Some content that appears in print may not be available in electronic books. For more information about Wiley products, visit our web site at www.wiley.com.

ISBN 978-0-470-50393-5

Printed in the United States of America.

10 9 8 7 6 5 4 3 2 1

Contents

Acknowledgments

I could never sufficiently acknowledge the people who put so much of their time, sweat, energy, and belief into this project. This, like everything else that I have been fortunate to have been involved in over the course of my career, has truly been a team effort. It takes teamwork to make the dream work, and this book is a clear example of that. The people I would like to acknowledge perhaps are not even aware of the difference that they are making in people's lives. I have the pleasure of hearing from the thousands upon thousands of people from all around the world who share with me the level of impact this information has made for them, but the people around me who are a vital part of the delivery of the method do not always get to be the recipients of the same level of gratitude that I am constantly blessed to be showered with.

So my acknowledgment here is but a small fraction of the gratitude that these amazing individuals deserve. I would like to start by acknowledging my wife Lauren. Lauren, I love you more than you could ever possibly imagine. You had the courage and patience to be with me through 14- and 16-hour days as I worked on this book over the four-month period beginning on our wedding date, and for that I am infinitely grateful. You, too, have invested much in the creation of this book, and I am truly blessed to have you in my life. Your belief in me and our marriage makes me a better man. I love you.

For my team of researchers and editors who worked around the clock with me, I am infinitely grateful—Gina Salvati, David Stanford,

Desiree Gartmon, Pina De Rosa, Jane Johnson, Alexander Davis, and Wellington. I never could have done it without you. Thank you, Ruth.

For my assistant Sally, you have poured yourself into this project more than anyone else, and I sincerely appreciate all of your hard work and dedication.

For the Gracie family, you have been the source of much of my inspiration, and without your teachings I would be a shell of the man I am today: Rorion, Rickson, Royce, Rener, Ryron, and Ralek. Thank you, from the bottom of my heart. I would be nothing without all of your powerful contributions to my life. And to Alex Stewart, my private instructor at The Gracie Academy, thanks so much, bro, for keeping it real! I thank you all for your belief in me and for your friendship.

To my research and training team at Christopher Howard Training, you are the ones who carry the message beyond me, and the world is a better place because of your presence: Duane Alley, Johnnie Cass, Peter Shaw, Annette Huygens-Tholen, Terriane Palmer-Peacock, and Leah Barton. Thank you!

Thanks beyond measure to Mark Victor Hansen, Robert Allen, and Gail Kingsbury for your help with the book. You are shining lights of inspiration with a spirit of giving that carries your powerful messages not only through yourselves, but through the legacies of all of those you touch.

To the team at John Wiley & Sons: Matt Holt, Dan Ambrosio, Christine Moore, Linda Indig, and Ashley Allison. Thanks for your patience and all of your hard work.

To my literary agent, Michael Ebeling: Thanks so much, Mike. I know you went well above and beyond on this one.

To Wendy Beacock: I couldn't ask for a more supportive best friend. You mean the world to me.

To my partner teams at Universal Events, Think Big Education, and Success Resources: You are the conduits through which we have the opportunity to change the world. Thank you, to Karen Corban, Ken Wood, Tamar Peters, Dina Bonke, Richard and Veronica Tan, and every member on your teams. You guys are like family, and I am incredibly grateful for your energy, passion, and belief.

To Matt McCullough and Vidi Chandra at Steamfish for your continual support in the best imagery on the planet.

Thank you to Bob, Cindy, and Nicole Shearin. You believed in me from the beginning, and you have taught me so much. My entire life took a new trajectory because of you. You are some of the most important people in my life.

Thank you to everyone who supplied stories for this book. Whether we used them or not, they were well appreciated.

To my home team: Robert, Triscka, Sarah, Terry, Paul, Carolina, Michael Silvers, The Christopher Howard Coaching Team. You are the engine that makes the whole thing turn. Heather Porter, thank you for your friendship and all that you have done with the Billionaire Adventure Club (BAC). I am proud of you and grateful for your contribution.

To all of our volunteer event crew around the planet, thank you for all that you do to help people claim the lives they really deserve. You make a huge impact!

To my family: Mom, Michael, Jill, Dad, and August . . . you're all the best! Thanks for your support and love.

Thank you also to every shining light of possibility who lit the way for my success: Tony Robbins, Robert Kiyosaki, Richard Branson, Warren Buffett, and all of the others who have been true inspirations for me and for a whole generation. Thank you, thank you, thank you.

And finally, to Mitch Sisskind: You are truly a professional and a lifesaver!

If I have missed anyone, please forgive me. Know that I am infinitely grateful for all of those who have helped to guide my life, and to guide this information into the hands of everybody on the planet!

You have truly made a difference, and the world is a better place because of it!

About the Author

Internationally acclaimed lifestyle and wealth strategist, Christopher Howard is a best-selling author, a prominent speaker, and the owner of Christopher Howard Training. For almost two decades, Chris has researched the success strategies of the world's greatest business, philanthropic, and spiritual minds. His extensive knowledge is shared through his books, home study courses, and public seminars worldwide. As a result, Chris Howard has helped hundreds of thousands of individuals create the wealth and engineer the lifestyle they truly desire. With operations in the United States, England, Ireland, Australia, New Zealand, and China, and further expansion scheduled for Europe, Canada, and Southeast Asia, Christopher Howard Training has become one of the fastest-growing personal development training companies in the world.

As a social entrepreneur, Chris Howard has made a philanthropic impact in developing nations worldwide. His endeavors include building a high school in the Huilloq Community in Peru, where previously education stopped after the primary school level. He brought a group of 30 coaches and mentors to work with hundreds of students at CIDA, the first free university in South Africa, supported by the likes of Oprah Winfrey, Nelson Mandela, and Richard Branson. In Cambodia, Chris helps raise awareness for the campaigns of social enterprise Friends International by sharing its messages throughout his global network. In addition to his own contributions to the Lotus Children's Centre in Mongolia, Chris also continues to share information about its sponsor-a-child campaign so others can follow.

Chris is also a master faculty member for Humanity Unites Brilliance (HUB), which is committed to making poverty history by creating opportunities through hundreds of millions of micro-loans.

Chris travels the world extensively with his wife Lauren, as they share the gift of transformation through education and entrepreneurial means.

INSTANT WEALTH
WAKE UP RICH!

CHAPTER

The Hidden Secret to Living a Life
of Untold Riches and Wealth

*"Our deepest fear is not that we are inadequate.
Our deepest fear is that we are powerful beyond
measure. It is our light, not our darkness, that
most frightens us.
We ask ourselves: Who am I to be brilliant,
gorgeous, talented, and fabulous?
Actually, who are you not to be?
Your playing small does not serve the world.
There's nothing enlightened about shrinking so
that other people won't feel insecure around you.
As we let our own light shine, we
unconsciously give other people permission to do
the same.
As we are liberated from our own fear, our
presence automatically liberates others."*

—Marianne Williamson

What are your dreams? What are your big dreams? What are the huge dreams that you want to bring to life?

I know you have dreams like that. We all have them—so right now I want you to think very clearly about those dreams of yours. Because in the pages that follow I tell you exactly what tools you'll need to realize your dreams, and then I'm going to give you those tools.

Are you ready to receive them? Please prepare yourself.

Even more important, prepare to use those dream-building tools, starting right away. Be prepared to put them into action—for yourself, for those you love, and ultimately for the world as a whole.

I think you're ready. I know you are.

Let's get started . . .

How to Make All Your Dreams a Reality

At the foundation of every dream lies a desire. Something you want to do. Or create. Or accomplish. But to achieve it, you've first got to believe it—and for many people that gets to be the hard part.

Dreams can appear so implausible. So *impossible*.

But how dreams *appear* and what they *are* can be two different things. In this book I show you how to wake up—not *from* your dreams, but *to* your dreams, and to the *Instant Wealth* that waking up brings. Dreams (and remember: within every dream is a desire) really *can* become realities. But true inspiration and deep commitment have to come into the mix—and that's up to you. With an inspiring dream and an extraordinary level of commitment, you can create even those things that most people would consider impossible.

You can turn visions and intentions into real world results. Many people have done it. Martin Luther King Jr. had a vision of the future that lived beyond his abbreviated time on the earth. His unwavering commitment brought his vision to America and forever transformed the nation.

So what's holding you back? What's keeping you asleep? What's separating you from the realization of your deepest desires? What's keeping you from being fully present and engaged in every moment?

This is a very important question, and there's more than one answer. Finding those answers requires insight, and facing them head on can take courage. If you're like most people, part of you *doesn't want* to achieve your dreams. Whether it's guilt or fear, or a profound inertia that builds up over the years, you may feel that you shouldn't really get what you want from life—that in some basic way your desires are wrong.

This self-restricting impulse is a huge barrier, so let's get it out of the way before it sabotages everything you're about to learn.

Think about the word *desire*.

De-sire: to me, it means "of the father." Sire is a term of fatherly respect. This is how we address a parent. This is how we speak to God.

Your heart's desire and God's will are one and the same. Follow your heart's desire, and you are following a divine inner intention. The moment you make a commitment to follow your inner voice, your life becomes the expression of the real purpose of your soul. You become the person you were meant to be. Every moment of every day becomes a moment spent in the embrace of God. There's nothing selfish or guilt-worthy about that.

The moment you make the decision to follow your heart and you cut yourself off from any other possibility, your experience of life becomes emotionally textured and rich, and this is the first key to *Instant Wealth*; this is the first key to living a truly rich life. A rich life can be yours in a matter of seconds. Financial prosperity will come second; *wealth* is something you experience right now. You can gain in the chapters that follow the power to achieve both a truly rich life right now as well as financial abundance beyond most people's wildest dreams.

So go for it! Picture this:

You have all the wealth in the world. You have the ability to create any experience of life you want. What will you do? What will your life be like? You can create any dream. What is it going to be?

Can you really believe what you've just read? Is it as real to you as the book you're holding in your hands? Be honest!

If you're not quite ready to believe it yet, let's see what's behind that hesitation.

The Only Thing Stopping You from Realizing All Your Dreams

What stops most people from following their heart, living their dreams, and creating a truly rich life is *fear*.

Answer these questions:

- Has fear led you to have a comfortable life—but at the price of your soul's true purpose?
- You may have lived this long by just playing it safe and you prefer to stay there, because it's comfortable. Do you play it safe? Do you play it safe by not pursuing your dreams?
- Do you play it safe in your career, by staying in a job that's going nowhere fast?
- Do you compromise in your relationships, by not really going after what you really want or by not realizing your true worth?
- At a level of consciousness that you often choose to ignore, are you afraid of actualizing your dreams?

Please hear this loud and clear. Every time you have an opportunity to broaden your life mentally, emotionally, spiritually, or financially, *and you don't do it because of fear*, you strengthen that fear and keep yourself trapped in mediocrity. You keep yourself in a comatose sleep, oblivious to your true potential, and oblivious to the rich and expansive life that you really could live.

Personal and professional growth starts to happen when you extend yourself to your personal edge every single day—and then go *beyond* that edge. You must lean just over your edge every day to live your dreams, and you also must lean just beyond your edge every day to really live your life full out.

Sustaining that "edge mentality" is *a major component of creating ever-expanding wealth*, financially and otherwise. You need the courage to push yourself beyond your own fears. You need to embrace your fears in order to make your life everything it was meant to be.

How I Conquered My Own Fear (And Why You Can, Too)

By the way, are you curious about my qualifications to speak so confidently about dreams, fears, and other immensely important life issues? Well, my qualifications are the same as everyone else's. I know fear from the inside out. I still confront fear every day of my life. On that score, the only difference between you and me might be *what* evokes our fears, not how strongly we feel them.

In other words, what frightens you might not frighten me, and vice versa. Which reminds me of a story. . . .

Not long ago I was in Europe finishing up my **Wealth Propulsion Intensive** seminar on a stage in front of thousands of people. I've led these kinds of events throughout the United States, Australia, New Zealand, England, Ireland, Hong Kong, South Africa, and many other countries. I've experienced the phenomenal pleasure of helping human beings wake up to their potential and live their greatest dreams. I've trained thousands upon thousands of entrepreneurs, executives, celebrities, public figures, psychologists, psychiatrists, artists, educators, and parents—and I've loved every minute of it. It has been my greatest passion to deliver the profound levels of transformation that people receive in the **Wealth Propulsion Intensive** weekends. This is what I've always wanted to do, and I was doing it!

As I approached the microphone standing on stage looking out across a sea of thousands of faces in the audience, I was ecstatic as I was about to live my greatest childhood dream. But I was also about to confront my all-time greatest fear.

What was that fear? I'll tell you a little further on.

That day my thoughts were focused on these people who were learning how to turn their grandest visions and intentions into real-world results. I said to myself, "They have obstacles preventing them from achieving their full potential, just like I've had. They have to confront those obstacles—just like I have to confront one of my own right now!"

Of one thing I was absolutely certain. I knew within myself that if I helped others wake up to their dreams, I could live my dreams as well. If I made my entire life's focus unleashing the potential in others, my potential would also be unleashed.

I thought of all the people who had told me of the extreme transformations they had experienced since getting involved with **Christopher Howard Training,** in which we teach the concepts that *you* may be discovering for the first time in *Instant Wealth—Wake Up Rich!*

I thought of the man who had stood up in the audience at one of our live events and emotionally shared the fact that he had already been a multimillionaire, but a year and a half after learning the information you will be presented within this book, he was able to increase his net worth to 57 million British pounds. . . .

I thought of Phil Anderson, from Australia, who when we first met had been stuck managing a health club, with no real prospect of freeing himself from the day-to-day operations. Phil diligently applied the secrets you can learn here and then expanded his mind so much so that he bought 20 health clubs, retired at age 38, started a television show, and was now buying up to 200 houses a year. He was truly living his dreams. . . .

I thought of the woman who had turned her struggling company into a dream business with $10,000,000 in sales, within just one year after she began to implement what you can learn in *Instant Wealth—Wake Up Rich!*

I thought of the man who had built a $200-million company who came up and hugged me. With tears streaming down his face, he said that although he had made a lot of money, he had never lived a *rich* life. He had always been gripped by fear and constant anger, but after studying with us, he at last felt wealthy beyond belief. He said we had helped him find the secret to genuine riches. . . .

I thought of the young woman in South Africa who, during one of our programs, had finally realized that she could let go of the emotional baggage she had carried for years after losing her parents to HIV and AIDS. She could be free to live a rich life and to make a divinely inspired difference in the lives of others. . . .

All these transformations were truly awe-inspiring, and over the years there had been many, many more.

As I stood looking at all the smiling, supportive men and women in front of me, they began to cheer. They rose to their feet, shouting and whistling and applauding. It was an incredible feeling to know that I had succeeded in my mission. I had developed a training team with the unquestionable abilities, tools, and strategies to help every one of those people wake up to *Instant Wealth*.

All this was true, and it was wonderful. Yet, it was not easy to bring myself to the microphone that day. However, I knew in my heart and soul that there was no other choice. For years, I had taught the concept that as entrepreneurs, our true business should be the expression of our soul's purpose—and to do that, it's necessary to live beyond your edge.

Now I had put myself in a position to practice what I preached. Although I was always too afraid to even admit it, my greatest dream had always been *to sing on stage for a huge crowd of people.*

Well, it was now or never . . .

When I was young, I was very much a social phobic. In school, I used to hide at recess and lunch, just to avoid having to interact with other people. Now, within just a few years, I had gone from being $70,000 in debt to making more than $22,000,000 in global sales in a single year. I had traveled the world (which is one of my greatest passions), staying in the magical overwater bungalows of Bora Bora, swimming in the pale, crystal blue waters of the Maldives, riding horseback through the rolling green hills of Mongolia, zipping through the vibrant streets of Cambodia in motorcycle-driven carriages, training in Brazilian jujitsu in the captivating city of Rio De Janeiro, trekking in safari Jeeps through spectacular reserves throughout South Africa, hiking the incredible waterfalls in Hawaii, and adventuring in many other places. I also had the opportunity to train with the best teachers in the world in martial arts and other activities that I loved. I often did all this and more in a single year!

I was truly living my dreams. But I knew that I had one more dream to go. One more fear to conquer. *One thing I didn't really believe I could do.* But if I avoided the things that I didn't believe I could do, I wouldn't be walking my talk. I wouldn't be practicing what I preach in my trainings. How could I look at a crowd of people and assure them they could do anything if I wasn't living at *my own* entrepreneurial edge and stepping up and going for it?

A little background. In 1968, music producer Steve Binder challenged the songwriter W. Earl Brown to compose "the greatest song he would ever write." This was in response to the assassinations of Robert Kennedy and Martin Luther King Jr. On a tight deadline, Brown created "If I Can Dream," which was indeed his greatest work. The song contained direct quotes from Dr. King's awe-inspiring *I Have a Dream* speech given in 1963. When Elvis Presley first heard the song, he was so moved that he said, *"I'm never going to sing another song I don't believe in."*

As the music began and I gripped the microphone, I thought of the people in the audience who didn't really believe that they could wake up to riches in their lives. I was totally determined, through living example, to reach into those people's very souls and give them my very best. My goal was to help awaken the inspiration for them to step up and live their edge, so that they would actually take the steps they were afraid to take.

I couldn't make any excuses. I *had* to do it.

As the crowd stood cheering wildly in front of me, I was terrified and exhilarated by what I was about to do. These people had experienced so many breakthroughs during the weekend. They had demolished so many of their previous limitations. They screamed their support as I got ready to break through limits of my own.

From there on, it was spectacular. All I remember is prowling the stage and belting "If I Can Dream," which I had chosen for the profound impact of its message and the inspiration that it stirred within me. Singing live in front of all those people was definitely facing my biggest fear head on. Yet the thought that I was able to truly express myself through the business I had built—while at the same time making a positive difference in people's lives—was beyond exhilarating.

Throughout the song, the crowd gave me their wild support and ecstatic cheers. How I was performing didn't really matter. They were supporting a fellow human being in the accomplishment of a lifelong dream. I was living a rich life in the truest sense, and my newfound friends and family in the crowd were there with me.

As I drew to a close, cheers and screams engulfed me as I was whisked off the stage. People were grabbing at me for autographs. Autographs? Mine? I was completely astonished by what was happening.

My staff hurried me down the stairs to my dressing room where I collapsed into a chair, having accomplished my greatest dream of all time. And just as if I'd come off an incredible ride at an amusement park, I thought, *"This is just the beginning!—I'm doing that again!!!"* I'm sure my performance was *far* from perfect, but I did it!

Lauren, my beautiful fiancée (and now my wife), was waiting for me backstage. She threw her arms around me and said, "You did it! I am *so* proud of you!!" Her eyes were wide and her smile was from ear to ear. My assistant, Sally, came backstage and said, "Chris, people are going crazy out there! They loved it!" Johnnie, one of our trainers, entered the room and said, "They're saying that you having the guts to do that has really inspired them to stop playing small themselves." It was exactly the effect that I had wanted, hoped for, dreamed of.

At that moment I thought, "My life is truly rich. This is wealth! I've really got everything I've always dreamed of. Rich relationships. A multimillion-dollar international company. A charitable foundation creating an impact in countries around the globe. I travel the world following my passions. I've done a best-selling book. I'm stretching myself toward ever-expansive riches and abundance and my business has really become the platform upon which I express my every heart's desire. And the best part of everything is that I'm making a profound and positive difference in the lives of thousands and thousands of people. I'm truly living my dream life!"

This was greater—much, much greater—than anything I had ever imagined.

Why Anybody—Including You—Can Be Rich

As I settled into the limousine and we drove back toward the hotel, I gazed out the window in contemplation and deep gratitude. I thought of how truly blessed I felt, and how truly amazed I was, that I had come this far.

It was hard to believe that not that long ago I had been living in the very worst part of town. The police were there every night to stop fights or to chase away the criminals who hung out on doorsteps. I was rationing myself to only $2 a day for food. I was $70,000 in debt in those days, with no real money coming in. My bills were piled up, and I had signed on with a consumer credit management service so I could avoid bankruptcy. Although I had the idea of launching my own business, the thought was very scary because I bore the scars of a previous entrepreneurial failure.

I had driven my first business into the ground so deep that I wound up living in a house that was being torn down *while* I lived in it. The gas had been shut off because I hadn't paid the bills in months. I was microwaving water one glass at a time to fill up a bucket so I could wash my hair. On the plus side, I was trying to keep a good attitude by reading books on how to "feel wealthy and abundant," and I was passionate about the path of living my dreams. I had discovered one component of *Instant Wealth*, but I was still broke financially and going nowhere fast. I was missing pieces of the puzzle. I was eating only every third day because I had *no money* at all.

At that point, out of desperation, I decided to go back into the workforce pool to learn more skills. I figured that if my life wasn't working, there must be something further I needed to learn. I made a strategic plan to work for a company that would increase my skills and the ability to live my dreams.

Specifically, I was committed to becoming a master of communication. I've always believed that this is the key foundation of personal success in life. Communication has two components: how you communicate with yourself by your thoughts, and how you communicate with others through words and actions. A person who creates truly amazing results in the world is someone who can get 10, 20, 30, or even a thousand people or more working together to achieve the success of a dream. That's called leverage, and communication mastery is the first step.

As my career path began to develop, I became recognized as one of the leading experts in leadership, communication, hypnosis, and neurolinguistic programming, or NLP, which is sometimes called the "psychology of excellence." Anthony Robbins had popularized NLP in the 1980s. He was a resource of inspiration and information as I began transforming my life. Whereas most psychological models study what's wrong, NLP focuses on what's right and how to replicate that. It's also known for its focus on the subjective experience of reality. How can you change your experience of the world? If you want to go from an experience of poverty to riches, or poor relationships to great relationships, or poor physical health to great physical health, what needs to be done? The answer is, *you must change your psychology*. NLP provides powerful tools for making those changes. I set out to master these tools, and **Christopher Howard Training** eventually became the largest school in the world teaching them.

I often point out in my seminars that the Dalai Lama and Donald Trump have two completely different psychologies, which give them two totally different life experiences—both of which deserve respect. But do you think that their psychologies have something to do with the amount of money they make? Of course! If you don't value money, you probably won't make much money. Your values are one of the major components that make up your personality. With the tools of NLP, we learn how to change the basis of personality to change the tangible results that you produce in the world. The same thing can be done with hypnosis. They are simply different modalities, different tools in the toolbox of change.

I sought out the best of the best of these tools. I was inspired by people like Dale Carnegie, Stephen Covey, and Napoleon Hill. I trained with every expert I could find. I worked for Dale Carnegie Training—phenomenal people—where I learned outstanding communication and leadership skills. I trained with psychologists and cutting-edge performance coaches throughout the country. I worked for the largest schools of clinical hypnosis and neurolinguistic programming in the world. I began to teach for them, and every weekend I was in a different city all across North America. I became very well known for my dynamic teaching style and also for my coaching.

The New Entrepreneurial Mind: The Secret to Creating Anything You Want in Life

Even though I was doing what I loved and learning a tremendous amount through teaching, I was still drowning in debt. Owing $70,000, I felt like I couldn't breathe. Every penny I made was going right out the window. When I realized that doing what I loved didn't necessarily mean "that the money would follow," I had no clue how I would go on.

At one point, I found myself on the floor of my apartment in tears. The worst part about everything at that time was that I had read hundreds of books on personal development. I had attended seminar after seminar after seminar, yet my life still wasn't working. I had studied how to *"think and grow rich,"* but *my* thinking had only amounted to a bunch of fantasies. I was still broke and deep in debt. I had learned from all the motivational "gurus," and I was motivated, but for some reason I just still wasn't able to make my life work.

For the time being, I wasn't able to apply all that great knowledge to my life. I hadn't yet discovered the one thing that would change everything. I had yet to gain an understanding of what would become the secret to my success.

I was frustrated and under a tremendous amount of pressure. Pressure however, is what it takes to transform carbon into diamond. And once the pressure has taken place, a diamond will never revert to its original form. In much the same way, I knew at the core of my being that I could no longer let scars of entrepreneurial failure stand in my way. I vowed to not be another statistic of business failure. I had to change and I had to change *now!*

It was at this extreme emotional low point that I made a decision that would change my life forever. I committed myself to not just making money, but to creating true wealth. I decided to use this emotional breaking point as the moment when I would finally wake up to enormous wealth.

At the time I had been reading Robert Kiyosaki's book, *Rich Dad Poor Dad*, and he had espoused the power of moving from the employee mindset to the **business owner and investor mindset**. He had adeptly taught how real financial opulence could *only* be created with this new mindset. This one concept gave me **a target**. I had to shift my thinking dramatically. I was fortunate to have already become an expert in the most powerful tools in the world for **Subconscious Reprogramming**; the most powerful tools for literally changing the basis of personality. It was time to put them to work! It was time to propel myself into a new realm of financial success by **installing the mindsets of the world's greatest business owners and investors**. For me, simply shifting to the **business owner and investor mindset** wasn't good enough. I needed to totally upgrade the wealth "software" of my mind. I got really serious about my approach to wealth creation. I mentioned earlier that I had been living in the worst part of town—but now I made a deliberate *decision* to do that so I could save the $5,000 necessary to launch my new business. I made a similar *choice* to spend two dollars a day for food as a way to save every penny I had for what would become my entrepreneurial path—my path to wealth in real financial terms.

I decided to become like the phoenix that rises from its own ashes. I had to change my life drastically, and I knew that the way to do it was to use every psychological skill I had learned over the years to totally replace my limiting financial psychology. In its place I would install a brand *New Entrepreneurial Mind,* I would *install* **the psychology of the wealthiest entrepreneurs in the world**. I would use hypnosis, NLP, and all of the other psychological disciplines I had been mastering. Whatever it took! I committed to the fact that my life would never be the same again.

In that moment of decision, I said to myself, "You must make the commitment to develop yourself and learn whatever is necessary to be the best! To polish up every weakness in your entrepreneurial game until it becomes your greatest strength!"

I would have to learn the right skills, strategies, and tactics to put a strong foundation underneath my dreams. My focus entirely shifted at that point, and I was more committed to this vision of the future than anything I had ever committed to before in my life. There was no doubt that I would accomplish it. Failure was *not* an option.

This commitment enabled me to go from $70,000 in debt to making that much money in a single day! That same commitment allowed me to do $3 million in sales in 24 hours! And in my mind, we hadn't even started: The best was yet to come. I don't say this to impress you. I want you to believe that you can do everything I've done and much more!

Just like all the great minds that have shaped the world, you have the potential to choose the extraordinary. It's up to you. In committing to *Instant Wealth*: *Wake Up Rich!,* and to *The New Entrepreneurial Mind* that underlies it, you are embarking on the journey to kick your financial evolution into high gear while simultaneously living every dream you've ever had. I came from a place where I knew nothing about business. Believe me: If I can do it, you can do it.

How Society Is Stopping You from Being Rich

For the most part, people in our society walk around in a state of disempowerment. They have been conditioned and programmed for scarcity, or even poverty, and to live lives that are devoid of real fulfillment.

In the movie *The Matrix*, the character named Morpheus explains to Neo that the world as he knew it was nothing more than an elaborate façade created by machines. The virtual reality of the Matrix gave humans the impression that they were living in a wonderful world, while hiding the truth that they were born into slavery for the survival of the machines. Once unplugged from the Matrix, one saw that the world really was in ruins. Humans appeared in their true condition, as withering bodies soon to be discarded by the machines once their energy had been depleted. In one scene, Morpheus holds out two pills to Neo. Morpheus tells Neo that if he takes the blue pill, he will go back to sleep and continue life as he had known it. Or Neo can take the red pill and wake up and learn the truth.

Similarly, a film called *The Island* is set in the future; the year is 2019. Most of the earth at this time has supposedly been rendered uninhabitable. Lincoln and Jordan are living in a confined, indoor, domelike community where they are encouraged to remain healthy, work menial jobs, and live mundane lives. The residents all hope to one day win the lottery and go to "the island," a beautiful paradise on earth, one of the last places capable of sustaining human life. But when Jordan wins the lottery to this island paradise, Lincoln stumbles upon the truth behind the Utopian prize. In reality, all the residents of their world are clones. They're harvested only to provide replacement organs and body parts to the residents of the world, which was never really incapable of sustaining human life. It was all a ruse. The promise of the island was fabricated to keep them happy and docile until they were required for harvesting.

Many people today, as a result of programming and conditioning, have a very inhibited and impoverished way of life. It's a disempowering social hypnosis in which they've been conditioned to believe that everything is "good enough." They are sleepwalking through life. Most people are taught to get a job, exchange their time for money, and spend 70 percent of their life in work they are by no means passionate about. They are taught to sell out on their dreams, to live in scarcity, and one day they will "win the lottery" of retirement. As in *The Matrix*, many are content to choose the blue pill, satisfied with the almost sheeplike existence that most of the population lives in.

But you're not satisfied with that. You've chosen the red pill, and that's obvious by your reading this book. Just as a diamond can never be changed back to its earlier form, *"A mind once stretched to a new dimension can never return to its original shape again."* Don't continue reading unless you are committed to *Instant Wealth*!

Why You Haven't Realized All the Riches You Want in Life

In *The Selfish Gene* (1976), the evolutionary biologist Richard Dawkins introduced the word *meme*. He defined it as a basic building block of our minds and culture, in the same way that genes are the basic building blocks of biological life. Memes are the fabric of the social hypnosis we live in. Like the DNA of human society, they influence every aspect of the mind, behavior, and culture. Too often, we allow ourselves to be hypnotized into believing that our dreams are not possible, or are unreal. I see this time and again in my seminars all over the world.

Consider these two contrasting life experiences to better understand how memes, the thought viruses of social hypnosis, can affect your choices in life:

Once there was a small boy whose mother always told him that he could be, do, have, and create anything that he wanted in life. She also taught him to follow his heart, be a nonconformist, and to do what really brought him the most joy. His mother and other family members nurtured his competitive spirit: they would sometimes even give him money to take on various physical challenges. Throughout his childhood, he was brought up with an appreciation for determination and unlimited thinking. I think you'll agree that when Richard Branson puts his mind to something—anything—he will find a way to achieve it.

Kim Browning, in contrast, was always told to get "her head out of the clouds" and to "get a real job where she would make real money." What's more, this was modeled by everyone around her as she grew up. Kim eventually found herself in a job she hated, and she stayed there for 10 long years because she was too afraid to leave. I first met Kim in one of our seminar programs on her thirty-fifth birthday, when she shared her story with me. Fortunately, she found the courage to believe in her dreams again and to wake up from her social hypnosis. She doubled her income in a matter of months, pursuing a path that she absolutely loves. Today, she owns her own business and says she'd never live another way.

Kim's story, for the first part of her life, is not an isolated event. I've heard similar stories countless times, and it breaks my heart to know that so many people have bought into disempowering social hypnosis. They have sold out on their dreams, sold their time for money, and allowed themselves to be robbed of the true joy and fulfillment they were really meant to have.

5 Little Known Ways Others Stop You from Having What You Want

Five major dichotomous ways of thinking create the social hypnosis that many people live with. These black-or-white, either-or beliefs keep people playing small and feeling impoverished. The interacting influence of these thought viruses locks people in a Matrix that holds them dazed in a disempowering trance. Within these pages, you can find answers to these issues and discover ways to break free from these illusions. Of the five dichotomies discussed here, I have personally been caught in all of them.

Dreams versus Obligations

Here, people feel they have to *either* follow their dreams *or* meet their obligations to other people. They feel they have to meet their obligations, and therefore can't pursue their own dreams. But the truth is that your biggest obligation to the people you love is to show them how to live a truly inspired life. Waking up to your heart's dreams—and transforming those dreams into *Instant Wealth*—is the greatest obligation you have in life. It's a fallacy to think that you can't provide for those you care about while simultaneously living a truly inspired and fulfilling life. At the time I launched my business, I had no obligations to anyone, so this dichotomy did not affect me directly. But as things grew, so did my obligations, and along with it my commitment to live my greatest dreams and the realization that my greatest obligation to the world is to live my dreams. It is true for all of us.

Spirituality versus Materialism

Over the years, I have been able to break free of the spiritual versus material dichotomy. I used to think that you *either* had to focus on being spiritually enlightened *or* focus your efforts solely on making money. Because I had this black-or-white type of thinking, guilt prevented me from moving powerfully forward toward my financial goals. I finally awoke to the truth that it's possible to be focused on both financial success and spirituality. What's more, the key to enlightened *Instant Wealth* is to channel your spiritual energies into the pursuit of all your goals. When you wake up to this realization, life becomes truly rich.

Passion versus Money

Before I broke free of the passion-versus-money dichotomy, I believed you *either* became a starving artist doing what you loved *or* you achieved wealth by selling out, joining the corporate world, and hating what you did. Again, I learned that I didn't need to choose between these goals. What assisted me in breaking through this dichotomy was the inspiration I received from other super-wealthy, super-successful entrepreneurs who were making money by waking up to what they loved.

Social versus Money

I used to believe that you *either* focused on attaining great wealth *or* on being a good person who contributes to the world. But those goals are not mutually exclusive. In these pages, you'll meet many people who have given so much of their great wealth to support wonderful and inspiring causes around the world.

Social versus Passion

Lastly, I was able to awaken from the social-versus-passion dichotomy. I once thought you had to choose between *either* making a difference in the world *or* following your heart's dearest, personal dreams. On one hand, Ayn Rand espoused the concept of pure individuality through her novels *The Fountainhead* and *Atlas Shrugged*. Other writers stressed the importance of being socially responsible, and praised the virtues of selflessness. I was lost between these two concepts until I learned that we contribute directly to the world through self-expression. By shining brightly, you give others permission to shine the same. As you'll see, many socially conscious entrepreneurs are simultaneously following their passion.

While these five major memes are very common, thousands of other derivative thought viruses keep people in trances of disempowerment as well.

Why You Are Dissatisfied with Your Life

People lack satisfaction in their lives because of social hypnosis, societal memes, and the conditioning of their youth. This artificial mindset is often accompanied by a lack of true fulfillment, or even depression.

Depression is a worldwide epidemic. In the United States alone, it currently affects more than 18.8 million adults.[1] Depression has been on the rise in the United States over the past few years, with external factors such as the economy affecting mental health. Depression is also on the rise in children: One million preschoolers are currently on antidepressants.[2] Virtually all of us will at some time be affected by depression in our life, either ourselves or as a result of someone who is close to us who is depressed.

Although women are almost twice as likely to be depressed as men, men are far less likely to report depression. Rather than seeking treatment, men typically keep it to themselves. They often feel discouraged or hopeless, which is expressed outwardly as anger or frustration. These negative emotions can lead to severe health challenges. Many people, both men and women, see themselves as simply stuck, with no options, having to take whatever comes their way. The problem is that they place the source of their power outside of themselves. They've plugged themselves into the Matrix. In most cases, they have given their power away to the economy and have also allowed their lives to be identified with their jobs.

In a more personal sphere, depression and stress can turn outwardly into anger and frustration. This is the real source of many relationship issues. At present, 50 percent of new marriages are predicted to end in divorce within two years' time. In his book *Why Mars and Venus Collide*, my friend, Dr. John Gray, states that the biggest problem relationships face is the difference in how men and women handle stress—and depression related to money or other causes is one of the biggest stresses people face today.

What people really want is greater meaning to their experience of life. Viktor Frankl, a Holocaust survivor and psychoanalyst, wrote in his book *Man's Search for Meaning* that "the people who emotionally survived the concentration camps associated greater meaning to their experience at the time." In other words, some people who were sent to the camps assumed it meant that people were inherently evil and life wasn't worth living. As a result, those people experienced a downward spiral of depression or resignation.

In contrast, others made the decision that their imprisonment *meant* they would have to keep their spirits high. If they succeeded, they could one day be reunited with their spouse who was in a different camp, or they could ensure that nothing like the camps would ever occur again. Even in the absolute worst circumstances imaginable, the meaning we associate with our experience causes us to spiral downward to despair or upward to greater heights of accomplishment.

So, if you want to change your life, you must find the courage to change your thinking. Courage is not the absence of fear. It's the realization that **something is more important than fear**: your dreams, your power, your life, and the lives of the people you care about. If you are at a place in your life where you are feeling pressure, that's great! Remember, pressure is how a diamond is formed. It was in one of my most high-pressure moments that I said to myself, *"Today is the last day you will live this way! Today is the day that you wake up to wealth!"*

Remember this:

***Your destiny is forged in the fires of your
determination.***

—Christopher Howard

8 Steps to Creating All the Wealth You Deserve and Realizing All Your Dreams

Now it's time to look clearly at what not really going for your dreams has cost you—mentally, emotionally, spiritually, and financially. It's very important that you give full attention and commitment to this exercise. It's vital for creating the kind of wealth that you deserve to have in your life.

Answer the following questions in just two or three minutes. Don't take a lot of time thinking about your responses. Just write the first thoughts that come to mind. But play full out! You have to really go for it.

1. What is the cost of playing small and not really going for your dreams and not really playing full out in your life?

2. What has that cost you so far in your life? What does it cost you spiritually? What does it cost you emotionally? Financially?

3. What would it continue to cost you if you were to carry on playing small and not really going after your dreams? What would it cost you over the next year? Over the next three years? The next five years?

4. Then what would it cost you *ultimately* in your life? What would you lose out on? What would you miss out on? What's

the ultimate price that you would have to pay for selling your-self short, playing small, and not going for your dreams?

5. What do you stand to gain by stepping up and making the commitment today to play full out, follow your heart, and live your dreams? What's the ultimate benefit?

6. When you achieve that ultimate benefit, what will that allow you to do or to have?

7. What's important to you about those benefits?

8. How committed are you to that?

The Most Important—Yet Least Known—Secret to Making All Your Dreams a Reality

Now you should understand the social hypnosis that most people are ruled by, and the value of waking up and making a shift today. You're ready for the most important commitment you can ever make.

It's the commitment to your dreams, to living your life on purpose, to making your life the expression of your soul's destiny, to becoming what you are really meant to be.

Think about it this way. Suppose you *really believed* that reading this book from cover to cover and going through all the exercises with full attention would change your life instantly? What if you could live every dream you ever had? What if you could truly create a shift in consciousness that brings *Instant Wealth* into your life? Would you go for it? Would you give everything it takes to open your eyes and wake up rich?

Then do it!

Very few people are really committed to anything in life. Yet we bring magic into our lives when we wake up to something inspiring. Fifteen years ago, when I set out to help people live their greatest dreams and create true wealth, I burned all my bridges behind me. I made a commitment that brought me the life I'm blessed to live today, and that shaped my long-term future as well.

With the following form, you have an opportunity to make this same commitment—not to me, but to yourself. You've got to hold yourself accountable. To really gain power in life, you need to maintain the integrity of your intentions. By sticking to your commitments—all of them—you will build a powerful psychological system for creating whatever result you truly desire.

Are you ready? Sign the following form and then continue reading on.

Commitment to *Instant Wealth: Wake Up Rich!*

I hereby commit to playing full out, reading this book from cover to cover, and doing all of the exercises at 100 percent. I will carry out my intentions as proof to myself of my commitment to my dreams, so I can create the wealth I deserve and desire.

Date: _____   Signature: _____

Fantastic! All great works began with a commitment like you are making now! But there is something else to realize . . .

Learn from the Best

There's another challenge as well. The first step is awakening from the slumber that obscures your own best interests. But even people who have the desire to fulfill their dreams lack the practical capability to make it happen. I want to change that—which is one of the major reasons that I am sharing the powerful tools I've discovered and used over the past 15 years.

Any speaker on wealth building will tell you that financial success is 80 percent psychology and only 20 percent strategy. Yet, most of them proceed to spend 100 percent of their time teaching strategy alone. What separates Bill Gates or Richard Branson or Oprah Winfrey from someone who merely longs for success? I'm absolutely certain that the difference lies in the psychological makeup of the individuals. Bill Gates could never go back to being *just* a millionaire; it's not in his design. Bill Gates's psychology is set for the billion-dollar-plus level. That's why this book deals with the most important aspect of success. Your psychology. Your thoughts. Your feelings. Your mind. Your soul.

> *Victorious warriors win first and then go to war,*
> *while defeated warriors go to war first and then*
> *seek to win.*
> **—Sun Tzu,** *The Art of War*

You will learn how to think like the most successful entrepreneurs in the world. In doing so, you will be empowered to make your unique entrepreneurial dreams come true. Your life will become truly rich in every sense of the word. Based on 15 years of research and the study of more than 1,000 super-wealthy entrepreneurs and phenomenally successful individuals, you can learn the secret psychology of true wealth from people such as:

Richard Branson	Oprah Winfrey	Steve Case	Michael Dell
Michael Eisner	J. Paul Getty	Jimmy Goldsmith	Estee Lauder
Martin Luther King, Jr.	Coco Chanel	Warren Buffett	Bill Gates
Sergey Brin	Jeong Kim	James Kimsey	Nelson Mandela
Mohandas Gandhi	Larry Ellison	Henry Kravis	Craig McCaw
Larry Page	Jeff Bezos	Carlos Slim Helu	Pierre Omidyar
Frederick Smith	J. K. Rowling	Beyonce Knowles	Angelina Jolie
Stephen Schwarzman	Martha Stewart	Donald Trump	Sam Walton
John D. Rockefeller	Sanford Weill	The Dalai Lama	Anita Roddick
Ted Turner	Simon Cowell	Rupert Murdoch	Rorion Gracie
Rickson Gracie	Royce Gracie	Anil Ambani	George Lucas
Steven Spielberg	Mary Kay Ash	Walt Disney	Henry Ford

Where you are now doesn't really matter. Do you feel your life is too small to really make a difference? Hundreds of people have said the same thing to me in my live seminars: *"Chris, I had no clue how small I was playing!"*—and many of these people were *already* multimillionaires! Whatever your starting point, you're right where you're supposed to be so you can dive in and really start upgrading your thinking toward the creation of serious wealth!

George Bernard Shaw said, "The reasonable man adapts himself to the world; the unreasonable one persists to adapt the world to himself. Therefore all progress depends on the unreasonable man."

All life is governed by its imagination. Einstein himself said that, *"Imagination is more important than knowledge."* It was with this mindset that my journey began, through the inspiration of those great entrepreneurs before me. It is my greatest hope that, through *Instant Wealth—Wake Up Rich!*, that you will embrace the secret of **The New Entrepreneurial Mind**—and that this will light a spark within you that can then spread like wildfire throughout the world!

Let the Adventure Begin!!!

■ ■ ■

If I Can Dream

There must be lights burning brighter somewhere
Got to be birds flying higher in a sky more blue
If I can dream of a better land
Where all my brothers walk hand in hand
Tell me why, oh why, oh why can't my dream come
true?

There must be peace and understanding sometime
Strong winds of promise that will blow away
All the doubt and fear
If I can dream of a warmer sun
Where hope keeps shining on everyone
Tell me why, oh why, oh why won't that sun appear?

We're lost in a cloud
With too much rain
We're trapped in a world
That's troubled with pain
But as long as a man
Has the strength to dream
He can redeem his soul and fly

Deep in my heart there's a trembling question
Still, I am sure that the answer's gonna come somehow
Out there in the dark, there's a beckoning candle
And while I can think, while I can talk
While I can stand, while I can walk
While I can dream, please let my dream
Come true, right now
Let it come true right now
Oh yeah

—Lyrics by W. Earl Brown

2

The Unbreakable Rule Every Massively Rich Person Knows and the Rest of the World Doesn't

I've come to believe that each of us has a personal calling that's as unique as a fingerprint and that the best way to succeed is discover what you love and then find a way to offer it to others in the form of service, working hard, and also allowing the energy of the Universe to lead you.

—Oprah Winfrey, founder of Harpo Productions, Inc.

Would you like to know the next step to create tremendous wealth in your life? Are you ready to catapult yourself to tremendous financial success? Are you ready to enter the fully awakened state where virtually any goal is within your reach?

In my work leading seminars and workshops around the world, I have met literally hundreds of thousands of people who have a strong desire to improve their lives and the lives of others. I have also studied many, many enormously successful entrepreneurs in a wide variety of industries. These men and women are using their wealth and their

27

skills to create positive change in our world. If you're interested in exponentially increasing your own wealth, and if you also have a burning desire to help others live better lives, then please read this chapter carefully.

> *Desire is the key to motivation, but it's determination and commitment to an unrelenting pursuit of your goal—a commitment to excellence—that will enable you to attain the success you seek.*
>
> **—Mario Andretti, champion race car driver**

Successful entrepreneurs are not primarily motivated by money. If money is your only goal, you will never stick with what you're doing long enough to become *truly* successful. Virtually all very wealthy entrepreneurs have embarked on the path of creation for love of the journey itself. They have had a passionate and unwavering commitment to forging a new future. They have had a commitment to being the best at what they do. They have been deeply committed to making a difference many generations to come.

I personally find it fascinating that so many super-wealthy individuals have an enormous desire to positively shape the world for those who will come after. Did they start out with that way of thinking? Or did they wake up to it later? Was it when they achieved their wealth that they realized they could make a greater difference? Or was the desire to make a difference part of what fueled them?

At the moment you commit yourself to a philanthropic intention, you embrace a much richer purpose than financial abundance for yourself. At that same moment, your desire to give back energizes you to achieve even greater levels of wealth. Channeling your entrepreneurial spirit toward worthy and inspiring goals provides incredible wealth-building momentum. It makes your passion and purpose far more meaningful. It clears the path for instant and sustainable wealth.

Instant Wealth: Wake Up Rich! proves that helping others is the *key* to creating enormous riches.

As an entrepreneur, your own wealth will always be a reflection of the value you create for others in your chosen marketplace. When you create value in the marketplace, you'll be rewarded with money—and as you intelligently create even more and more value, the floodgates will fly wide open. You'll be tremendously rewarded.

When you truly grasp the concept of passion and purpose—when you really embrace **The New Entrepreneurial Mind**—you will have all the motivation you need to create absolutely anything that you desire. When you wholeheartedly commit to following the path of your entrepreneurial dreams, you'll become stronger, bolder, and even invincible. You'll wake up every morning exhilarated, enthusiastic, and energetic—ready to start the day on the inspired path of your entrepreneurial destiny. The dual factors of passion and purpose will unite to create a combustion effect that turbocharges you toward the life you were meant to live. It's like stepping into a Lamborghini, pushing the pedal to the metal, and watching the sparks fly off the guardrail of life as you move powerfully forward!

So how can you embrace these concepts in your own life?

First, realize that the meaning and purpose you bring to your business and your life are directly related to how explosively and passionately you pursue your goals. When you're passionately doing what you were really born to do, you can amass wealth that can powerfully serve generations to come. By channeling your wealth in philanthropic directions, you can create a legacy that makes your quest far more meaningful and far more motivating.

When you're following your passion, you can fall in love with the process of creating everything you've always desired; you can fall in love with the journey. When you fall in love with the journey, that's when you wake up to amazing results.

The One Common Money Secret of the Rich

They say, "Do what you love and the money will follow." But that's not true! Following your passion is the entry ticket. Doing what you were born to do is the essence of a passionate life. But lots of people are very passionate about what they do—yet they never make a dime.

You've read this far, so I know you're committed, really committed to growing your wealth. But money is not an end in itself. It's a means to an end, and the end is the ultimate vision of two concepts: your passion, and the expression of your soul's purpose in the world. When you combine these concepts, you create a truly powerful propulsion system to drive you toward your entrepreneurial aspirations.

What would happen if you were to embrace these concepts now? What would happen if you followed your passion, learned to monetize it, and created a far grander purpose to everything you were doing?

Imagine for a moment that you threw yourself passionately into the pure ecstasy of your entrepreneurial dreams and infused joy— *en-joyed*—the process so much that you channeled your focus in an extraordinary way. Therefore, you became the best in the world at your chosen enterprise and, as a result, created wealth beyond your wildest dreams!

Now, imagine that you also committed to give that wealth back through a charitable foundation. All the wealth you built doing what you were born to do will also make a difference in the lives of others and change the world for the better.

- What do you think you would be *capable of* doing in the world then?
- How much more *motivation* would you have?
- How much more *energy* would you have?
- How much more *excited* would you be to go out and tackle huge challenges?
- How much more *exhilarated* would you be to be the pioneer or the explorer on the quest to create your ultimate vision, your divine destiny?

The most important keys to creating great wealth are **passion** and **purpose**. When you learn to monetize your passion, and you combine your passion and purpose with a powerful conviction in the vision of the future you will create, your potential becomes unlimited.

How to Be Truly Unstoppable in Your Pursuit of Wealth

*I never wanted to be a businessman; I just
wanted to change the world.*
> **—Richard Branson, founder of
> the Virgin Companies**

*Allow your business and your life to be the
expression of your soul's purpose.*
> **—Christopher Howard**

Every human being has something to give to the world: ideas, inventions, humor, talent, buildings, books. We're all blessed with gifts we sometimes don't even know we have. We all have a driving purpose in life, a dream to fulfill, and a path to follow. Many people know this at some level, yet have an aching, empty feeling when they realize they are not fulfilling their destiny, or contributing to the world as they know they could.

Instant Wealth: Wake Up Rich! helps you in two ways: to embrace your purpose in life, and to actively put together a plan that moves you powerfully toward the riches that are your divine destiny.

At the moment Oprah Winfrey got off the air after her very first morning talk show appearance, she thought, "Thank God, I've found what I was meant to do." She said it was "like breathing" to her. Oprah is a person who lives with great passion. That's so clear on camera and in all of her business endeavors. She is also very strong in her belief that when **you** do work that you love and that fulfills **you,** the rest will come.

Oprah knew from an early age where her passion was. From the age of three, she was reciting speeches in churches. She stood up in the podium and declared, *"Jesus rose on Easter day, Hallelujah, Hallelujah, all the angels did proclaim."*

She also listened to people in the congregation tell her grandmother how talented she was. The more she heard that, the more she began to believe it. Oprah is convinced that you know you're doing the right thing when you would do your job and not even be paid for it. She says that she would do her job even if she had to work a second job to support it.

Oprah's absolute passion for speaking and teaching led to her broadcasting career, and later propelled her forward to the number one talk show in television history. She masterfully learned to put a business structure underneath her greatest dreams. Her **New Entrepreneurial Mind** allowed her to become the first African-American woman to hit billionaire status. She looks at her talk show as a ministry through which she can preach her mission of transformation.

Oprah says the reason she was able to create so much financial success is that her main focus was never, ever, *ever* on money: in fact, she was surprised when the money started flowing. It's true that she was very attentive to managing the bottom line, but her primary motivation was to make a difference in people's lives through media.

Consider also the story of a young film student who mostly just followed his heart and passions along the path. As he kept moving forward, he thought, *"I like this, and I like this,"* and he *"just kept going to where it was warmer and warmer, until it finally got* hot.*"*

When he realized in film school that he could actually learn how to make movies, he loved the idea. Once he actually got there, he found that all his talents and all his passions collided in a powerful way. He said to himself, *"Hey, this is it. I can do this really well. I love to do it."*

Today, the life of George Lucas, creator of the *Star Wars* series, is all about making movies and telling stories. His dream is to tell *all* the stories that are in his head. Every day he pours his love into what he was born to do. His entrepreneurial mindset allowed him to assemble the right business team and learned how to monetize his dream—but his passion is what keeps fueling it all.

When you commit to following your passion and you allow it to unfold along your path, you'll have all the fuel you need to go the distance.

7 Steps to Uncover Your Life's Purpose

Many of us do not have the clarity about their passion that Oprah Winfrey possessed even at the age of three. Sometimes we have no idea what our passion is. Maybe we haven't discovered it, or maybe we have lost faith that we could ever live our passion. We give up on the idea of waking up to our dreams before the dream has even begun.

With that in mind, take a few minutes for an exercise that will help you identify and connect with whatever you're really passionate about. This exercise will clarify where to best focus your energies so you can make your life emotionally rich and textured, and to create the extraordinary adventure that your life has the potential to be. That's accomplished by waking up rich and creating *Instant Wealth*: This exercise will help you do both.

First, answer the following questions in as much detail as you like. Take at least two minutes to answer each question.

1. What were my dreams when I was a child around 10 years of age? What and who did I want to be?

2. What have been the greatest moments of joy and fulfillment in my life?

3. What are the greatest sources of joy in my work?

4. What activities do I absolutely love in my personal life?

(continued)

---

5. What are my greatest talents and natural abilities?

6. What is the single most important thing I would like to accomplish in my career?

7. What is the one most important thing I would like to accomplish in my personal life?

Before reading any further, think about the connections and relationships between your answers. As those relationships become clearer, you'll begin to gain greater clarity on your true purpose in life. How much more would you enjoy your life if you committed to your true purpose and true passion? What if you were to commit *today* to following your heart?

If you commit to doing all the exercises as you continue through this book, you'll begin to notice shifts in your consciousness and your awareness. And you'll gain far more and more clarity on your passion and your ultimate destiny.

Now you're ready to continue on your journey!

The One Essential Ingredient to Fulfill Your Dreams

Suppose you had asked Bill Gates, while he was on his path of wealth creation, to choose between his work and his money? He would have chosen his work in a heartbeat, because his has inspired him above all else. As he's said, *"It's a much bigger thrill to lead a team of thousands of talented, bright people than it is to have a big bank account."*

More than by money, Bill Gates has been motivated by love for creation. He's passionate about technology, he's *passionate* about expansion, he loves to play the game of business, and he *loves* to manifest his dreams! There were great risks involved in the founding of Microsoft during a time when personal computers were in only a few households. But with motivation and dedication on the part of Bill Gates and his long-time business partner Paul Allen, Microsoft grew into the multibillion-dollar corporation it is today.

Think of business as a good game. Lots of competition and a minimum of rules. You keep score with money.
—**Bill Gates, co-founder of Microsoft**

The Hidden Force that Influences All Your Decisions

Human beings are capable of doing things they don't want to do, but only when there's a clear sense that a specific action is *important*. When you clarify your values and what's important to you, you get a much deeper understanding of why you're currently getting certain results in your life. Once you've done this clarification process, you will begin to see how you can gain momentum and propulsion to produce more spectacular results. You'll see how you can direct your experience of life much more powerfully.

To help with this, please complete the values elicitation exercise that follows. It's basically very simple. It's just a matter of asking yourself this question:

What's Important to Me in the Context of My Life?

When you think about your answer to this question, a series of words will appear in your mind. Just allow the words to flow freely. Write them down as they occur to you and a list of your values will begin to emerge. If you find yourself drawing a blank, push through it and look deeper for more values. With a little effort and concentration, you'll gain awareness of the values that are the true unconscious drivers of your behavior.

If you find you've got six or seven values on the page and you can't think of anything more, simply say to yourself:

What Else Is Important to Me? Or What *Could* Be Important to Me?
Now list your values by asking yourself that all-important question, "What's important to me in life?"

_____	_____	_____
_____	_____	_____
_____	_____	_____
_____	_____	_____

Once you've got an entire list of your values, it's time to review them and list them in order of importance. Don't list them in order of how you *wish* they were, or how *you would like them to be*. Order them according to how they really and honestly have manifested themselves in your life right up to this moment. Be brutally honest with yourself!

It's very likely that you won't be happy with the ordering and sequencing of your current values. For example, you may want more money, but if money is in the number 12 spot on your values list, this could be a very clear indication of why you don't currently have more money in your life. This exercise may dig up some emotional issues. That's okay—because transformation will occur as you go forward in the book. This is just a starting point. It's the *before* picture.

You need an accurate assessment of where you are, if you intend to get to where you want to go.

In the following space, arrange your values in the order you *really* have been living them, based on the results you're currently getting in your life.

Ready? Go!

_____	_____	_____
_____	_____	_____
_____	_____	_____
_____	_____	_____

Once again, I want to stress that you might not be happy with the order of values that's been expressing itself in your day-to-day experience. Just see this as a wake-up call that prepares you for the next step.

At the same time, consider what would happen if you really took charge of your internal propulsion system? What if you were to shift values now so that they drive you forward with greater congruency, power, and ease? That's exactly what you're going to do!

You're about to begin a truly turbocharged goal-setting process. You're going to get clear on everything you want to be, everything you want to do, and every dream you want to manifest in your lifetime. It's important that you cast off any and all limitations you might feel. Run with the power of your imagination. All great things begin as thought. Thought is the seed of actual creation and of tangible results. Think like a kid again: *"If I could be, do, and have anything that I wanted in life, what would I be, do, and have?"*

- Start with *be*. The best way to do this is to take about five minutes now, and list out all the things you want to be in your lifetime. Do you want to be somebody who is strong?
- Do you want to be someone who is capable?
- Do you want to be an incredible entrepreneur?
- Do you want to be intelligent?
- Do you want to be someone who is financially intelligent, with incredible business acumen and financial literacy?
- Do you want to be someone who is kind and gentle, who is caring and giving?
- Who do you truly want to be?

Take five minutes to write down your thoughts:

Now follow the same procedure with *do*—everything you want to *do* in your lifetime.

- Do you want to travel the world?
- Do you want to create a charitable foundation?
- Do you want to sail a boat around the Tahitian islands for two weeks?
- Do you want to get a black belt in martial arts?
- Do you want to learn a new language, or maybe two?
- Do you want to climb the Himalayas?
- Do you want to visit Tibet, the Taj Mahal, the Pyramids ... ?
- Do you want to have lunch at the Great Wall of China?

For the next five minutes, list everything you want to do.

Now list all the things you want to *have* in your lifetime.

- Do you want a home of your own?
- Do you want several homes of your own?
- Do you want to have a Lamborghini? A helicopter? A chauffeur?
- Do you want a private jet? Your own island?

Think like a child! Write down everything you want to have.

What Must Happen Before You Can Have Riches

When you've finished these exercises, be aware that super-wealthy, super-successful people are truly *purposeful* about the things you've just been writing about. The irrefutable basis *Instant Wealth*, as well as long-lasting success, is doing what you were born to do. This is the first step to infusing the creation of your future with passion and purpose. It's the essence of living a wealthy life every instant of every day. It's totally different from seeing wealth as a milestone that one day in the future might somehow come your way. When you're experiencing *Instant Wealth*, your daily experience becomes emotionally textured, your journey becomes rich, and every moment of every day becomes as if it were a moment spent in the embrace of God.

Unfortunately, most people live with a mentality of *scarcity*. They live in fear. They feel impoverished. They focus on all the things that they *don't* have. They chase fearfully after wealth, which is a constantly moving target in front of them. They say, "One day, when I make $50,000, or $50 million, *that's* when I'll feel wealthy." But if they're lucky enough to make it there, they never experience the elusive *wealthy* state because there's always another goal out in front of them, and another one, and another one. They don't realize it, but what they're really looking for is not a number but a *feeling* of wealth and success.

When you wake up to what you're born to do, there's magic. When you're appreciating what you have, you experience the magic of wealth in every moment because you have a rich life. What's more, when you have a rich life, you become a more powerful magnet for people, resources, and opportunities that will help you achieve your goals faster than ever before.

Oprah Winfrey is doing what she was born to do. Pierre Omidyar, the founder of eBay, is doing what he was born to do. George Lucas and Steven Spielberg are doing what they were born to do. All of these people are actualizing their purpose to the fullest extent. They pour so much love into what they're doing that they create something much grander than the money they've earned—and they've got the rocket fuel to continually propel themselves forward.

You too can access this same rocket fuel through a simple commitment to live your passion. *"Entrepreneurs* must *be passionate,"* says

Michael Dell, founder of Dell Computers. His company suffered great setbacks during the mid-1990s, causing Dell Computers to lose its market share to Gateway. But his continuing passion and motivation helped Dell Computers become the world's second-largest computer manufacturer, with revenues close to $62 billion in 2009.

Michael Dell was always an entrepreneur, building computers from his dorm room at the University of Texas. He has said, "People who look for great ideas to make money are not nearly as successful as those who say 'Okay, what do I really love to do? What am I excited about? What do I know something about? What's interesting and compelling?'"

The #1 Reason Traditional Goal Setting Doesn't Work (and What to Do About It)

In the following exercise you'll paint a picture of what you would like your ideal day to look like 5 years or 10 years in the future. Describe this in full detail. Envision how you wake up on your ideal day, what you're doing, and what you've created in your life. Fully imagine your ultimate vision through all five senses. Write this in the present tense.

> What would you like your life to be 5 or 10 years in the future?

My Vision:

> Entrepreneurs are visionaries, with the ability to turn their visions and dreams into realities and results. Many people, and perhaps yourself, have set goals that were successfully reached. Maybe you have also had the experience of setting goals that you did *not* achieve.

To help with the latter situation, I have included a link to a *free* mp3 download of The **Strategic Visioning** Process. This is a technique that is taught in our **Wealth Propulsion Intensive** weekend seminar. It allows you to navigate the future with precision and accuracy. It allows you to program your mind for total success as you're creating any goal that you desire. **Go to: www.chrishoward.com/strategicvisioning.** Download the process now.

Think of any specific entrepreneurial goal that you have and listen to the file. When you have mastered this process you will become truly powerful in regard to making any goal you want a reality!

© 2009 Christopher Howard's Academy of Wealth

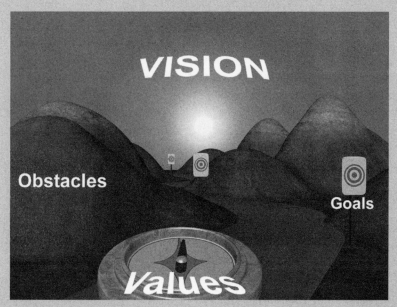

Go to: www.chrishoward.com/strategicvisioning. Download the process now!

Some Cases in Point!

Rupert Murdoch, owner of News Corporation, says, *"It's no good to start a business just to make a bit of money. You've got to believe in what you're doing."* Murdoch began his business career by acquiring one newspaper and then eventually acquiring multiple newspapers and publications in Australia. Rupert Murdoch is now the proprietor of one of the world's largest media conglomerates, with holdings in *HarperCollins, The Sun, The Sunday Times, The New York Post, GQ,* and Twentieth-Century Fox.

For Sir Richard Branson, founder of Virgin Records and Virgin Atlantic Airways, business is an adventure. Branson began his first business at age 16 with a magazine called *Student.* With his unique and highly competitive style, he has expanded his business into industries ranging from music to airlines. Branson understands that you don't have to love whatever specific business—Branson doesn't have to be passionate about cell phones—but you *do* have to be passionate and purposeful about what you're doing. You need to channel the energy of your heart for your success to be long term, consistent, and to create the snowball effect that the next entrepreneur espouses.

Warren Buffett knows that success in life (and business!) requires only "a really long hill and some really wet snow." At the age of six, this young visionary purchased six-packs of Coca-Cola from his grandfather's grocery store for a quarter. While other neighborhood kids were out playing, Warren Buffett sold the bottles of Coke for five cents each. At age 11, he had saved enough money to purchase three shares of Cities Service Preferred stock at $38 per share. This stock quickly fell to $27. Frightened, but determined, he held the shares until they rebounded at $40, when he quickly sold them. He would later come to regret this decision, as that stock eventually skyrocketed to $200 per share. That experience taught him a lesson that he holds as truth today: Patience is a virtue! At the time this chapter was written, Warren Buffett had an estimated net worth of $37 billion—and he has pledged to give away 85 percent of his entire fortune to the Bill and Melinda Gates Foundation.

Your takeaway from all this should be a very powerful realization. The foundation of success is the ability to be driven by something grander than money. Warren Buffett, for example, enjoys the "process much more than the proceeds," but he playfully admits that he has "learned to live with both." Buffett describes money as a by-product of something he loves to do and does extremely well: analyzing businesses and making the right choices to grow wealth.

How I Transformed My Life from Over $70,000 in Debt to Earning Over $10,000 an Hour

As I've mentioned, I was once in a job that gave me a good income, but I hated what I was doing. I stayed at that job for security, but eventually I realized I was selling out my dreams. I wasn't listening to my heart and standing up for myself. I wasn't doing what I *really* wanted to do.

I was finally able to make a leap and be true to my heart. When I did that, I made far more money than ever before. My life completely changed when I found the *courage* to take that leap.

I began enjoying my work so much that I poured endless hours into it. It didn't even seem like I was working. When I was preparing my career path as an entrepreneur, public speaker, and teacher, I knew I had to educate myself to do what I wanted to do. I went into an intense mode of education and learning. I read anything and everything I could find about conveying information. I studied, I read scripts, and I practiced the most famous speeches of all time—speeches by Martin Luther King Jr., John F. Kennedy, and many others.

I practiced those speeches as if they were my own. Seven or eight hours a day I did *nothing* but practice. I used anything I could find to help me become more powerful on a platform and more effective as a coach. I had to bring out the best in myself in order to bring out the best out in other people. For 15 full years, I read *everything* about communication and leadership. I *enjoyed* it! The time I spent studying and practicing was a gift, not a burden.

When I wasn't studying, speaking, teaching, and coaching, I was out building my business. I went to training seminars, attended Toast-masters meetings, networked, cold called, and did public speaking anywhere and everywhere I could. I also coached all my friends and family. I did it for nothing at first, and then I began coaching for a fee. Because I'd put so much time and effort into my development, I quickly surpassed most other people who were doing coaching or speaking. In fact, my private coaching rates increased from $300 an hour to $500, and eventually to $10,000 an hour!

When the attendance at our seminars jumped from 30 people to more than 4,000 people at a time, I was often asked how I became so successful so fast. What they didn't know was how much work I had been putting in. I grew the largest company of its kind in the world. I worked seven days a week, 14-hour days, but I was building my dream—so it didn't seem like hard work at all. It was a great time in my life because I had really found my heart's purpose.

How to Be Rich

When you commit to *Instant Wealth*, you too can lose yourself power-fully in the magic of waking up rich. But it doesn't happen by itself!

When I teach seminars all over the world, I ask my audiences, *"How many people here would love to be rich?"* Everybody in the room raises their hands. When I ask, *"How many people would love to have a great relationship?"* Everybody raises a hand. I ask, *"How many people would love to have great physical health?"* Everybody raises a hand.

Then I ask the next question: *"How many people are willing to do whatever it takes?"*

Inevitably, far fewer people raise their hand for that. So, you know, everybody and their mothers are in love with an end result, but that's not what produces the end result. It's being in love with the *process*. If you were to fall in love with only the *process* of working out and eating right, you'd get in better shape. If you were to fall in love with the *process* of fulfilling your spouse, you'd have a better relationship. If you were to fall in love with the *process* of selling and marketing your business, you'd create more income. If you were to fall in love with the *process* of investing, and the *process* of developing your financial literacy and your financial intelligence, you'd make more money.

Summing up, the key is not falling in love with the end result. It's falling in love with the process that leads you to the end result, and when you fall in love with the process and you're passionate about the process itself, your dreams will surely come true.

When Oprah Winfrey was asked by a reporter if she was a worka-holic she responded, "Yes, ma'am, I am. This is all I do. I do this and I do it till I drop. I work on weekends. I go as many places as I can speak."

Oprah loves the process. When you love the process you will be instantly wealthy, and if you do it intelligently you will create ever-expansive wealth. Get excited! It's time to embrace *your* entrepreneurial passion!

Chin-Ning Chu, the author of *The Art of War for Women*, said that, "The entrepreneur is a person who, in order to avoid working eight hours a day, works sixteen hours a day. And these entrepreneurs fight with great strength and determination against all odds."

CHAPTER

How to Create Unstoppable Momentum to Grow Your Wealth Faster than Ever Before

The Future is an empty canvas or a blank sheet of paper, and if you have the courage of your own thought and your own observation you can make of it what you will.

—Lewis Lapham, American writer

The Alchemist is a wonderful, inspirational book by Paulo Coelho, one of the world's best-selling novelists. The story is a parable about an Andalusian shepherd boy who dreams of finding treasure near the Egyptian pyramids, so he leaves his native Spain to literally follow his dream. He has many adventures, but he learns most about life when he meets an alchemist. Alchemy was believed to be a method of turning lead into gold; however, the people who were interested only in gold never succeeded as alchemists. Only those who loved the pursuit and the process ever achieved success—because *love* is what makes all things great.

Channeling your love and your passion in a consistent direction is what will turn lead into gold in your work and in your life. Coelho's novel is about discovering your heart's purpose. He says that finding what he calls your *personal legend* is your only true obligation.

Jeff Bezos, founder of Amazon.com (which is worth more than $15 billion today), likens the pursuit of money just for the sake of money to the Gold Rush in 1849. People from all over the country headed to California to strike it rich quick. Doctors, lawyers, and all kinds of professionals left whatever they did well, and in many cases loved, to go pan for gold. But that didn't work for most people in 1849, and it rarely works at any time. Even when there is a payoff—when someone is lucky enough to win the lottery—Jeff believes that ultimately this won't be fulfilling. Following your heart and learning to monetize your passion is the real key.

People who have a spiritual approach to life often believe, "Oh, I can't be spiritual and make money too," or "If you're politically and socially active and aware, you have to give up making money." But the truth is just the opposite. Having a grander purpose *empowers* you to help others, to live a spiritual life—even a heroic life—and to make a difference in the world.

The first essential step toward helping the poor is to not become one of them. You can fuel your contribution and give back far more when you create huge wealth.

As my own path has evolved, one of my personal goals has been to eliminate poverty through educational and entrepreneurial means. That goal must begin on the individual micro scale and then expand to the macro, global environment. We can hardly teach people to become wealthy if we're living with scarcity ourselves. If we want to heal the world, we must first heal ourselves.

The idea that you must choose to be either spiritually aware *or* financially successful is totally wrong. You're not required to take a vow of poverty to have a positive impact in the world. Dichotomous, black-and-white thinking has nothing to do with what life is really like. Life is composed of many shades of gray. It's certainly true that Mother Teresa was a woman with a heart of gold and a message of love who touched many people's lives in a powerful way. But someone like Bill Gates, with his vast resources and entrepreneurial approach to health issues around the world, has a far greater chance to create a legacy of saving millions of lives.

How to Be Spiritual and Rich at the Same Time

Oprah Winfrey is well known as a generous philanthropist. One Christmas, she helped the Glide Memorial Church with a donation of $50,000, for distributing meals to families in need. And in 1998, Oprah founded Oprah's Angel Network, which has raised over $80 million for improving education and leadership development. She has often been cited as the country's most philanthropic celebrity, donating hundreds of millions of dollars to a variety of different causes.

You can do it, too! In writing *Instant Wealth—Wake Up Rich!*, one of my goals is to show you that wealth creation does not have to be a self-centered, ego-based pursuit. It can be a very spiritual, people-centered quest as well. You can *use* your money and your skills and everything you create to serve a grander purpose. Don't be imprisoned by black-or-white-type thinking, in which you *either* have a wealthy lifestyle *or* make a societal contribution. You truly can have it all!

Instant Wealth—Wake Up Rich! intends to empower you toward living every dream you've ever had—and at the same time to accelerate a wave of higher awareness that's sweeping the planet right now. In the future, we will look back on this time as a major turning point. The new generation of entrepreneurs realizes that their talents not only can create wealth, but can also bring innovations that elevate the standard of living for all. You're part of this revolution!

What is *Instant Wealth*? For me it's an awakened state, where you lose yourself completely in the pursuit of your passion. You lose yourself completely in the love of the moment. And the moment itself is made ever richer and more meaningful because not only are you doing what you were born to do, but you are on a powerful path to making a great difference in the world through the ultimate effect of your generosity. *Instant Wealth* is being fully present in the moment, and in the moment feeling gratitude for all that you have. What we appreciate appreciates. In his book *The Way of the Peaceful Warrior*, Dan Millman looks to teach the powerful lesson of being fully present every moment of every day rather than living in the past or living in the future. "There are no ordinary moments" is the powerful message that the reader is urged to wake up to. Being fully present is an awakened state. When you add to this the concept of being on path and on purpose, and also gratitude and appreciation, you are instantly wealthy. This state becomes far richer and more meaningful when everything that you are doing will ultimately serve an even grander purpose in the world. Not only does your life become meaningful and rich in the moment, but being on path toward an inspiring legacy provides an incredible propulsion system to pull you powerfully forward. It's been said that the past and the future don't exist as anything other than constructs of the mind; there is only the now. This is true. There is only the now. From a quantum physics perspective the past and the future could be considered like wave patterns that collide in the now, and we *create* both the past and the future through our observations in the now or, in other words, our perspectives, mindsets, and actions in the now.

When your ultimate destiny is aligned with a greater purpose of making a positive impact in the world, then every self-indulgence as you are building your business or following your dreams could actually be saving lives *in the moment*, or eradicating poverty *in the moment* that you are pursuing your most personal dreams, because everything that you do in the now has a ripple effect that can change future generations to come. The money that's made today by Sergey Brin and Larry Page, the co-founders of Google, is making an impact for generations to come *in the moment*, because they are setting aside millions upon millions of dollars to help change the world for the better. By "singing your unique song," you could be saving the world *in the moment* when its purpose is *ultimately* to leave a powerful legacy. In this way truly "there are no ordinary moments." Every moment becomes emotionally textured and rich, and your business and your life can become a heroic adventure!

A Radical Evolution of Thought that Can Grow Your Wealth Exponentially

Are you ready to kick your wealth to the stratosphere? Then we need to radically change your thinking. Read this section with ferocious curiosity about how you can grow your wealth exponentially.

Earlier, we discussed personal values—what you want to do, be, and have. You identified and explored the values that are most important in your life. Many people aren't aware of the *value themes* that run through families, societies, and nations. Thematic values for a society emerge from many factors, including the geographical location, the economic conditions, and the historical period. Individually, our value themes develop from our family situation, the type of schools we attended, and many other factors. And today, values are strongly influenced by the powerful and almost universal presence of the media in one form or another.

Value themes are a good example of what Richard Dawkins calls *memes.* They enter our consciousness and cause us to make conscious or subconscious choices. More specifically, value themes are a major determining factor for the money we make and the overall richness of our lives. They determine whether we live a life of opulence or scarcity, and they influence the entire mosaic of the inner and outer world we create for ourselves.

In the 1960s, Dr. Clare W. Graves was a professor at Union University who did psychological research with the students in his classes. He published his findings in the *Harvard Business Review* in 1966. Through testing and surveys, Dr. Graves found that a variety of values levels appeared in different people—and from this he created a system for effectively understanding human psychology and evolution. It appears there are eight different value levels of thought and consciousness. These aren't intended as stereotypes, but they are systems of thought that may be present within an individual. They can change over time or even from moment to moment

Values Evolution
1. Survival
2. Tribal
3. Aggression and Power
4. Hierarchy and Rules

(continued)

5. Achievement
6. Group and Cause Oriented
7. Systemic Results
8. Global Interdependence

© 2009 Christopher Howard's Academy of Wealth

While Clare Graves looked at his system of values from a research standpoint—and stopped looking for any real meaning beyond Level Seven—we can look at the system as an evolution of consciousness that we can experience simply by learning more about them. I also touch on a deeper postulation of Values Level Eight here than Graves himself considered.

As you progress through the levels, look for types of psychological and emotional challenge that occur at each level. Try to relate them to your own situation. How could they potentially impede your financial success and your life fulfillment? Also be aware of the evolution of thought from one level to the next—and how by moving forward yourself you can be very powerfully propelled toward your dreams.

When a person living at a certain values level recognizes the deficiencies at that level, a crisis or some other dramatic event can cause a change in consciousness that moves them up to the next level. As Einstein said, "The significant problems we face cannot be solved at the same level of thinking that created them."

Values Level One is the level of survival. Because today only newborn babies or animals would really fall into the category of being at Values Level One, we will primarily take a look at Values Levels Two through Eight. When people are at Values Level One or the survival level, they soon realize that it's tough to survive alone. As a result, they begin to band together and we get to Values Level Two, which is the tribal level.

The Tribal Level is one of those that express group-centered values. The successive levels alternate between those that are *egocentric* (self-centered) and others that are *sociocentric* (group-centered). Levels One, Three, Five, and Seven are *expressive* values levels, while the *even* number value systems, Two, Four, Six, and Eight, are considered *sacrificial*—in which the locus (center) of control or power is in the group rather than in the individual.

Level Two, tribal values level, is sociocentric. It's tribal in the sense that people band together and sacrifice themselves for the good of the chief, the one who makes the rules and oversees the tribe. Family and familial bonds are also in the realm of Values Level Two.

Within the tribal systems described by Values Level Two, challenges to the power structure may emerge. They often come from younger people within the tribe, who in effect say, "I don't want to sacrifice myself for the good of the chief. I want to be my own chief." They strike out on their own and arrive at Values Level Three.

Values Level Three is power-driven. It's an *expressive egocentric* level. Here might is right. All that matters is who's the toughest, because the toughest and the strongest get to rule. It's all about having power over others.

But, as with the gunslingers of the Old West, there's always somebody bigger, badder, and tougher coming along. The young gunslingers become aging gunslingers and decide that rules are needed to govern the newly emerging generation of tough guys. So, a retired gunslinger becomes the sheriff, and we have the emergence of Values Level Four, the rules-regulated value system.

Rather than might is right, Level Four represents might *for* right. Chivalry and honor are Values Level Four concepts. We realize, for example, that we can't have people shooting each other for no reason, and we put laws in place. The new generation of gunslingers are seen as criminals. We're going to put them in jail. Values Level Four brings the emergence of hierarchical organizations that are rules-governed and fundamentally conservative, such as organized religions and military organizations.

In Values Level Four thinking, there is one way. It's the organization's way that is correct, and all others are wrong. Level Four is a sacrificial values level in which you subordinate yourself now for the promise of some later reward. The self-sacrifice might be for the promise of an afterlife with 72 virgins, or for the promise of a gold watch. Corporations are Values Level Four structures, in which workers sacrifice now for future retirement.

A problem with Values Level Four is the frustration of waiting for a reward that often turns out to be less than expected. Change takes place when someone says, *"I don't want to wait twenty years for my gold watch. I want my gold watch now. I want my Rolex now."* This is the emergence of Values Level Five thinking, which is achievement and goal oriented.

Many entrepreneurs are at Values Level Five thinking, in which they strike out on their own and launch their own corporations. Values Level Five is for creation or achievement of any kind, including the creation of wealth. Values Level Five thinkers are very status conscious and brand conscious. They want only the best in life. They also want to be the best.

The deficiency of Values Level Five is that people become human *doings* rather than human *beings*. There's often a *need to prove*, and a feeling that nothing is good enough. Level Five people may reach the end of life feeling like there's an emptiness in their souls. They've never discovered who they were in relation to other people. They may have sacrificed relationships, or sacrificed their own physical health, in the pursuit of some material achievement.

What's Ethical?
1. Whatever keeps us safe and secure while respecting the family, our customers, and traditions.
2. Ethics, shmethics. I'll exploit whatever I want to get what I want, right now.
3. What our higher authority states is ethical in accordance with the rule of law, promoting good and shunning evil.
4. Whatever suits my strategy to stretch myself and accomplish goals in pursuit of a better life.
5. Whatever group discussion agrees will lead to harmony and inner peace without hurting others or their feelings.
6. Whatever intellectual exploration suggests is best under these conditions, knowing that life is full of contradictions.
7. The world and I are one, and therefore I would never do harm to others because in doing so I would be harming myself.

© 2009 Christopher Howard's Academy of Wealth

Unlike Level Five, Values Level Six isn't expressive. It's once again sociocentric, or group centered. This values level includes organizations like Greenpeace and other environmental groups. New Age thinking is at Values Level Six, although not all Values Level Six thinking is New Age. This level is centered on giving, sharing, contributing, and making a difference.

Unfortunately, not a lot of action happens through Level Six thinking. It's more about discovering *who you are* in relationship to other people. It's an internal journey that's sociocentric. There are a lot of people feeling great and meditating, but they're not getting material results in the world. In a Values Level Six gathering, things are very slow. Nobody can be in charge because *"everybody*'s equal." Eventually people can become frustrated with that ineffectiveness and move into Values Level Seven.

Values Level Seven is very results oriented. It's the first values level that has the *flexibility* to move through the range of all the other levels with ease. For example, someone at Level Four would be very rigid in her thinking because Values Level Four says, "There's one way, the right way, which is the only way." It's a very rigid way of thinking. Values Level Five says, "My way's the only way. I'm going out and I'm creating my way in the world." Values Level Six says, "No, it's all about the group, and that's the only way." Values Level Seven says, "No, all those things work *when* they work—and they don't when they don't. I'm going to use my flexibility of thought to operate within *any* values system as long as it produces results."

Along with producing results, Level Seven is very oriented toward sustainability. Level Seven thinkers can be socially conscious, primarily because they are natural problem solvers and they are intellectually stimulated by applying their systems thinking to **big** challenges. We'll be discussing secrets of wealth creation from many great visionaries and philanthropists whose thinking was at Values Level Seven.

Values Level Seven is, once again, an expressive values system, in which people's true fulfillment *may be* lacking. They may not feel *a part of* something grander than themselves because Values Level Seven thinkers often have a lone-wolf mentality. Level Seven people *can be* very uncommitted and transient. If a job or a relationship is no longer working for them, they'll just move out of it.

The pains of feeling *alone* on the journey and the lack of a much deeper sense of fulfillment then leads to the emergence of Values Level Eight. As in Level Seven, we have here the ability to move throughout the entire range of the other value levels—but Values Level Eight experiences a deeper sense of *inner peace*. There's an even greater capacity to have a deep sense of *fulfillment* in life at this level. At Level Seven, people may begin to find greater meaning by tackling global problems, but at Eight, people have the capacity to do the same as Seven and also simultaneously seek an inner sense of spiritual peace and oneness. There's a global consciousness. Values Level Eight thinkers consider themselves to be like eddies or whirlpools in a stream, and there's a consciousness and awareness of the planet being an interdependent *living* entity.

Leadership
Level 8 TURQUOISE Oneness driven
Anyone can be the leader because he is a different expression of
    me.
Level 7 YELLOW Knowledge and experience driven
Whoever is the most effective and best for the talk at hand can be
    the leader.
Level 6 GREEN Relationship and community driven
There are no leaders because we are all equally valued; no individual is better than any other.
Level 5 ORANGE Ambition and achievement driven
I'm the leader because I claim it and I'm the best, therefore I'll
    utilize other people to achieve my goals.
Level 4 BLUE Duty and rule driven
Seniority and loyalty results in authority and promotion within
    the hierarchy.
Level 3 RED Power driven
The toughest and strongest rules. Whoever had the most recent
    conquest will be respected and feared.
Level 2 PURPLE Safety and security driven

When Clare Graves (who was a self-proclaimed Values Levels Four and Five person) described Values Level Eight, he simply alluded to it and said that a few individuals are *different*.

From *my* perspective, Scientific Buddhism could be considered Values Level Eight, although individual practitioners could fall at either Values Level Six or Eight. While we don't generally think of the Dalai Lama as somebody who's producing a lot of material results, integrated Level Eight thinking can be very useful for living a *rich life*. Values Levels Seven and Eight have *the capacity* to think of global welfare, of making a difference, of improving sustainability—and the ability to *produce results from an entrepreneurial perspective*.

Someone who is primarily Values Level Eight in thinking could also have a secondary strong suit of Values Levels Two, Five, Six, or Seven, which could determine how she expresses her Eight.

There is clearly more flexibility of thought and action at Values Levels Seven and Eight, and as each shift in Values Levels is a reaction to the challenges faced at earlier levels, it would stand to reason that an admirable goal could be to move up toward Values Level Seven or Eight. **The New Entrepreneurial Mind** can operate especially effectively at either of these levels.

While the values levels could be considered hierarchical, to avoid posturing as to which is best, Clare Graves's values are also represented by colors. Values Level One is Beige, Values Level Two is Purple, Values Level Three is Red, Values Level Four is Blue, Values Level Five is Orange, Values Level Six is Green, Values Level Seven is Yellow, and Values Level Eight is Turquoise. It's worthy to note that Nelson Mandela talked about the Clare Graves system of values in his book, *A Long Walk to Freedom*. He gave it credit for helping to shift South Africa from apartheid to democracy. Because both numbers and colors are used, people who learned the model were able to see each other not as black or white, but in terms of the value system's colors. Instead of saying, "*He's black*," or "*She's white*," they would say, "*He's thinking in red*," or "*She's thinking in green*."

How to Be Truly Fulfilled on Your Path to Riches

Andrew Carnegie was clearly a Levels Five and Seven thinker, with a sustainability consciousness. He is universally revered as the originator of modern philanthropy. In his essay "Wealth," Carnegie taught that "with great wealth comes great obligation and great responsibility." The obligation of great wealth is to channel much of it back into society—to use that wealth, as an entrepreneur is powerfully equipped to do, to tackle social problems and change the world for the better.

The evolution of thought has allowed other entrepreneurs to wake up and begin thinking of the riches of the planet. Some of these have come from a place of true Level Seven thinking with genuine concerns for sustainability; others have come from a Level Five need to be the best, even in philanthropy. But true fulfillment comes from a Level Seven or Level Eight approach, in which the emotional rewards are inherent in the giving.

I believe the power to make money is a gift from God. To be developed and used to the best of our ability for the good of mankind. Having been endowed with the gift I possess, I believe it is my duty to make money and still more money and to use the money I make for the good of my fellow man according to the dictates of my conscience.

—John D. Rockefeller

What the World's Wealthiest Individuals Know About Wealth You Don't

In 1998, when Ted Turner pledged a billion dollars (nearly half his wealth at the time) to the United Nations to pay off the debts of the United States, he threw out a challenge for others to put their fortunes to work. Two people he mentioned by name were Warren Buffett and Bill Gates.

Bill Gates then made it clear that his charitable contributions would be at the same level of Ted Turner's, or would even eclipse them. Shortly thereafter, Gates began turning more of his attention toward philanthropic interests.

Then a real turning point happened as a result of a series of events that occurred between 2006 and 2008. First, Warren Buffett, who was inspired by Andrew Carnegie's writings, pledged $31 billion to the Bill and Melinda Gates Foundation, which had been set up to address major educational and public health issues. Buffett's donation set the record as the largest charitable donation ever. In 2006, Bill Gates announced that he would step down from Microsoft in two years' time to concentrate on his foundation and some of the biggest social challenges of our time.

These moves and the commitments of many others—such as Richard Branson's pledge of $3 billion to combat global warming—have set a very powerful example for the next generation of entrepreneurs. Right out of the gate, these entrepreneurial minds are finding ways for their wealth and to take on even bigger challenges for the good of all. For example, Sergey Brin and Larry Page of Google, each with a net worth of more than $18 billion, have begun to set aside huge amounts of their wealth for alternative energy solutions and other global concerns.

Larry Page has said, "Sergey and I founded Google because we believed we could provide an important service to the world—instantly delivering relevant information on virtually any topic. Serving our end users is at the heart of what we do and remains our number one priority: Our goal is to develop services that significantly improve the lives of as many people as possible. We are proud of the products we have built, and we hope that those we create in the future will have an even greater positive impact on the world."

Many of the world's older fortunes were born in the Industrial Age, through oil or railroads. Today, wealth is being made very differently, and by a younger generation of entrepreneurs than ever before. In 1986, there were only 140 billionaires in the world; in 2008, there were 1,125, according to *Forbes* magazine. One of the reasons for this incredible growth of wealth is the Internet; people who used to reach thousands of customers can now reach millions. For example, Mark

Zuckerberg launched Facebook from his dorm room at Harvard. At first, it was used only by Harvard students, until Mark saw the larger potential. Facebook is now the most-visited social networking site in the world. Mark Zuckerberg became the world's youngest billionaire at the age of 23.

This rapidly expanding next generation of entrepreneurs—including **you**—has been foreshadowed by the previous generation. Your challenge is to begin thinking even earlier of ways to apply your wealth and your entrepreneurial spirit to bigger and more meaningful challenges. The fact that you're reading *Instant Wealth—Wake Up Rich!* and embracing **The New Entrepreneurial Mind** means you're heeding the call. The exciting part is that the linking of your entrepreneurial dreams and growing wealth to making an even bigger global impact and being a force for good just increases your motivation exponentially. If you're up for the challenge, it's time to ride the huge wave that's coming!

What will it take for you to become the type of person who is going to achieve every goal you have? The following exercise will help answer that question.

Imagine a blank movie screen. Now, on that screen picture the ideal, perfect you—the person who has already achieved every goal you have, and who has already realized the grandest vision of life.

Now, as you imagine that ideal person, take two minutes to write down what must have been important to this person to allow him to accomplish every goal that you want to accomplish. Write down what this person's values must have been. What was number one? What was number two? What was number three? What drove this person on a daily basis? (Remember, values are single words or short word phrases, a maximum of three words.)

Go ahead and list the values of the person who has already achieved your goals.

_____   _____   _____

_____   _____   _____

_____   _____   _____

_____   _____   _____

_____   _____   _____

If You Want to Be Rich and Happy Follow this Idea

From Andrew Carnegie, Warren Buffett borrowed the idea of giving his kids enough money so they can do anything but not enough so they can do nothing. Buffett believes that, if you've made a lot of money in your lifetime, you should not turn all that money over to your children. That can cause a dependency on inherited money that actually *unmotivates* people and robs them of ambition to make something of their lives. Buffett, a Values Level Seven thinker like Carnegie, also believes that the mass retention of generational wealth creates deeper divides between the rich and poor, and can lead to major problems in society as a whole. It is therefore preferable to redistribute that wealth in intelligent ways. These super-effective visionaries have believed that entrepreneurs can be far more capable of making the intelligent choices for how to channel that money than the government.

"The man who dies rich dies disgraced," said Andrew Carnegie, who abhorred charity and preferred to give his money to help others help themselves.

I, too, was inspired by these concepts in 1999, when I first committed to changing my world financially. As I began studying the most successful entrepreneurs and investors in the world, I read a book about Warren Buffett and was fascinated by his views on philanthropy. One thing about Buffett really impressed me: He always fully intended to give virtually his entire fortune to society in the form of a charitable foundation at the end of his life. He wanted the wealth he had created to help solve major world concerns. He also knew that the longer he waited to give it back, the more he would have to give—because *he knew how to grow it* better than anyone else on Earth. I thought that if I were to do the same thing, then every apparent self-indulgence in building my own business, following my dreams, and creating wealth could serve the greater purpose of saving lives in the world or eradicating poverty. Whenever I earned money, it would give me greater leverage to make a difference to society at the end of my life.

When I had that realization, I made a decision that permanently eradicated my own conflicts about money and gave me tremendous motivation to make my own entrepreneurial dreams come true. It was then that I launched my business, and I've never looked back. Linking my business with that greater purpose gave the enterprise far more meaning. It also provided far greater motivation, because it radically shifted my thinking toward building my business from a philanthropic perspective. That was really a turning point for me. My wish is that it will be the same for *you.*

You are about to gain a mindset that will allow you to propel yourself to incredible financial success. Moreover, you will learn how to channel your new entrepreneurial mind to tackle ever greater and more worthy challenges. As this happens, you'll be able to contribute in meaningful ways that will really make your life a heroic journey! I'll show you examples of entrepreneurs—not only young entrepreneurs, but those of an older generation also—who have developed what I've called **The New Entrepreneurial Mind.**

Regardless of your age or your present circumstances, you can join a new generation of entrepreneurs who are thinking in a new way. You can realize every dream you've ever had, build enormous wealth, *and* have a grand impact on the world! Fasten your seatbelt, as you're about to embark on an extraordinary journey of transformative consciousness!

Your New Entrepreneurial Mind
1. Commit to following your passion
2. Pour love into the creation of your dream
3. Fall in love with the process
4. Create propulsion by having a heroic grander purpose of making a difference in the world

Our Goal at Christopher Howard Training is to put these tools in the hands of everyone on the planet. For an incredible **Gift** so that you and all the people you love can create all the wealth that you want, go to: www.chrishoward.com/instantwealth. This gift is a limited opportunity, so, go now!

CHAPTER 4

The Money Secret History's Richest People Use to Create Wealth that Lasts for Generations

Millions of men have lived to fight, build palaces and boundaries, shape destinies and societies, but the compelling force of all times has been the force of originality and creation profoundly affecting the roots of human spirit.

—Ansel Adams, photographer,
environmentalist

Start with a dream. Maybe a dream that is personal and small, but worth doing. Then dream a bigger dream. Keep dreaming until your dreams seem impossible to achieve. Then you'll know you're on the right track. Then you'll know you're ready to conjure up a dream big enough to define your future and perhaps your generation's future.

—Vance Loffman, chairman and CEO
of Lockheed Martin

Alexander the Great was one of the most successful military leaders of all time. At his death, three centuries before the birth of Christ, his conquests stretched from Egypt to India—and his overriding goal was to unite all the peoples of the world. In a similar way, the modern conqueror named Bill Gates had his own global vision. Gates boldly asserted from the very beginning that the goal of his Microsoft Corporation was to "put a computer on a desk in every home." He has traveled all over the globe in this quest for expansion. He sees lesser-developed countries as the greatest opportunities:

"That's where we'll get our growth in the coming years. These countries are only just getting started buying personal computers in big numbers. . . . Everything's about big horizons at Microsoft. We love big horizons."

The Almost Instant Way to Massively Increase Your Fortune

Sam Walton also had a global vision, or even an obsession. He opened the first Wal-Mart store in 1962. When he died in 1992, the company was the biggest retailer in the world. Jack Welch, the legendary former chairman and CEO of General Electric, described Sam Walton like this: "He went into one of the most mature industries and found a way to make it grow, grow, grow, double-digit, month after month, year after year."

Robert Falcon Scott, better known as "Scott of the Antarctic," led two expeditions to the Antarctic regions. On his second expedition he arrived at the South Pole on January 17th, 1912, only to find that he and his team of five had been beaten to the Pole by another explorer's group. Scott and his entire team did not make it back on the return trek because of exhaustion and extreme conditions. Many people would see this as tragic—but it might honor their memories more to recognize that these were true adventurers who were fortunate to live their entire lives right up until the end in pursuit of their grandest dreams.

In much the same way that Scott was willing to risk everything, his distant relative, Sir Richard Branson, also continually expands his entrepreneurial dreams. The ultimate of this is Virgin Galactic, "the world's first space line." Richard describes this as "the start of a new era in the history of mankind . . . making the affordable exploration of space by human beings a real possibility."

Once an organization loses its spirit of pioneering and rests on its early work, its progress stops.
—**Thomas Watson, founder of IBM**

Grand visions inspire. *Spirit* infuses emotional texture and richness into our dreams and our lives. Character traits that have powerfully shaped our past can also help forge our entrepreneurial futures.

One of my own direct ancestors, Nathan Hale, was a soldier for the Continental Army during the Revolutionary War. He was captured by the British while on an intelligence-gathering mission and hanged on September 22, 1776. Nathan Hale fought for a dream of the future that he held with every fiber of his being. At the time of his execution, his final words were, "My only regret is that I have but one life to give for my country."

I feel like a kindred spirit of Nathan Hale when I think of my own dreams. Just as Nathan Hale had an unwavering commitment to his vision, today's super-successful entrepreneurs are visionaries with total commitment and faith. They are sometimes described as risk-takers, but for the real entrepreneur, failure is not an option. They will put everything on the line in the name of their entrepreneurial freedom and dreams.

What Super-Affluent People Have in Common

Super-affluent entrepreneurs are obsessed with expansion, pioneering, and delivering more and more—and even *more*—value. They have an unwavering commitment to resculpting the world in the likeness of their dreams. They're pursuing their passion in every present moment, not just in some vaguely defined future.

I have a friend whose dance studio has $50,000 of debt. She's constantly thinking, "How can I pay off my debt? How can I pay off my debt? How can I pay off my debt?" She's absolutely frantic in her thinking, and therefore in the way she runs her business. She's playing a really small game, instead of thinking, "Where can I expand my business? How can I expand my business? How can I dwarf my debt by creating so much revenue that this debt is nothing?"

What takes most businesses down is not debt, but their debt-to-income ratio. If your revenue is increasing so much so as to dwarf the debt, it's not that much of a problem. But focusing on massive expansion is a totally different mindset from that of the average business person.

How to Create Wealth Beyond Even Your Wildest Dreams

Yesterday's military empire builders are today's expansively thinking entrepreneurs. When you embrace expansive thinking, you will add a vital element to your ability to create ever-increasing financial opulence. And you can create wealth beyond your wildest dreams. Rupert Murdoch's global vision took him from owning a small newspaper in Adelaide, Australia, to multiple newspapers within Australia, and then the United Kingdom, the United States, and Asia. From newspapers, he made the leap into other forms of media. He built Sky Broadcasting, and then Fox television. Today, Murdoch has moved into satellite television, the Internet, and the film industry. With a personal net worth of more than $4 billion, his company, News Corporation, is truly a media *empire*, with an unrelenting commitment to expansion.

Now Murdoch is considering the positive global impact his empire can provide. In 2007, he pledged to make News Corporation carbon neutral by 2010. He has committed to fight global climate change by weaving environmental themes through all of his media outlets. Rupert Murdoch says his audience's carbon footprint is 10,000 times that of News Corporation: "That's the carbon footprint we want to conquer."

Would you like to be able to create material wealth beyond your wildest dreams? Would you love a way to hit ever-larger financial targets so that you have a prosperous life on every level, including lots of cash in the bank? If so, the following information is vital for you to grasp.

Human beings have the capacity to think at various levels of abstraction, from the very abstract (for example, the universe), to the very concrete (for example, a grain of sand). Many people don't understand that thinking at greater levels of abstraction is directly related to *income level*. What do I mean by that? Some people are very detailed thinkers, some are big-picture thinkers—but who makes more money? The foot soldier or the general? The general makes more money because the general sees the big picture. Who makes more money: the janitor or the CEO? The CEO makes more money, because, once again, the CEO sees the big picture.

Thinking abstractly and expansively is directly correlated to the value we create and the money we make. But operating throughout the range of abstraction—from more abstract to more specific—is also vitally important. People who are massively wealthy not only conjure a big-picture vision, but also turn it into real-world results. Plenty of big-picture thinkers aren't sufficiently grounded to produce results in the material world.

Regarding this, let's look at a concept called *chunking*. This is simply a way to think of information: Are you thinking *detail* or thinking *abstract?* If you are committed to making more money, ask yourself, *"What must I do to create more value?"* If you are selling your time for money, there is only so much value you can create because you have only so many hours in a day. You need to be more expansive in your thinking. You need to chunk up to deliver more expansive value to the world.

> To chunk up your thinking, ask yourself, "What is this an example of?" or "For what purpose?"
>
> Or, if you're already thinking of the big picture, you need to chunk down. Ask, "What specifically?" This will help you become more detailed.
>
> You can also chunk laterally by *first* chunking up one level and *then* asking yourself, "What are *other* examples of this?"

Consider the work of a massage therapist. To chunk up, you might ask, "What is this an example of—and for what purpose?" You could answer, "Well, massage therapy is an example of body work" or, "It's an example of stress relief." Stress relief or body work are both larger-level chunks on massage therapy. If you wanted to chunk up even more on that, you could chunk all the way up to personal development or helping others. You will find yourself in an entirely different field but coming from the same genesis. You could consider launching an online school of instruction in mind-and-body medicine. You could think, "I'm not just a massage therapist, I work in the field of relaxation and inner peace. I am going to create a series of relaxation products, or I am going to open my own spa resort where people can go to find the peace of mind they really crave, and I will have other massage therapists who work for me at the resort. Perhaps I'll launch an entire chain of resorts." Chunking up means wider and more expansive thinking. (See Figure 4.1.)

The important thing is to listen to your heart each step of the way. Thinking more expansively for expansion's sake is not the point. You need to ask yourself each step of the way, "Is this particular expansion effort really what's in my heart?"

For example, I visited a resort that is part of a major chain with more than one hundred locations. I had known for a while that I wanted to get back into the resort industry because it was one of my passions. As I stood in the lobby with a view overlooking the beautiful property, I considered the thought that I could launch my own hotel resort chain with as far of a reach as the chain that I was visiting. It felt good to be thinking so expansively, but then I did an internal check and thought, "Is this what I really want?" And I got that it wasn't something that I really desired.

What I really wanted was to launch a smaller chain of boutique hotels. That really appealed to me; far less expansive with this particular expression of my soul, but spot on in the form of what was really in my heart. With real desire, you'll have all the motivation you need to see a project through and realize your dreams.

The expansion of Amazon.com is another example of chunking up. When Jeff Bezos launched Amazon.com, he began by selling books online and grew the company to a value of billions. Then he began

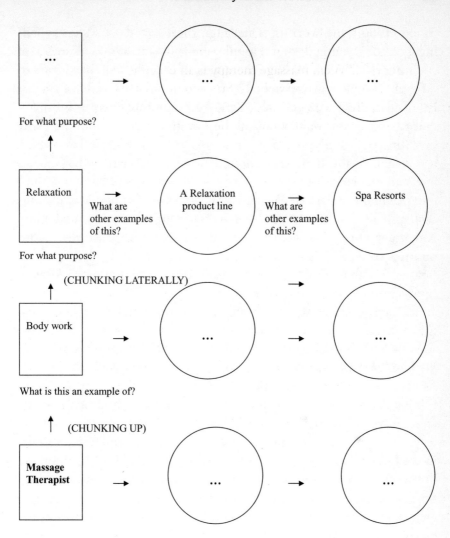

Figure 4.1

to chunk up. He thought, "Okay, I am selling books. What is selling books an example of?" He answered, "Well, it's an example of **e-commerce.**" Now, Amazon.com has expanded to selling all sorts of different products and services. It's an e-commerce hub rather than just being an online bookstore valued at over $15 billion today. It is important to note that it was a vital step for him to have started in the niche of selling books before moving into general e-commerce because he was able to establish his brand dominance and then parlay that success into a more expansive vision.

Remember that Sir Richard Branson started at age 16 with *Student*, a small magazine to give teenagers a political voice in the United Kingdom. Then he decided he was going to launch a mail-order record business, and this was followed by record stores. He then launched his first recording studio, because he realized that the real money was in production.

Branson was continually thinking of growth and expansion along the way. And he parlayed each success into even greater, more expansive success. So, continue to chunk up by asking, *"For what purpose?"* and *"What's this an example of?"* Many entrepreneurs say, *"The secret to success is to Think Big,"* but they never teach you how to actually do it. Chunking is the process for thinking expansively—which is really another way of saying, *Dream.* (See Figure 4.2.)

Think of your current business or occupation, and write it down in the box on page 72, Figure 4.3. Then begin chunking up, chunking down, and chunking laterally, filling in the boxes with potential answers to each of the questions you ask yourself.

The exercise that you have just done allowed you to identify elements of what you're currently doing and chunk up on it—that is, expand your thinking to gain flexibility and see other places you can direct your energy. As you advance, you create more wealth than you could possibly imagine. And once again, your wealth is a reflection of the value you create in the eyes of the current marketplace. If you're thinking expansively and thinking of delivering more and more value, you can conquer the world.

Oprah Winfrey says the best way to bring expansion to your life is to "create the highest and grandest vision possible...because you become what you believe." Oprah describes her own focus on

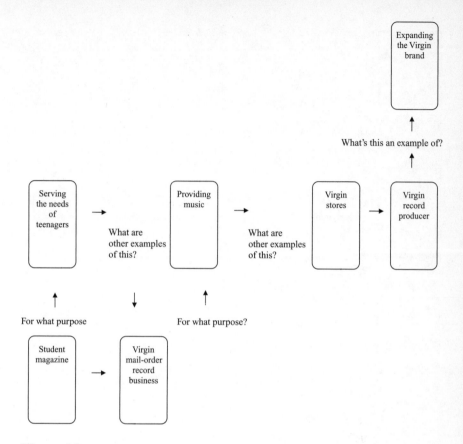

Figure 4.2

expansion in this way, "I do everything to the absolute ultimate. I grow until I can't grow any more in a certain position, and then another door opens."

Both Microsoft and the Bill and Melinda Gates Foundation are great models for expansionary thinking. Microsoft employs more than 55,000 people in 85 countries. The Bill and Melinda Gates Foundation has donated $11 billion since it was founded in 1994. With the foundation, Bill Gates still has that conquer-the-world mentality, but conquering with an altruistic purpose. Once I adopted that mentality, my business, as well as the value I was delivering, grew exponentially. Yours can, too!

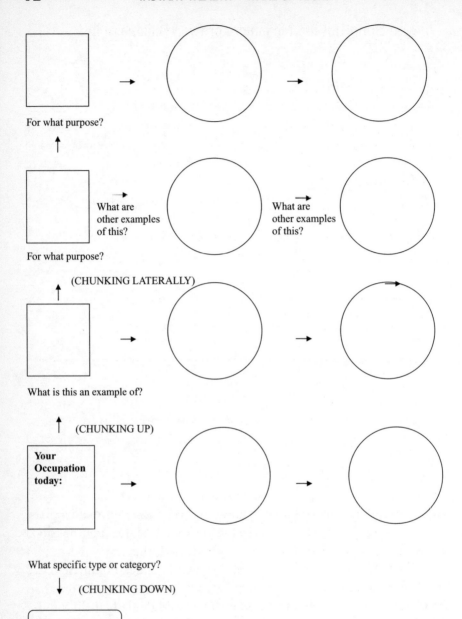

For what purpose?

For what purpose?

What are other examples of this?

What are other examples of this?

(CHUNKING LATERALLY)

What is this an example of?

(CHUNKING UP)

Your Occupation today:

What specific type or category?

(CHUNKING DOWN)

Figure 4.3

How to Bring Out the Millionaire or Even Billionaire Inside You

When I first made the commitment to embrace the **New Entrepreneurial Mind,** I realized that there was so much to learn. But I had no clue how to learn everything I needed to know. I found an expert in speed reading and accelerated learning who helped me to absorb information as rapidly as possible. With the assistance of those advanced learning processes, I created a unique system I call **Cognitive Reimprinting.**

This is *reimprinting* your mind to expand beyond anything that you ever thought you could do previously, while simultaneously installing the road maps at the subconscious level to get you from where you are financially to wherever you want to go.

Einstein said that "we are boxed in by the boundary conditions of our thinking."

As they get older, people tend to think within certain limits and certain boundaries. Those boundaries represent the difference between thinking and dreaming. As children, we go through an imprinting phase of intellectual growth in which beliefs, values, and viewpoints are absorbed without much mental exertion. We neurologically imprint the information. All our habits and reflexive behaviors are the result of actualized neural networks. These are like finely grooved roads in the neurology of our brain. You have more potential neurological connections inside your mind and body than all the grains of sand on the entire planet, and more than all the visible stars in the night sky.

Your brain is redundant on a scale of three to one, which means you have three times the potential in your brain than you will ever tap into. The human nervous system is redundant on a scale of 10 to 1, which means you have 10 times the potential that you will ever tap into. It's just that the neural networks eventually stop expanding as quickly as our exposure to all of the stimuli around us. It happens around the age of 9 or 10, when we develop predisposed biases and ways of looking at the world. By this time, much of the social hypnosis that people live with has already set in.

There was an experiment done with two kittens about 40 years ago. Even though I'm totally opposed to the aim of the experiment, its results are worth studying. The kittens were raised in special environments in which their vision was impaired during their imprinting phase. One kitten's vision was hindered so that it could see only horizontal lines. The other kitten had its vision hindered so it could see only vertical lines. When the kittens were released into a typical indoor environment, the kitten that had its vertical vision impaired had trouble avoiding objects, yet never jumped on to tables or countertops. The kitten that had its horizontal vision impaired was constantly bumping into furniture legs, yet never jumped on to tables or chairs because its blind spot had become hardwired into its way of thinking.

This is exactly how many people live their lives. Everything we experience in the imprint phase gets wired in. People begin to operate on past biases, past values, and beliefs that have already been formed. We become hardened in our views—even in what we can actually see—and the learning rate very dramatically slows down. We need to wake up from that!

Our eyes have to be *trained* to see. Our perceptions are **learned** perceptions. But this doesn't mean that if we weren't born to multimillionaire parents we would never have any clue to how to make wealth; it just means that we need to upgrade our entire mindset. The good news is that with today's tools and technologies for facilitating psychological change, we can reimprint subconscious programming in the blink of an eye. We can wake up to the potential for wealth that really exists in the world. We can figuratively install a **New Entrepreneurial Mind.** It's the key to embodying *Instant Wealth*.

An Easy Way to Adopt the Mindset of the Most Successful and Wealthy People Who Ever Lived

This upgrade is what I mean by **Cognitive Reimprinting.** It's taking the sponge of your neurology, wringing it out, and then resaturating it with the mindset of the most successful and wealthy people who ever walked the Earth. I personally used accelerative learning techniques to accumulate information on more than 1,000 very rich entrepreneurs and superstar creators. Then I used the psychological processes of neurolinguistic programming to break down the psychology of these super-wealthy individuals. I also studied people who were emotionally super-happy and super-rich.

Finally, I used hypnosis and other tools for accelerating transformation to install a brand new entrepreneurial mind in myself. It was very much like being reborn and raised in an entirely new way. All of this happened within a very compressed amount of time. I upgraded my mind and then totally transformed my financial results!

While you learn about the information gleaned from this methodology in *Instant Wealth—Wake Up Rich!*, you can experience it firsthand in our Wealth Building seminar series.

As I was studying super-super-successful people, the richest of the rich, I saw that every one of them was obsessed with expansion. They were constantly focused on growth. This concept of obsession with expansion changed my whole life.

I immediately began to think in an entirely different way about my business. I became very clear that my mission for my training company was to put the *tools of accelerating human transformation into the hands of everyone on the planet.* I knew that if we did that, the world would be a better place by helping millions of people make their dreams come true. I also decided to continually look for, and act on, opportunities to leverage my brand and to think bigger. My goal became to constantly launch new businesses, products, and services that would make a difference in the world. And, of course, I'd be rewarded with wealth, wealth that I could use to fuel my dreams and ultimately give back in even more compelling ways.

As I began to think bigger and bigger and bigger, some of the ventures that I launched were successful and some weren't. If you have failures along the way, always remember that every successful entrepreneur fails at some ventures. Your next win is certainly around the corner!

Now I own several businesses and a charitable organization, and I see more opportunities on the horizon. I know that the best is yet to come! Once I had thought only of teaching. Now I think of living my heart's every desire by creating new businesses. I've expanded my wealth and my dreams beyond what I ever thought possible. Just as my businesses are the scaffolding underneath my dreams, your enterprises can be the support for any dream that you've ever had!

The Most Common Mistake People Without Money Make

When I first got into personal development, I wanted to be a teacher and a speaker. But that wasn't all I wanted out of life. I knew how important it was to find my true purpose and to go after it. I also knew how critical it was to keep going, to have a single-mindedness of purpose on my path. I realized that throughout my life one of the major reasons for my lack of success had been because I had jumped from interest to interest without giving any real momentum to any one thing.

For example, I had worked years before for a major international hotel resort, and I worked my way up into management. But I stopped before I made it to executive manager, before I had attained what I had thought of as real success. I also finally got my black belt in martial arts, but then I stopped practicing altogether for a few years before eventually starting up again.

There were many things like that in my life that I started and then stopped along the way. I was clearly not staying clear in my purpose or staying focused on leveraging and expanding my success. Time and time again, I prevented myself from getting the momentum to create amazing results in anything. I knew I was capable of so much more than I was exhibiting.

And so are you!

Singleness of purpose is one of the chief essentials for success in life, no matter what may be one's aim.

—John D. Rockefeller

The Secret Andrew Carnegie Used to Create— A $300 Billion Empire in Today's Dollars

Single-minded purpose, channeling your attention, and focusing in one concentrated direction is the key mindset for expanding your empire. Some people say the key is, "Don't put all your eggs in one basket." Andrew Carnegie said, "The wise man puts his all his eggs in one basket, and watches that basket."

Carnegie fits into the idea of **The New Entrepreneurial Mind** even though his life was mostly lived in the nineteenth century (from 1835 to 1919). He is estimated to have been the second-richest man in history, with a net worth equivalent to more than $300 billion in 2009 dollars. He was, of course, extremely generous with that money, donating almost all of it to establish more than 2,500 public libraries as well as establishing schools and universities in the United States, the United Kingdom, and other countries.

Following Carnegie's suggestion of so many years ago, I decided to change my life and be single-minded and focused. I wanted to put all my eggs into creating the best personal and professional development company in the world. I realized that my training company wasn't *everything* I wanted to do in my life, but I decided to pursue that course while still listening to my heart along the way. I decided to become *really* single-minded.

I made that choice 15 years ago—and the time for you to choose a single-minded purpose is *right now*. "Some day" doesn't exist in the realm of *Instant Wealth*. It's the moments of decision that shape our lives, so make the choice to be single-minded in your purpose. It's the key to the doorway of freedom and wealth beyond your wildest imagination!

It's kind of fun to do the impossible.

—**Walt Disney**

Why You Can Do Anything You Set Your Mind To

As with any entrepreneurial venture, I encountered tests along the way. Early on, someone offered me a job to run an unrelated company for $80,000 a year, more than I had ever been offered in the business world. Of course, my reaction was to think, "Wow, should I take this job?" But I *knew* what my passion was. While the offer was attractive, I wouldn't have been following my heart.

The tests are there to remind you of the importance of staying your course. Actor Harrison Ford said he figured out how to succeed in Hollywood early on. It was simply a matter of outlasting everyone else, because so many actors came and went. When the tests come, let them remind you to *stay the course*.

Stick with one thing long enough until you can get some serious momentum; *then* you can parlay it into other types of success.

How to Turn Your Life Around, Get Rich, and Stay Rich for Life

When you're just starting, make sure that you're successful at *something*. Then you can expand into the other things that you also want to accomplish and achieve. If you attempt to pursue too many interests prematurely, you're just spreading yourself into too many directions. More often than not, that diversification prevents people from really succeeding.

The biggest fortunes in the world—such as Wal-Mart, Microsoft, and even the Virgin companies—were **not** made through diversification. They can be *preserved* through diversification, but they are *made* through a concentration of efforts and energies. Richard Branson may have created many different companies, but the *one thing* on which he's concentrated his energies is the business of "branded venture capital"—that is, lending the strength of the Virgin brand to a multitude of different companies that benefit from the strength of the one brand.

So I decided to stick with one career path—but when I began to see some positive results, I thought, "Wow, I can take the success that I've created through this single-mindedness of purpose and now expand the scope of my single-mindedness, and I can parlay what I'm doing into *many different* realms, which, from a larger perspective, are moving in the same direction. In order to grow, I **can't** limit myself to simply speaking on a stage, because there are only so many people I can help at one time."

For my business to continue expanding—and for my message to reach more people—I began to develop audio programs, books, and other ancillary products. I also hired trainers to teach the powerful tools and technologies that I had been researching and creating. Today, at any time, three or four of my trainings are taking place somewhere in the world, without requiring my physical presence. There's no way we could reach as many people as we do without this kind of leverage.

If a thing is humanly possible, consider it to be within your reach.

—Marcus Aurelius, Roman emperor

The Secret to Creating Forward-Moving Momentum in Your Life

Constant movement, which is necessary to generate momentum, is a requirement of expansion. If you throw a pebble into a pond, what happens as a result? The ripples in the water are an example of a concept that comes from physics known as *precession*. If the pebbles that we throw are value-driven by positive values, then the precessional events to follow will be ripples of happiness, joy, abundance, and fulfillment. Alternatively, negative actions with unethical intentions will cause emptiness, depression, and even legal troubles. When we take the divinely inspired actions that come from following our hearts and living our dreams, the precessional effects will be divinely inspired as well.

Robert Allen and Mark Victor Hansen refer to precession in their book, *The One-Minute Millionaire:*

> *Enlightened millionaires know that they must create wealth where everyone wins. When they focus on adding value, what happens precessionally will be positive. They may not fully understand or appreciate all the precessional events as they occur. They just know that* unexpected *positive things will happen as long as they focus on adding as much value as possible.*

Notice the word *unexpected*. The precessional events that follow your actions may not always be what you feel has a direct connection with your ultimate goal or dream, causing you to possibly not even recognize the opportunity. But keep this in mind: when you throw the pebble, you have no idea exactly how far the resulting ripples will go.

How to Move Toward Your Destiny in Only 10 Minutes

I want you to take 10 minutes for a fun exercise. You are going to rewrite the story of your own life and gain a greater perspective on the precessional events that have shaped it and can lead toward your ultimate destiny. Think of four or five events from your past that you can weave into the story. Be sure to pick some negative incidents so that you can use them in your new story as learning opportunities and obstacles you overcame.

This is going to be a heroic, epic fairy tale. What have you always imagined your life to be? Make it fun! With each experience you include, ask yourself, "What would a prince or princess do?" or "What would a rock star do?" What did the prince do as he made his way through this situation? What was the princess experiencing? What were the lessons that the heroes learned? What were the positive, empowering lessons that allowed them to fulfill their divine destiny?

Bring your imaginary life story up to the present, and extend it off into the future. Make sure it's an inspiring and captivating story with powerful lessons and end results. This is one of the exercises that I did in Hawaii years ago. I thought of it while creating one of our trainings called "**Rich Heart—Wealthy Mind.**" Then I did the exercise myself.

When I left Hawaii at the end of that week, my life was never the same again. I truly woke up to the magic of life. Since then, every moment of every day has been spent in the embrace of God. I'm not saying that I haven't had problems. I have. I'm not saying I haven't had challenges. I have. But I woke up to my grander purpose and life has been truly magical. I have truly lived a rich life since then, and that is exactly my goal for you.

Rewriting the story of your life can reframe your basic relationship to your grandest dreams and ambitions. So right now, take 10 minutes for this exercise. See yourself on a wonderful and magical adventure, on the journey of a lifetime! When you have finished, continue on. There's a lot more to empower you on the path to claim your *Instant Wealth!*

_____

_____

_____

_____

_____

_____

What 1,000 of the Richest People in the World Know About Success that You Don't

Maintaining focus is essential for success. Understand your circle of competence, the one thing you're good at, and put your time and energy there.

—Bill Gates

Anyone who truly intends to make a huge difference in the world—and create massive amounts of wealth in the process—is never thinking, "One day I'm going to retire." Ask self-made, wealthy, successful people if they're working so eventually they can retire, and they'll laugh at the idea. Their work is their *love*. Their desire to continue to expand their interests is an expression of who they are at the core of their being. It's in their genes!

Warren Buffett has often been asked the secret of his success. It's the same thing that makes a Tiger Woods or a Michael Jordan. It's the uncanny ability to *channel focus in a singular direction*. To focus is a two-part process: it's a clear vision, and it's waking up as the person who can make the vision occur.

Warren Buffett reads over 2,000 annual reports a year. His extraordinary power of focus makes him a master of analyzing businesses and discovering the best choices to expand his portfolio. If you want to grow your dreams to the fullest extent and make a difference in the world, you've got to cultivate the ability to channel your focus like Warren Buffett.

I had an Olympic gold medalist volleyball player in one of my seminars recently. I asked her, "How focused are you?" And she said, "Very. Nothing has been more important to me than my dream." I then asked her, "How competitive are you?" She replied, "I love to win. I live to win." I asked, "How hard do you work?" And she said, "Incredibly hard. I train harder than anyone I know." She is focused on her sport, she is driven to do better, she is single-minded in her purpose of becoming great at what she does, and she is obsessed with expanding—in her case, from being the best player in her city, her state, her country, and then in the world.

What makes Olympic athletes extraordinary is the fact that they channel their focus more than other people. What works for them will work for you.

How Going Slower Can Make You Richer

My friend Keith Cunningham, a pioneer in cable television, who structured hundreds of millions of dollars for his various business ventures, uses the analogy of being in a lunch line when he talks about success. If you're in a really long lunch line, it seems like it will take forever to get to the food. Of course, you will eventually get to eat if you just wait long enough. But most people start looking around and thinking, "Maybe I'm in the wrong line. This line is moving too slowly." So they jump out of one line and into another. Then they realize the other line is also moving just as slowly, and they're not still happy, so they jump to yet another line.

Keith says, "That's how most people live their entire lives. They jump from lunch line to lunch line. What they have to realize is that if they had just stayed in the first line, they would already be eating."

People let mistakes knock them off their path. Then they give up and quit. But if you are pursuing the right goal—*if you do what you were born to do and follow your heart's desire*—then patience becomes a nonissue. And if you've made a commitment to yourself that you're going to follow your passion, that you're going to follow your heart unwaveringly and forever, single-mindedly and obsessively, it becomes easier and easier to achieve your goals.

My good friend Eric Lochtefeld launched a business back in 2000 called University of Dreams. The business helped college students find summer internships at top companies in the field of their choice, while simultaneously running a summer curriculum of street-smart life education. Eric had $200,000 in debt at the time, but he had a huge dream. He had found his passion and he had a desire to really make a difference in people's lives. For Eric, failure was not an option, even though it would take a lot of patience and persistence to reap rewards.

It took seven years, but today the profits are in the seven-figure range, and Eric has 52 full-time employees with operations around the world. He's been contacted by more than 50 private equity firms wanting to purchase his business with bids in the $20 million range. But Eric has no intention of selling because, from his perspective, he hasn't even started the *real* expansion yet. Channeling his focus certainly paid off over time.

In addition to patience when you're working toward your long-term goals, it's also important to live in the present rather than in the future. I've always been keenly aware of the goals in front of me. I have a vision of what I want to create in the future that goes beyond my training company into the many expressions of things I'm passionate about. But I'm not preoccupied with the future; I live in the current moment. When I get on stage, I'm very present and passionate about teaching. I live my life day to day, and it's the love of the journey that really helps me realize my goals. So enjoy the process of what you're doing. Fall in love with your entrepreneurial journey!

Simplest Way to Make Your Success A Self-Fullfilling Prophecy

You need to know in your gut, with absolute certainty, that there is no other path than the journey of creating your entrepreneurial dreams. You need to have so much faith that your success becomes a self-fulfilling prophecy.

Michael Dell, founder of Dell Computers, stayed the course and his entrepreneurial dreams paid off. This allowed him to create the Michael and Susan Dell Foundation, which has a global philanthropic reach. They have contributed more than $1.2 billion toward education and child development programs in Texas alone! They also donated $5 million to help victims of Hurricane Katrina. They have contributed generously to microfinance lenders in India's six largest cities in an effort to alleviate the poverty of millions of people.

You too can achieve amazing things through the powerful use of your imagination and the sheer force of your will. Certainty of that came for me when I first decided to develop a transformational training business in 1994. I made a commitment to make speaking and teaching the expression of my soul. I burned all of my bridges. When you are incredibly committed, you take bold steps.

I was a personal trainer at the time. I found the trainer I trusted most and transferred all my personal training clients to him. Of course, this cut off my income. I don't necessarily recommend anything that extreme. You may find it prudent to simultaneously preserve some cash flow for yourself as you are launching yourself toward *Instant Wealth*. But burning the bridges was the path that I chose to take, and I couldn't have done it any other way. It forced me to figure out how to make my new business work.

Although I wouldn't have done this any other way, it also wasn't always comfortable. I had challenges and times when I struggled, especially in the early days. I remember people asking me, *"What are you going to do now?"* But I didn't think about anything else except making my new direction in life work. I was on a mission. I could be a shining light of possibility, and by changing my life radically I could help others do the same. Thoughts of self-doubt never ever entered my mind. They couldn't enter my mind. I knew that there was no turning back.

Magic comes with that level of commitment. I was absolutely certain that I could and would do what I had set out to do, and it has become a self-fulfilling prophecy. I once thought I would make $1 million in a year and be speaking around the country. Now I've done that much in a *day* and I'm speaking around the world. I've accomplished things I could not have even dreamt of before. But the feeling of certainty that I would make my dreams come true was always there. That certainty will come to *you* when you make the maximum commitment to *Instant Wealth*.

How to Adopt Unwavering Self-Confidence in Yourself

My certainty and my willingness to do whatever it takes came across as brash on a couple of occasions in the early days, before I knew how to temper it with humility.

I remember applying for a professional speaking position when I was about 25 years old. I walked in and sat down for lunch with the man who ran the company and one of his managers. I basically said, "I'm the best. You've got to hire me." As soon as I said it, I saw that my bold statement had shocked the manager a little bit. But the owner of the company turned to her and said, "Don't be put off by what he just said. A good speaker *needs* to have a healthy ego."

Still, I was worried. I left the interview thinking I might have been a little too self-assured in my presentation. I didn't convey what I had really wanted to say—not that I was "the best," but that "I have the *heart* to be the best speaker on your team. I'll pour so much of my heart and spirit into this job. I will work harder than anybody in the world. I am so committed to do whatever it takes. I'll work around the clock to be the person who shines as the best, who excels, and stands out at this." I knew those things about myself, but I didn't communicate them very skillfully. I had to learn to temper certainty with humility.

Fortunately, I got the job, anyway. Heart, spirit, and willingness to work harder than anybody else are all part of the "do whatever it takes" attitude. You have total certainty that you'll accomplish your goals and achieve what you want in business and in life. You will make it happen. There is no other option. You will wake up rich!

Tiger Woods was perceived as being cocky by the media when he first gave interviews after his initial success. When reporters asked, "Aren't you lucky?" Tiger outright rejected that idea. He said his success had nothing to do with luck; to be extraordinary took vision and a willingness to work harder than most people would ever dream of doing.

This is the attitude of every highly successful person. What people might perceive as arrogance isn't *always* boasting. It can come from a strong commitment to yourself and to your dreams. That's the foundation of your certainty, your belief, and your patience. The key, once again, is to temper this certainty with humility. Be committed and certain—but play yourself down, not up.

True confidence comes from the certainty of your unwavering commitment and your willingness to do whatever it takes. When you're coming from this place, you have nothing *to prove*.

Let Go of Attachments

There's one final point I want to make here about how to expand your entrepreneurial empire: to be successful, you must release the fear-based attachment to be something that you're not, or to be further ahead than you are. Many people struggle with this neediness to be further ahead than they are.

Challenge: For the next five days, take five minutes each day with your eyes closed in silence imagining being the ideal you. Imagine going through your day with all the traits and characteristics that you would deem to be ideal. Remember to do this exercise as if you are looking through your own eyes, seeing what you would see as the ideal you. Enjoy the results!

One of the secrets of success, which may seem paradoxical in relation to what I just mentioned, is to project yourself up to the level that you want to be, or to imagine yourself being the highest ideal of success you desire and *live* in that place of imagination. When you do that, you will eventually become what you consistently imagine yourself to be. They say that God made man in his image. So who do you *image* (or imagine) yourself to be?

The other side of the equation is the absolute necessity of releasing *fear-based attachment* to being, doing, or having anything that you don't perceive to be currently in your experience. This ties in to having patience, to living in the moment, and to pouring heart and soul into every minute of every day. That doesn't mean you should rest on your laurels, but you need to appreciate the moment because what we appreciate appreciates. It's a fine balance between certainty of the future and connection with the present.

An exercise designed to create what I call **Expanded Awareness** is a highly effective way to eliminate negative thoughts about past, present, or future. **Expanded Awareness** is a relaxed state of mind that creates a mental condition of both total focus and receptivity to new information. **Expanded Awareness** takes place when your attention shifts from foveal, or single-focused, vision to peripheral vision. We're going to use this exercise to obliterate old attachments and to create new mindsets and choices.

As soon as we describe and define a problem, we put boundary conditions on it. We can then shift our attention from the *content* of the problem to the *context*, using **Expanded Awareness**. We can move from the *problem* to the *not a problem*, which is where the solution can be found.

You will need seven or eight minutes for this exercise. Read the exercise all the way through to be sure you understand the steps before beginning. The best results often come after running through the whole exercise three or four times in a row.

1. Find a spot on the wall in front of you, somewhere above eye level. Focus all your attention on that spot.
2. Think of all your fear-based attachments to be something that you are not. Think of the ways you *need* to be further ahead than you are. Think of your attachments to *having to have* your visions and dreams fulfilled.
3. Keep your eyes on that spot on the wall, but shift your attention and your awareness toward the periphery. In other words, go into expanded awareness. While you're still looking at the spot on the wall, shift *every* aspect of your focus and *every* aspect of your awareness to your peripheral vision.
4. Now think of all your fear-based attachments to "needing to be anywhere" you are not. Think of the ways you need to

be further ahead than you are. Think of your attachments to having to have your visions and dreams fulfilled.

5. And as you remain in expanded awareness, pour out all of your fear-based attachments and all of your fear-based needs on that spot on the wall.

6. As you direct all your attachments to that spot, it's time to preserve that positive experience, and to learn from it. When you do this now, you will be free from those old attachments in the future. As you do this, what do you feel you are learning? Make sure you answer this question with highly positive statements.

7. As the exercise ends, project your consciousness forward to some indefinite time in your future. Then turn and look back toward the moment when you let go of your fears, of your *needs* and attachments. Notice how much better and stronger you look in the future after making that change now.

Repeat this exercise whenever you want to reinforce the experience of being at ease in the moment, while at the same time moving confidently toward your dreams.

How to Win by Losing

To further explain the target of this meditation, I want to share some experiences from my martial arts training. I have always loved the martial arts for the discipline and character they have built in me. I've been a student of martial arts for most of my life, and I got my black belt in Twin Dragon Kung Fu in the early 1990s. But when I was 25, I started training in Gracie Jiu Jitsu, a grappling art with joint locks, submissions, and chokes that have proven incredibly effective as a combat art. My teacher and dear friend, Grand Master Rorion Gracie, has shown me so many metaphors through Jiu Jitsu. These have mapped across into my development as a person and an entrepreneur.

One lesson stands out in my mind. Although I had already attained my black belt in another art, the belt ranking system in Jiu Jitsu is white, blue, purple, brown, black. When I began Jiu Jitsu, it was with the beginner's mind. I was given a white belt.

One day, after I had attained the rank of blue belt and had maintained that rank for a couple of years, I was wrestling, or rolling, with Rorion and I was fighting hard. I was really struggling, like I was fighting for my life. Then Rorion stopped me. He said, "Chris, I know you want to move up. I know you want to beat the purple belts so you can be promoted. But you need to *relax*."

He knew exactly what was on my mind. I had been beaten recently by a few purple belts, and I desperately wanted to move up in rank. My only goal was to get the purple belt. But Rorion went on: "I'm afraid that your need to beat the purple belts will stop you from getting what it really takes to beat them. You have a fear of losing. I can feel you struggling and burning yourself out way too early. You're so focused on wanting to win that you miss all the opportunities to win that are actually there."

I've heard it said that how you do *anything* is how you do *everything*. That was certainly true for me, because my life issues were playing out in the same way I played my game of Jiu Jitsu. I had a fear of losing, a fear of not being good enough, or not being the best. I was living in this needy, stressed-out place. I was struggling on the mat, just like I was struggling in my business and my life. It was ineffective and exhausting.

Rorion told me I had to relax. He actually *forbade* me to win—initially for three months, and then for an entire year. I was traveling around the world training with other people in Jiu Jitsu, and he told me, "I don't want you to win anywhere you go. You can't attack. You can't try to make the other guy tap out. But I also want you to do your best not to lose. If you do tap out, that's okay. But find out what led you to that point and never let it happen again. Pretty soon you won't be tapping out with purple belts, or brown, or black."

I continued traveling and training with the best instructors all over the world, knowing all the time that I would never win. So I didn't try to win. I just did my best not to lose—and when I did, I thought about how I got in that position so it wouldn't happen again. That made me a very defensive player. Then, all of a sudden, I saw that Rorion had been right. The brown belts, and sometimes even the black belts, people who were ranked much higher than I was, weren't making me tap out. I wasn't giving up anymore, and I had a very relaxed game.

I was very excited and called Rorion, and left him a telephone message. When I realized this, I was in Australia. He called back with a message, "Chris, I got your message, and I'm impressed! But I'm not surprised."

When I came back to practice with Rorion again, he presented me with another challenge. He called in his son, Roron, and told him to lie on the ground. Then he told me to get in Roron's guard, which is one of the Jiu Jitsu positions. He told me to try to choke his son—but not to hurt him, of course, because his son was only six years old. Once I started to roll and play with his son, Rorion said to me, "This is how you have to be *all the time*. You have to be this relaxed all the time to conserve your energy. Then you wait for the right move to win."

Shortly after that, he brought in a purple belt, and he handed it to me. He said, *"This is a long time coming, but I wanted to make sure you were ready."* Over that year when he forbade me to win, he taught me to **let go** of my attachment and my neediness. He taught me to get rid of my fear of losing by ***being willing to lose***—and to learn from every loss how to avoid it the next time.

The most important thing that Rorion taught me, though, was to let go of my fear, enjoy the game, and relax. I was able to keep this state in training situations with guys twice my size who were coming after me hard and wanting to beat me up. I let go of all attachment. I could finally play a relaxed game.

This Simple Mind Tool Eliminates Stress from Your Life

Entrepreneurs face what they perceive to be life-or-death struggles all the time. Many live in a constant state of fight or flight. I know, because I lived that way myself. I was constantly stressed, and I took it out on people I cared about because I wasn't willing to face my own fears. The relaxed attitude that Rorion taught me is the same mindset that Richard Branson has when he's lying in his hammock talking about fuel emissions for Virgin Galactic, trying to make sure that his fleet is green enough.

It's easy to see his relaxed state of mind. I asked Richard, "How do you handle stress?" He replied "Chris, I don't have any stress. Nothing can go wrong in business that's worth worrying about. If something were to happen to my health or the health of someone in my family, *that* would be a real problem. But if the Virgin companies were to fall apart today, I'd just move to Bali or something."

Please hear this loud and clear. There is no place "you have to be." Many hugely successful people have a playful attitude about their lives, and it's not just because they have money. They've learned to let go of attachment to outcomes. They keep moving forward with fierce dedication, but they have peace of mind as well. It's a dual process of loving the journey rather than the destination while at the same time remaining obsessed with realizing their dreams. This is truly **The New Entrepreneurial Mind**.

This kind patience goes hand in hand with being a pioneer. It doesn't mean losing focus on your dreams. Steve Case, a co-founder of AOL, had the patience to see his dream through. It took nine years to get one million subscribers on AOL; then it hit a critical mass. In the next nine months, AOL went from 1 million to 35 million subscribers.

Many people tried to dissuade Case along the way, but he had faith in his vision. He enjoyed the pioneering aspect of creating his business. He had studied the history of innovation and he knew that success often takes years before suddenly the floodgates fly wide open and with tremendous rewards. This driving commitment, combined with infinite patience, was the key to AOL's success, and allowed Steve to live in a much clearer space of mind while continually moving toward his goals.

So many people are wrapped up in the fear-based need to be somewhere. The lives of so many stressed-out people are shortened because of the high levels of adrenaline that their bodies constantly create. Even Richard Branson said that creating his Virgin companies was "a struggle to survive" all along. I believe the release of attachment, loving the journey rather than the destination, really allows you to channel your concentration for the long haul.

Now, with that said, it's time to reveal the mindset that will allow you to take your life up to a whole new level. It's time to discover the *one* thing that will change *everything*. . . .

YOUR New Entrepreneurial Mind
1. Commit to following your passion
2. Pour love into the creation of your dream
3. Fall in love with the process
4. Create propulsion by having a heroic, grander purpose of making a difference in the world
5. Be obsessed with expansion
6. Be single-minded in your purpose
7. Have extraordinary focus on your dreams and on becoming the person who can make them happen
8. Release attachment to the outcome; fall in love with the journey of your dreams

CHAPTER 6

How to End Financial Sabotage and Instantly Turn Your Life Around

If you're committed to achieving the results you're seeking in your life, the single most important thing you must do is take *personal* responsibility for all that you create.

So many people try to shift responsibility for their circumstances to some outside source. It might be their job, the economy, their spouse, or dozens of other possibilities. But entrepreneurs who create extraordinary results—the super-wealthy and super-successful—take complete responsibility for all aspects of their lives.

Warren Buffett is a great example of this. In 1987, just before the Black Monday stock market crash, Buffett acquired a 12 percent stake in the Salomon Brothers brokerage house—only to find that the federal government was investigating a trading scandal within the company. The banks were going to call in $146 billion of loans, the doors would be shut, and 8,000 employees' jobs were on the line. Because of Buffett's reputation for integrity, Salomon Brothers was told that they would be given the chance to turn things around *only* if Warren Buffett himself were put in charge. Buffett became interim chairman despite the fact that this wasn't his typical role as an investor.

This heroic move of taking the personal responsibility saved not only Buffett's stake in the company but the jobs of everyone involved. It was possible only because of Buffett's reputation. Buffett's sense of responsibility is also demonstrated in his annual reports to the shareholders of his holding company, Berkshire Hathaway. He communicates with absolute candor, and he says it's more important to talk openly about mistakes than successes. Every year his report includes what he calls the "mistake du jour," in which he gives all the details of the biggest money management error he made that year. This level of frankness, combined with his extraordinary results, has made Warren Buffett one of the wealthiest people in the world.

Take responsibility for results on the personal level, the professional level, and even on the global level.

How to Develop a "No Excuse" Attitude

You can be on the cause side of the cause-and-effect equation, or you can be on the effect side. The person on the cause side has a no-excuses attitude. That person says, "I *create* the circumstances in my life." And that person is the most empowered. Oprah Winfrey puts it this way: "I take full responsibility for my success or failures, from what happens on my talk show to losing my luggage on a trip."

I believe I'm at cause for everything that happens in my world— whether through the things that I do or the things that I fail to do. And when I choose that belief, I know how important my belief really is. Our beliefs determine our actions, and they therefore also determine our results. When you choose to believe that you are responsible for everything, either through your actions or your lack of actions, you have maximum power to change your own behaviors and produce powerful results.

In contrast, people on the effect side of the equation have lots of excuses for why they can't get the results they want. They'll say things like, "I can't be successful because..." and then mention something (or anything) as the reason. For example, "The economy is the reason I can't succeed." But isn't everyone living in the same economy? The truth is, a lot of people right now are successful regardless of the economy!

Shifting economic conditions are nothing more than the tide coming in and going out. Anybody can make money when it's high tide, but must have a no-excuses attitude that it is impervious to market conditions or economic downturns. Because the tide comes in and it goes out. That's what the tide does.

It's only when the tide goes out that you learn who's been swimming naked.

—**Warren Buffett**

Why the Rich Look Forward to Obstacles and How They Turn Them into Opportunities

Part of truly being at cause is using anything and everything that occurs to your advantage. For example, while the media hypnotizes society to believe that the world is coming to an end, and while most of the world is complaining about the economy, true entrepreneurs are actively taking steps to become hugely wealthy.

Many people are saying the markets are terrible. But if I were to show you a piece of property for $30,000 that was previously valued at $300,000, you would say, "Wow, what a *great economy!* What a *great market!*" But most people don't see it that way.

The same is true of the stock market. Right now, with so many stocks popping up, essentially with "for sale" signs on them, or "for a limited time, you can find the best prices on all your favorite stocks." The opportunities are huge. All it takes to claim a brand new future is to stop making excuses and seek out those opportunities! It's never a question of resources; it's always a question of resourcefulness. As I like to say, "You can either make excuses or make a fortune. It's up to you."

From a business perspective, the world is rapidly changing and we've got to wake up to its riches. *Time* magazine predicts that by 2019 the segment of the U.S. workforce made up of independent contractors will increase from 26 percent to 40 percent. Employers are looking to outsource work so they can keep expenses down. This means more people must take responsibility for their own businesses. It would be easy to complain or feel fearful about this change, but it's far better to adopt **The New Entrepreneurial Mind** and use the circumstances to wake up rich. If you're in a position in which you think you may lose the stability of a full-time job, get excited and ask yourself the question: "What do I need to do so that I will be in the top 1 percent of the wealthiest and most successful people in that newly evolving outsourced group?"

My dear friend, entrepreneur and best-selling author Robert Allen, knows very well the power of taking personal responsibility. He graduated with his MBA during a severe recession, and approached 30 top corporations with his resume. He got letters of rejection from all 30. He *could have* wallowed in excuses. Instead, he made a conscious choice to use the situation to his advantage. He focused on *Instant Wealth*.

Robert Allen found a mentor who had made a fortune in real estate, which soon became Robert's passion. With his mentor's coaching, he bought his first duplex. Within three years, he made his first million dollars. Within six years, his first book, *Nothing Down*, became the all-time best-selling real estate investment book. Today, he has one of the most successful real estate training companies in existence and a multimillion dollar net worth.

Sometimes difficult situations are the catalyst for taking responsibility, adopting a no-excuses attitude, and using the circumstances of the moment to propel you forward. Difficult situations can also be the opportunity for changing the world around you. I personally believe small business owners are the people who will turn the economy around. Entrepreneurs will make their businesses succeed by delivering more value, and by setting the prices at a point at which people are going to pay for that value. When I lost my job, *that* was when I launched my business. I did it out of *necessity*. I thought, "This can be a great opportunity for you to launch something of your own. You can *choose* to make this the opportunity to embrace your dreams!"

Sometimes during my career I've seen people view the economy as really down. They saw things from a *"Poor me, this is the worst of times"* mindset. Right after the September 11th attacks, people were saying that the aftermath would simply shut down their businesses, that everything in the world (once again) was coming to an end. At that time, people needed the messages of *Instant Wealth—Wake Up Rich!* more than ever:

- You can make your dreams come true regardless of the circumstance.
- Listen to your heart and know that you can grow your wealth.
- You can make a difference in the world.
- It all starts with you! It all starts now!

In times of crisis it's often time to expand rather than contract.

—Chris Howard

What to Do If You Want to Turn Your Life Around Immediately

I personally experienced some of my worst times back when I was living in that house that was being torn down while I was living in it. At that low point, I said to myself, "You have to find the courage to step up and take charge of your life! You need to focus all your resources right now!" Of course, if you had checked my bank accounts or my wallet at the time, you would have seen that I had no resources. But in difficult times, it's absolutely imperative that you adopt a no-excuses attitude. You absolutely must not rationalize or blame others for your circumstances. If I had done that, there is no way I would be where I am now.

Instead of remaining stuck in excuses, I did what I had to do. I got credit cards, I took loans, and I stayed focused so I could continue to learn, train, and educate myself. I had to become the person who could make my entrepreneurial dreams come true. I had to do this even more fervently in "the worst of times." So do you!

Think about this: In what areas of your life do you need to stop making excuses and start investing more in your dreams? What opportunities can unfold as a direct result of the current circumstances that can launch me to greater levels of success? Where is *Instant Wealth* waiting for you?

Right now, take two minutes and use the following space to write out all the reasons or excuses why you can't achieve what you want to achieve in your life. I don't know what those reasons or excuses are going to be; I don't know if they're going to be not enough money, limited time, obligations to family, or not having the contacts you need. Just list everything that's preventing you from achieving your greatest entrepreneurial dreams. Write down those reasons, and then we'll move on to the next step.

I can't achieve what I want in life because:

_____

_____

_____

_____

_____

Now that you've listed all your reasons, I want you to recognize them for exactly what they are: *excuses!* It's not the external circumstances that determine our results in life; it's how we deal with those external circumstances. Keep reading and we'll deal with these reasons or excuses as we move forward.

Entrepreneurs who aren't successful, who aren't making things work in their lives or businesses or careers or relationships, find an infinite number of things to blame:

"My employees are not effective."
"The team wasn't motivated."
"My business partner didn't do his job."

"I don't have the right education."

"I'm the wrong sex, color, religion, or ethnic background."

"My parents didn't teach me how to be successful."

"I have a learning disability."

And many more . . .

I had the good fortune to take a group of 30 coaches and mentors from my philanthropic enterprise, The Alliance for Global Wealth, to South Africa to work with a group of students at CIDA University, the first free university in South Africa. I was inspired to go to CIDA after spending a few days with Sir Richard Branson on his private island in the British West Indies. Richard mentioned his work in Africa to help eradicate poverty through education and entrepreneurialism. Because that was in complete alignment with my mission, I soon found myself on a plane to Africa to see how we might be of assistance. While at CIDA, my friends and fellow mentors worked with a group of 400 students to help them develop new empowering mindsets and make their entrepreneurial dreams come true. Fully half of these students had lost their parents to AIDS. But their spirit to succeed and make something of their lives was incredible. One of the young women in the group approached me and said, "Chris, I really want to make my life work. I want to be extremely successful as an entrepreneur. I feel that I have so much to share with the world—but I feel stuck. I lost both my parents to AIDS and my uncle, who raised me, raped me repeatedly. How can I forgive? How can I move on?"

Do you think she deserves to live a good life? Do you think she deserves to move beyond the challenges of the past to step up and embrace her own dreams? Do you think that she deserves to share her gifts with the people within her own country and the world so that she can make the difference that she wants to make? Of course, she does. But the fact is, "deserving" will not make the difference. What makes a Mahatma Gandhi or a Nelson Mandela, or a Martin Luther King Jr., or what defines any great leader is the ability to refuse any and all excuses.

That young woman has an opportunity to become a shining light of possibility for the millions of South Africans who have perhaps found themselves in similar situations. That opportunity springs from her capacity to free herself from the shackles of the past with a vision of a world where things like that could never occur. She deserves this, don't you think?

A Navy SEAL's Secret to Getting the Results You Want Now

I was fortunate to start learning this whole concept of no excuses when I was 12 years old and beginning to study martial arts. One of my first instructors was Owen Watson, a tough former Navy SEAL, very intimidating to a 12-year-old. What really stood out were the dragon tattoos on his forearms and the big samurai sword he would wield around class while putting us through drills and exercises that would make *grown men cry.* Anyone who dared come to class late had to do 500 pushups. If you were late and had an excuse it was 1,000 pushups.

On the very few occasions when I was late to class, I would just say, "I'm late, no excuse"—and I would drop immediately into the pushup position for my 500. No excuse was good enough to miss a scheduled class. "Even if someone in your family had died," he said, "their condition wouldn't change one iota with you stepping out of the situation to go to class for an hour or two, so you had better be there. No excuses."

While I describe him as tough, he also had a heart of gold. I attribute much of my success in life to the disciplined attitude that he instilled in us. He was my first spiritual mentor. He called us *"God's Warriors,"* and we were taught to live with a very strict code of honor and to help our fellow person. I learned a lot from my early martial arts training. I wouldn't train in that same militaristic type of school today, but those early studies shaped who I am from a character perspective. "No excuses," is one of my greatest lessons—and there really are no excuses. Reasons or excuses box us into mediocrity, but they often *seem* good; they *seem* justified. That's the challenge. I learned at the age of 12 that I couldn't use excuses or reasons, even good reasons, to get in the way of the results I wanted to achieve in my life. And neither can you.

But while I learned the concept of no excuses early on, it didn't always translate automatically to everything. Sometimes I had to be slapped around a bit by life first. Perhaps you can relate?

There was a time when I was totally broke financially. I was eating only every third day. I was searching for change in the sofa to buy doughnuts. I was sleeping on a mattress on the floor. The ceiling leaked and there were floods in the house every now and then. I had rescued a little puppy from the streets that slept in a little cage by my mattress, and he and I would lament together at night. I felt more sorry for him having to live in those conditions than I did for myself. I had gotten to the point where I was just throwing my bills away, because I was completely overwhelmed and I knew I had no chance of paying them. It wasn't a great way to live.

Then my friend Jim Gillespie called to remind me about a training seminar that he and I had discussed. It was a training course for becoming a professional seminar leader, and that was my real vision. I had been educating myself in psychological, leadership, and coaching skills to bring out the best in people for several years as part of my career transition to my dreams. I had earned the ability to coach people through a considerable investment of money and years of intensive education, and I was already working with friends, family, and even doing some professional coaching with really great results. But there was definitely some lag time in regard to making my own life work. I had already invested what seemed like a lot of money at the time. I was like the college student just coming out of school and desperately needing to create some cash flow.

Jim asked me, "Chris, have you registered for the professional seminar leader training yet?" I really wanted to be a presenter and a speaker, but I knew the course was $5,000 and I didn't have a dime left on my credit cards. I was overwhelmed with debt and I wasn't eating or paying my bills. He was adamant that I go. I told him, "I can't. I have no money." Still, he pushed: "Chris, you *have* to go." I repeated, "I can't. I have no money."

I had all the reasons in the world for why I couldn't do what I really wanted to do. What I really *needed* to do. At the time, my reasons were good. Lots of people would have agreed with them, especially my family—and while I love them with all my heart and they often have good advice, the people in my family are not entrepreneurs.

I was so angry with Jim, because I felt he just didn't understand how dire my financial situation really was. But he continued to push me. He said, "Chris, to say you can't go because you don't have the money is a limiting belief. It's not real. It's just an excuse." So I told him yet again, "Jim, I have no money." And by that point, I was so mad that I hung up the phone on him, and I didn't talk to him for three months.

But he had started me dreaming, and I was getting ready to wake up rich. I said to myself, "Wait a second. I coach people to move beyond their limiting money issues; it is ridiculous for me to say I don't have the money and to use that as the excuse for not advancing on my dreams." At that point, I started to ask myself better questions, like "Where could I get the money? How could I do this?" That was the beginning of a whole new life. Most people spend their lives justifying why they can't or shouldn't do something instead of just asking themselves how they can. And if you ask better questions, you get better answers. There's no doubt about it.

I called American Express, where my card was already over the limit, but I was able to persuade them to extend my credit a bit. Within 24 hours, I was enrolled in that training class—and when I finished the class, my whole life turned around: I started speaking to groups, which gave me greater exposure to more people. A friend then asked me to co-teach a program on communication and leadership and I was paid $35 thousand for about two and a half weeks of work! Coaching clients started flooding in, more people wanted to see me, and my business started to expand wildly. It was a brand new and thrilling story for me.

But before that, I had bought into the excuse that I had no money and therefore couldn't take the steps to live my entrepreneurial dreams. Jim was a good friend to me during that time, because he pushed me *beyond* that reason or excuse. We all have reasons or excuses in our lives, and they'll hold us back, unless we become aware of them. It's when you think they're the real reason that you have to challenge yourselves. It's when you think your reasons and excuses are *most* real that you've *really* got to challenge yourself.

What do you find yourself saying that prevents you from living your entrepreneurial dreams? Is it that you don't have the money, or the time, or that you have to ask someone else's permission, or that you can't meet your obligations and also follow your dreams? Is it that you can do it, but you just can't do it now? Is it that you don't know how to do it? When you move beyond these reasons and excuses, you'll get the biggest breakthroughs.

Why It Takes Only 2 Minutes to Take Charge of Your Future— and How to Do It

I have always done my best to think, "Regardless of external circumstances, what do I need to do for taking charge of my future?" It doesn't mean I haven't made mistakes. I have. It doesn't mean that there aren't blind spots in my life; there are. It doesn't mean that I don't have even greater levels of transformation on the horizon; we all do. But continuing to focus on taking responsibility—often with the help of good coaches, mentors, and friends like Jim—has allowed me to continually expand my business in greater and more impactful ways. It's allowed me to move from living in that house that was being torn down to a point where at the time of writing this book, **Christopher Howard Training** has become the number one personal development presence in Australia and the United Kingdom. As a result of our taking responsibility for our circumstances, rather than clinging to reasons or excuses that would keep anybody boxed in to mediocrity, we've continually grown at a rapid pace regardless of market conditions.

Now I want you to review what you wrote earlier in this chapter: all the reasons and excuses that were preventing you from achieving your greatest dreams, and the results that you want to produce in your life. Look back over everything that you wrote on that page.

Once you've reviewed everything that you wrote on that page, take two minutes to answer each of the following questions:

What is it costing you in your life right now to hold on to these reasons or excuses?

What has your acceptance of these reasons or excuses cost you in your life up until now?

(continued)

What do they cost you emotionally, what do they cost you spiritually, and what do they cost you financially?

What would be the cost of holding on to these reasons or excuses over another year?

What would be the cost of holding on to these reasons or excuses over three years?

What would be the cost of holding on to these reasons or excuses over five years?

What would be the ultimate cost of holding on to these reasons or excuses in your life?

What would be the benefit if you were to step into your power and release these reasons or excuses today?

Ultimately, how would that improve your life?

What would that get for you or allow you to do?

What is important to you about that?

How committed are you to that outcome?

Fantastic! Now that you have written your answers to those questions, we're ready to continue. Look back to page 100, where you listed the excuses that were preventing you from achieving your dreams. In the spaces that follow, briefly note your excuses one by one, and then write down their opposite. For example, if you said that lack of money was stopping you from achieving your dreams, write the opposite of that old excuse; for example: *"It's never a question of resources, it's a question of resourcefulness. And I'm totally resourceful."* If the old reason was that you didn't have the time, you could write, *"I'm a master of time and space. I create my time. It's born from my thinking."* If you previously wrote, that you didn't have the contacts to be successful, now you can say, *"I'm a master connector. Whatever people connections I need to make, I can do it by reaching out and drawing those people into me."* For every one of the reasons or excuses you wrote before, there is an opposite point of view that you need to embrace.

Find that opposite for each of your excuses and write it down now:

Old excuse

Polar opposite

Old excuse

Polar opposite

Old excuse

(continued)

Polar opposite

Old excuse

Polar opposite

Old excuse

Polar opposite

Old excuse

Polar opposite

As you complete this exercise and look over your responses, keep in mind that the experience of living with no excuses is not something that anyone does alone. The people and places in your life have a huge influence on your thoughts, feelings, and actions. That can be both good and bad.

As you embrace **The New Entrepreneurial Mind,** you will run into dissenters along the way. They're like crabs crawling out of a bucket. One crab crawls out, and all the rest try to pull it back. Even people who love and care about you very much will try to keep you boxed in. They have bought in to the social hypnosis that *you* can't do what you want to do, because they believe *they* can't do what they want to do.

Reality is created by validation. It's your job to surround yourself with people who hold you to a higher standard, like my friend Jim. These are people who anchor you into the reality that you want, rather than the social hypnosis that the rest of the world lives in. Accept your family for who they are, but choose your friends. Surround yourself with others who also embrace **The New Entrepreneurial Mind.**

What to Do If You Want to Be Rich and Don't Want to Work Too Hard

Knowing what it takes to create at the level of super-entrepreneur is essential, but whether you put that knowledge into action is entirely up to you. I've worked with people who say, "I want the finances of Bill Gates, but I don't want to work hard, I just want to work smart." Or, "I want to be rich like Warren Buffett, but with a four-hour work week." That's kind of like saying, "I want six-pack abs, and I want to eat this whole pizza all by myself." Extraordinary people pour an extraordinary amount of energy into what they do, and they produce extraordinary results. Just as these super-entrepreneurs do not use "an unwillingness to work" as an excuse for their lack of success, nor would a desire to work "as little as possible" ever be the goal.

I've met thousands of people all over the world. Whenever I'm working one on one with someone, I am totally committed to helping them actualize their fullest potential, and to assist in this process, I'll listen to the reasons or excuses that underlie the descriptions of their problems. Then I almost always look to reframe them or turn them around. A large part of coaching is assisting entrepreneurs in changing their thinking, in opening up their minds so they say, "Wait a second, maybe that really isn't a problem. I really can go out there and do what I want to do." That sense of inspiration can fuel powerful action. It can awaken you to the fact that your destiny is here for you right now. You just need to seize the moment.

Many people in the world look for an easy way to wealth. They see work as the enemy. Their mantra often is, "You don't have to work *hard*; you just have to work *smart*." Actually, you have to do both. I guarantee you, the smart workers are channeling their hard work in a smart way that allows them to become super-successful in a financial way. If you could get considerable results in a "four-hour workweek," what do you think you could get in 50 or 60 hours?

Richard Branson puts it brilliantly when he says, "I don't think of work as work and play as play; to me, it's all living." I've also heard people say, "I've never worked a day in my life, because I love what I do so much." When you're following your heart's purpose and channeling your energies in the right way, then you're playfully creating your own success. This is when you can really begin to embrace the artistry of living. If you can play at becoming successful and if you can enjoy the game, that's when you get real magic. That's when you get *Instant Wealth*.

In my own life, almost every job I had felt like play to me. There were only a couple of jobs that I took over the years when I was working just for the money. I worked at Pizza Hut when I was a teen, and I worked as a landscaper for one whole day. I had a lot of odd jobs when I was young. I was always interested in working because I always wanted to have my own money. But I still tried to plug myself into fun jobs. For example, I remember working at a movie theater as a projectionist, and I loved that job because I was being paid to see all the movies.

Working in hotel resorts for several years was an amazing experience because I traveled all over the world, meeting different people and experiencing different cultures. My biggest worries during that time were what was for dinner that night. That job was truly a *lifestyle*, and I think that's where I first got the idea that I could connect a particular lifestyle with my entrepreneurial path. I have always pursued my passions, I have always pursued my dreams, and I have loved every minute of it. That doesn't mean I haven't had hard times or challenging times, but for the most part, I've just had a blast in everything I've done, and that's what has allowed me to create financial success and to stay on my entrepreneurial path. I could never imagine working at something that I hated or going into a job just to make money or working from nine to five. When I tried that in a couple of circumstances, I didn't last long.

A real entrepreneur is somebody who has no safety net underneath them.
—**Henry Kravis, financier and investor**

What Everybody Must Know—Including You—About Creating a Life of Untold Riches and Wealth

If you are committed to your dreams and you are committed to embracing **The New Entrepreneurial Mind** so you can obtain *Instant Wealth*, you must take hands-on responsibility for your finances. Oprah Winfrey signs every check that goes out from her company. She understands the importance of the total responsibility and accountability for the lifeblood of the business and the lifeblood of the dream. People often try to deflect responsibility for their finances to others because they just don't want to deal with it personally. But what happens if those others don't manage your money well? In that case, is there still someone else to blame? If you get 20 or 30 years into the future and you don't have the financial success you desired, having someone to blame doesn't help much.

All of this is especially important for those who are relatively recent arrivals to the entrepreneurial lifestyle, such as new arrivals in this country, young people, and women. In the past, many women gave up their power by letting men in their lives take responsibility for their finances. That choice often had disastrous results.

I remember a woman who came to one of my **Billionaire Boot Camp** classes, where we teach participants how to expand their entrepreneurial minds and their wealth. I usually ask people about their goals for attending the class, and this woman—who, by the way, I now consider a friend—replied, "I want to get really, really rich." So I then asked, "Okay. How do you plan to do that?" She admitted, "I don't know. Somehow, money will just come to me, or I'll marry a rich guy."

I was a bit taken aback by her viewpoint. First, she was taking zero responsibility for achieving her own goals—but there was also the fact that she had come to the class with her boyfriend who had never made a lot of money. I soon found out that she was hoping to manipulate her boyfriend into changing who he was, so that he would go make the money she wanted him to make so that she would not have to work and could live what she called "the good life."

I've seen many variations of this same scenario, in which one person wants to change another. It's not always an issue of gender. I've met men who want their wives to support them; I've met adults who want their parents to support them; I've met parents who want their children to support them. But the problem is always the same: that approach to life puts 100 percent of the power to live your dreams in someone else's hands.

So I told this woman, "You have to take responsibility for your *own* finances if you're serious about being rich. I can tell you this right now: Money is not going to simply come to you. You have to *do* something. If you want to marry a rich guy, that's your prerogative. Maybe you need relationship coaching instead of wealth-building coaching right now, though I think that money is probably the wrong reason to marry someone. Still, if you want to marry someone who's well off, then you're in the wrong relationship. On the other hand, if you look at the wealth of the man you want to find as being a product of his *ambition*, and you really value ambition in the person you want to be with, I can respect that. But you still have to make a choice: Are you going to take your financial success into your own hands, or are you not going to do that?"

She said she understood what I was explaining to her. But I know when someone is actually understanding something or just listening without really hearing. I could see that she hadn't really owned the reality that she needed to wake up to. During that week, however, she began to change the way she viewed the situation and even how she had lived her entire life up until that point. At the end of the course, she came up to me and said, "You know what? I've never taken responsibility for my own money before. I've always been taken care of—not well taken care of, but I've always waited for a man to handle things for me."

She later wrote to tell me that she had just launched her own business. She had embraced a whole new level of commitment to taking responsibility for her own financial success. She really did love the man she was with and wanted to stay with him, *and* she was committed to living a better quality of life through her own efforts. She was no longer saying to her boyfriend, "*You* have to go out and do this." Instead, she was stepping up and saying, "I'm going to do this. I'm going to take charge of *my own life.*" Even in marriage you need to take responsibility for your own finances. It's fine if there's a joint account, but you have to take responsibility for knowing where you would be if, God forbid, something were to happen to the relationship.

There are three things you don't want to leave in the hands of somebody else: your health, your finances, and your children.

An Overlooked Money Idea Rich People Never Make a Priority

There have been times in my life when I haven't taken full financial responsibility. At one point in my business, the financials were outside my awareness. I wasn't taking responsibility for understanding our cash flow. We had a financial team and a CFO, so I left all responsibility to them. Since I was the CEO, and I was on the road teaching, I assumed they would handle our finances. But as CEO, I still needed to know what was happening, and I finally realized I was too much out of touch; I didn't have my finger on the pulse of the organization. That got us into trouble a few times, and I had to raise money when we were under tight time constraints because we needed it quickly.

Always raise money *before* you need it, so that you are continually in a position of strength. I wasn't taking enough responsibility for knowing exactly where we were, and that weakened my ability to go out and grow the business as effectively as I could. I woke up to that, and I shifted my thinking to, "Well, I'm the one who's growing this business, so I have to take 100 percent responsibility."

The moment that I made that shift in my thinking, I started throwing myself into the financials. I wanted to know exactly where we were. I asked better questions. I made myself able to anticipate well in advance what our cash flow needs were going to be. That changed my entire way of looking at the business, and transformed my ability to grow the business effectively. As a result, I've become a much more mature business person.

Understanding your business's financials is one of your most important responsibilities as an entrepreneur. Do you want to take greater responsibility for your finances in your business and your life? If so, what can you do right now to reclaim your power?

The 7-Day Process that Eliminates All Obstacles and Negatives From Your Past

Before I launched **The Christopher Howard Companies** and **Christopher Howard Training**, I had been working for several other seminar companies. When it came time to leave them, I immediately called Bob Shearin, my current business partner, to talk over what I might do after leaving my old job. Bob was married to a close friend of mine and he was the most successful entrepreneur I personally knew. I explained to him that I had to make a shift in my life and I laid out the possibilities before me: I might teach for other companies while I took the time to write a book, or I might launch a business—which seemed like a huge commitment and a lot of work. I was waffling a bit. I really didn't know what to do.

Bob's response to my indecision was very interesting. He didn't try to talk me into starting my own business. He knew I would have to come to that decision completely on my own, because you can't launch an entrepreneurial venture half-heartedly. He considered, unbeknownst to me, investing a small amount of money in my business to get it started, but he wasn't going to do that unless I proved that I was a self-starter.

After chatting with Bob and thinking about it a bit, I called again and I told him that I had totally committed to striking it out on my own. I was going to be launching this business. At that point, he agreed that if I put some money into it—if I had some skin in the game—he would also invest. That's how Bob became my partner. But it never would have happened if I hadn't taken responsibility and made the decision on my own to start the business without knowing whether I would have any help from anyone else.

I had to be a self-starter committed to success, and take to-tal responsibility for that success. So do you. I didn't have anybody nudging me along, or trying to talk me into starting a business or helping to motivate me. The motivation and commitment had to come from within me. Likewise, your motivation must come from within you!

So here's your assignment. For the next seven nights, you're going to program yourself at the subconscious level to move beyond the reasons or excuses of the past. I call this *Subconscious Reprogramming*.

I've taught clinical hypnosis, Ericksonian hypnosis, and **Subconscious Reprogramming** for years. In fact, I've created the largest company in the world for teaching these techniques. **Subconscious Reprogramming** really boils down to just one thing. You have a conscious mind, and you have an unconscious mind. What separates the conscious mind from the unconscious mind is what we call the critical faculty. As we discussed in an earlier chapter, before the age of approximately nine years, you're in what's called the imprint period. Like a sponge, your neurology is just soaking in the beliefs and the values of your parents and other important people in your life.

After this age, you develop a critical faculty that distinguishes fantasy from reality. This is the part of you that says, "Yes, I buy that" or, "No, I don't buy that." It's a good thing. When I was a kid, for example, I thought I could fly and so I jumped off a two-story building. But when the critical faculty began to develop in me, I stopped jumping off of buildings.

However, the critical faculty can also assert itself in ways that are self-limiting. You may say to yourself, *"Yes, I can do this"*—and your critical faculty says, *"No you can't."* You may say, *"Yes, I can find the money to make my dreams happen."* The critical faculty says, *"I don't buy it."*

Have you ever had those dialogues within yourself? Fortunately, there's an easy, effective, and efficient way to reprogram your subconscious mind so the critical faculty doesn't intrude on your positive intentions. Once you've done this, a positive self-suggestion will go straight to your subconscious mind. That way, you'll be able to align your conscious intentions with your unconscious resources. You gain power in your life when you give direct commands to your subconscious and you follow through. All you have to do is *suspend disbelief.* **Subconscious Reprogramming** is basically *just imagining and pretending.* Here's a very brief overview of the process.

First, you will close your eyes. Then you'll to try to open your eyes and find that you cannot. What does that mean? You'll simply close your eyes and pretend that you cannot open them. You'll try, but find that you can't. Your eyes will remain closed because you're pretending that you can't open them. As you do that, you're automatically in a state of suspended disbelief—that is, in the hypnotic state.

I taught hypnosis for years, and during that time, I would tell the story I learned from hypnotist Dave Elman. What Elman found was that if he would put the children who were afraid of getting vaccinations in this imaginary state—the state of suspended disbelief—it would be very simple. He would just say, "Close your eyes and pretend you can't open them." The child, just playing, would close his eyes and pretend he couldn't open them. Essentially, they were getting rid of the critical faculty instantly. At this point, Elman would give them direct suggestions. He'd say, "Now you may feel me working but this won't bother you." He would then give them a shot, poke them, stitch them, whatever he had to do; the children wouldn't feel a thing. Why? Because when they were in that state of suspended disbelief, they had gotten rid of the critical faculty at the moment he gave them the suggestion.

For the next week, before you go to sleep, I want you to devote seven minutes to this exercise. Seven nights, seven minutes, as follows:

Sit in a quiet place.
Close your eyes and pretend you can't open them.
Try to open them and find that you can't.

You will then give yourself what I call direct commands from the conscious mind to the subconscious mind. You should prepare these commands in advance. You may want to look back to the exercise in which you wrote down the polar opposites of the old excuses that were preventing you from achieving your goals.

You're going to just tell yourself all the things you need to know. For instance: "*I have all the resources in the world. . . . I'm master of my time and space. I create my own time—it's born from my thinking. . . . I'm responsible for my success. . . . I have all the resources in the whole universe at my disposal.*"

You may want to address yourself in the second person, which is my own preference: "You are totally powerful. . . . You have all the resources in the known universe at your disposal."

Bear in mind that the magic number in any suggestion is three. So when you give yourself a suggestion, phrase it three times in three different ways. In this way, it will enter your subconscious mind much more deeply.

For example, you might say, *"You have all the resources in the known universe at your disposal. You're totally resourceful. You realize that success is never a question of resources. It's always a question of resourcefulness. You're totally resourceful and you have all the resources at your disposal. It's born from your will."* Layer the suggestion in multiple ways.

When giving yourself suggestions, it's important to focus on the positive end point. You wouldn't want to say, *"I have no fear."* Instead, use a positive phrasing: *"I am totally confident. I can do this. I can achieve my dreams easily and effortlessly."* Say it the way you want it. That's imperative!

You can also access what I call *end-result imagery*. This is not a requirement, but it adds a lot of power to the process. End-result imagery is done by visualizing what you will ultimately create as a result of your acceptance of your self-suggestions. This visualization can be done before and after the direct suggestions, or interspersed among them.

The whole exercise is easy. Here's a quick summary:

- Close your eyes and pretend you can't open them.
- Try to open them and find that you can't.
- Stay in that state of suspended disbelief and begin to layer in your positive self-suggestions.
- *You may choose* to intersperse these direct suggestions with end-result imagery.
- Then go to sleep and enjoy the results!

The Unusual Wealth Secret that Works Faster than Anything Else You've Ever Been Told

Warren Buffett was once asked, "What does somebody have to do to be really rich?" He answered, "Invest in your own education, number one." Time and time again, hugely successful people are those who have done exactly that. It doesn't have to be traditional education. In fact, in the 2008 *Forbes* list of billionaires, 73 of them had not completed traditional schooling. Li Ka-Shing, Hong Kong's richest person (worth over $26 billion today) dropped out of school at age 12, and began selling plastic flowers. And as is well known, Bill Gates dropped out of Harvard to launch Microsoft.

There are three things you can do with your time. You can waste it. You can sell it. Or (by far the best choice) you can invest your time, and that means you never take a job just for the pay. Work because you have a dream, and because you're committed to your dream. Or take a job because it adds to your skills. One way or another, work should be an investment in yourself.

Most successful entrepreneurs don't come from inherited wealth. Most don't come from poverty either. They usually came from middle-class families and build on the work of previous generations. Most of them, however, deeply believe in educating themselves in a variety of ways. Hugely successful people enhance their ability to succeed by getting out there and just start *doing*. But they're rapidly learning at the same time, by seeking out mentors, guides, and sources of inspiration from the marketplace.

Do you live by the philosophy that *you* are your best investment? What extraordinary investments have you made in yourself and your education that have caused you to produce spectacular entrepreneurial results? What specific results have you produced as a result of your investments in yourself?

The Only Investment Guaranteed to Make You Money

Would you be willing to invest 10,000 hours in yourself? In his book titled *Outliers*, Malcolm Gladwell writes, "Ten thousand hours is the magic number of greatness." Gladwell refers to a study performed in the 1990s by psychologist K. Anders Ericsson and two of his colleagues at Berlin's Academy of Music. They gathered the school's violinists and divided them into three groups:

1. Those with amateur talent
2. Those considered to be merely good
3. Those with expert abilities

Among these three groups, the difference proved to be the amount of time spent in solitary practice in the course of their skill development. The amateur group totaled around 2,000 hours of practice by the age of 20. Group two, the good violinists, averaged around 5,000 hours by the age of 20. Group three, the group with the ability to be concert violinists, totaled around 10,000 hours by age 20. The level of performance they had attained was closely linked to the amount of practice accumulated.

Along the same lines, neurologist Daniel Levitin states, "In study after study—of composers, basketball players, fiction writers, ice skaters, concert pianists, and chess players—this number comes up again and again. Of course, this doesn't address why some people get more out of their practice sessions than others do. But no one has yet found a case in which true world-class expertise was accomplished in less time. It seems that it takes the brain this long to assimilate all that it needs to know to achieve true mastery."

But 10,000 hours is an enormous amount of time. In most cases it would take about 10 years to accomplish. You may not want to become a concert pianist, basketball player, or a fiction writer—so how does this apply to your entrepreneurial dreams?

Consider this: To be able to play a violin—not necessarily well, but to even get a sound out of it—you must know several things: for example, how to hold the violin, how to position your hands, and what amount of force you'll need to make a sound. Each element, regardless of how small, needs to be learned through spending time practicing before you can play well.

Now relate this to all the smaller but still important elements that make up your entrepreneurial dream. No matter what your dream is, time would be definitely well spent attending classes or seminars or in an apprenticeship in which you can model successful people, read, and study the many aspects that make up your entrepreneurial intention. Every hour will lead you closer to the 10,000 hours it takes to have the expertise in your field that would allow you to live your entrepreneurial dreams to the full.

For example, even after earning $87 million in one year and ranking fourth on *Forbes* magazine's list of 100 celebrity top income earners, Beyonce Knowles still spends tireless hours practicing. She believes in "repetition, repetition, repetition." While on tour, after every performance she spends two hours reviewing the tapes from the show, even when she's performed it 100 times, in an effort to constantly improve herself and her performance. She says, "I'm never satisfied."

Beyonce is an inspiring example of someone who is committed to making it and falling in love with the process (way beyond her 10,000 hours), while at the same time remaining humble: "Like everyone else, you work really hard and you want it to be great; you want your friends to like it. What makes me comfortable is practice and knowing I'm prepared. But I still get nervous!"

This Amazing Secret Will Shortcut Your Path to Wealth

One of the best ways to rapidly study and assimilate the highest quality learnings, and to insure that your 10,000 hours are played at the greatest level of perfection, is through mentoring. By connecting with someone who has already awakened to great riches, your own eyes will be opened too.

When Warren Buffett was starting out, he wanted Benjamin Graham as his mentor. Graham wrote *The Intelligent Investor* and is considered to be the founder of value investing. Buffett, who was Graham's student at Columbia, made a proposal he thought Graham couldn't refuse: "I told him I'd go work for him for free. And Ben Graham, being the very intelligent man that he is, did a quick cost-benefit analysis on the proposal I was making, and decided to turn me down."

Eventually, Ben Graham did ask Warren to come work with him, so Warren did get some real-life education. Warren learned Graham's investment style forward and backward before going out on his own and launching his first investment partnership. He learned an enormous amount from Graham, yet he began to formulate his own ideas about how to apply Graham's philosophies even more effectively. Buffet's philosophies continued to evolve as he sought out more mentors and found other sources of inspiration such as Phil Fisher, author of the book *Common Stocks, Uncommon Profits.*

It's vital to continually seek out those mentors who will help you take the next giant leap forward.

I once hired a publicist who, when we first started working together, asked me, "Chris, who do you want to bring into your life this year?" We made a list of 20 people. Within six months I had gotten to know 10 of them. In fact, six of the people on that list became great personal friends.

My publicist was a fantastic networker. He called everybody he knew and said, "Who do you know who knows this person?" Or, "Who do you know who might know someone who knows this person?" He called and called and called. That's how I met Richard Branson. Within six months of putting him on my list of people I wanted to meet and get to know, I had met Richard, I had spent some time with him, and I was even going to South Africa to do work with some of his philanthropic interests.

Among many others within that same six-month period I met Mark Victor Hansen (who had also appeared on my list), co-creator of the *Chicken Soup for the Soul* books, which have sold more than 150 million copies. Because of the relationship I was able to forge with both him and Robert Allen, co-author of *The One-Minute Millionaire*, both of them helped me to prepare this book. Today, they are both close personal friends.

Unfortunately, most people never create a networking target list. You need to do that before you can hope to make any progress toward finding a mentor. And when you find the right mentors, you can truly tap into *Instant Wealth*.

The "Magic" Question that Compels Rich People to Be Your Mentor

After creating your list of names, a second key step is correctly approaching a possible mentor. The worst thing you could say is, "Will you be my mentor?" That's like going on a first date and saying, "Will you marry me?" It's just too big a bite. Just start with something simple, like, "May I ask you a question?"

That's exactly the approach I took with Richard Branson over the course of a few days I spent with him on Necker Island, his private resort. I asked, "May I ask you a question? How do you do this? How do you do that? How do you manage this company? How do you handle stress?" He joked, "The next time we meet, I'm going be asking you these same questions." But by the end of my stay, I felt like I had really learned so much. Soon after I was going off across the globe to explore how **Christopher Howard Training** might work with the Branson School for Entrepreneurship so it could help eradicate poverty in South Africa.

Once you've met someone on your target list and established a preliminary relationship, the best way to proceed is "easy does it." You might ask, "Would you mind taking a look at this business plan?" If you develop the relationship correctly, the individual may become interested in helping you. Moreover, if you're taking the person's advice and showing that you're a quick study of the advice you're getting, your new contact may invest in your work, or even become a partner.

That's exactly what happened with my current business partner. When I launched my company, I had good skills in several areas. I had been doing training and development at various companies. I was a teacher of neuro linguistic programming (NLP) and clinical hypnosis across North America for some of the biggest companies in the world, and I was working for Dale Carnegie Training at the same time. But I had no background in business whatsoever. Before I could start a company that would take advantage of all my skills and experience, I needed someone who knew something about business.

As previously mentioned, I started an extensive study of billionaires, using our unique methodology of breaking down their values, their belief systems, and the way they make decisions. Then I used hypnosis to instill all of these ideas in myself, to expand my mind and create *Instant Wealth*. I found that I was suddenly thinking like a business owner. But I still didn't have any real-world, practical experience of running a company.

The richest man in my life when I was growing up wasn't someone I knew personally, but my parents knew his wife. We went to an occasional Christmas party at their beautiful home in Manhattan Beach, California. One day, I was at my parents' house when this very wealthy woman was visiting. When I mentioned my potential plans for creating a million-dollar business, she said, "You should talk to my husband." I was surprised that she said this, because for years I had never really spoken to him directly. I had the impression that he was a standoffish guy who didn't talk to anybody. But his wife said, "Let me set you up to meet with Bob."

I mentioned Bob Shearin earlier. Bob, who got his MBA from Harvard when I was just four years old, built a $70 million wholesale clothing business. He's now semi-retired, though he still has multiple investments. Bob had a wealth of experience that came from his years of experience in the realm of business. Bob didn't try to encourage or discourage me about launching a business. He simply said, "What do you want to do?" Then he helped me think it through and gave me a bit of coaching. He told me I absolutely needed a business plan.

As I followed all of Bob's suggestions, I realized I was in a mentoring relationship without even knowing it. Then Bob said, "I'm not going to put any money into your business unless you have some skin in the game." He told me I would need $5,000. At the time I didn't have a dime to my name. I went into a austerity mode to come up with the money. I rationed myself to $2 a day for food; McDonald's had a special of three burgers for $2, and that's all I ate. I lived in a cheap, rundown apartment to save up for the magic $5,000 figure.

Eventually, we made it. Bob invested a small amount of money, and we launched **Christopher Howard Training**. In the early days, I primarily trained coaches, educators, and therapists in tools for accelerating human transformation. Since then, knowing and working with Bob has been the best thing in the world for me. When he came on board, I had no business acumen at all. I had to learn the language of business and how to communicate with business people. Bob really helped me out along the way. He had a lifetime of experience that I didn't have. If you don't have business expertise, yet you're committed to growing your entrepreneurial dreams, it's absolutely essential, in my opinion, to bring in a mentor like Bob. You just need to find that person and enroll him in your vision!

I've seen so many entrepreneurs fail because they just didn't know how to run a business; they didn't have the experience. If you don't have that, you can borrow somebody else's experience if you bring them in. That's what I did when I partnered with Bob Shearin, and we've been together now for nine years. I can say without a doubt that I would not be in business today had it not been for his presence in my life. I'm infinitely grateful for that.

Tom Kiblin was another mentor who had a big impact on my life. Tom owned a Dale Carnegie franchise in Southern California, and was my boss for a year. He taught me so much from a leadership perspective. He had a heart of gold and the ability to champion people, to see the best in them, to bring out the best in them, and he did that for me. Tom passed away in 2007, and it really shook my world when I heard that, because he was truly a great man. And in part, this book is dedicated to Tom. There are a few people in my life who have helped me so much that I wouldn't be where I am today without them, and Tom is one of them.

Sir Isaac Newton said, "If I have seen further it is because I stand on the shoulders of giants." I'm infinitely grateful for everybody who has made an impact on my thinking and on developing our business and helping others to wake up rich.

How to Accelerate the Wealth You Create to a Fraction of the Time

Conversations with high performing men and women are some of the best ways to rapidly learn and elevate the level of your game.

In *Think and Grow Rich*, Napoleon Hill introduced the concept of creating "a mastermind alliance"—a small group of mentors who can help you elevate your game. I've worked at that over the years. Bob Shearin has been my most important mentor, but I've had many others as well.

For example, I was doing relationship coaching with a woman named Joanne Mednick, whom I really adore. I was talking with Joanne almost every day, and she often mentioned her husband. His name wasn't familiar to me, but I eventually learned that her husband, Scott Mednick, was a producer of many films, including *300*, *Superman Returns*, and *10,000 B.C.* Scott's attitude is "any friend of Joanne is a friend of mine"—so we met to talk one day, and we started thinking about how I could raise money, how I could build my brand, and how I could grow my business in various ways.

Many entrepreneurs want to launch huge dreams, but Scott had actually done it. He was a co-founder of Legendary Pictures, where they raised $500 million to launch. This was something I needed to learn about, so I asked for insight and advice.

Having the right mentors is the key to learning anything you need to make your entrepreneurial dreams come true.

Scott told me, "Chris, raising money is just like pitching a movie. If I'm going to pitch a movie with two unknowns as the stars, nobody's going to care about that. But if I've got an all-star cast, with Tom Cruise and Angelina Jolie, and if we've got Steven Spielberg attached to it, then all of a sudden it's easy. You've got to have a team worth betting on. Your proposition has to be very attractive to investors. If you don't have all of the necessary elements, then all you need to do is assemble your cast or bring in team members who do have the elements that will give you the credibility you need."

Finally I asked Scott, "Have you ever bootstrapped a business before?"—meaning picking yourself up by the bootstraps, using credit cards and personal loans, refinancing your house, and doing everything you can to raise cash. He said, "Most of us have done that at one time. It's an incredibly valuable learning experience." But when I asked if he would ever do it again, he said, "Never. Not knowing what I now know today."

My Gift to You!
For an incredible online source of mentors so that you can develop a master mind alliance including people like Scott Mednick, go to: www.thementorscircle.com and accelerate your success a thousandfold!

Scott helped to change my thinking immensely in terms of how I would go about growing many projects. Spending time with him supercharged every one of my 10,000 hours. My meeting with Scott Mednick was a case of "luck is preparation meeting opportunity." I had been preparing all my life to ask the right kinds of questions, and to ease my way into a relationship without overstepping the boundaries. Scott is a great mentor and a dear friend, and he's helped me out tremendously by accelerating my business education and growth.

I have many more such friends. Rorion Gracie, and all the Gracie family, who are my martial arts instructors, are incredible mentors to me—not just about business, but also about life. The lessons I get in jujitsu about how to be relaxed, how to breathe, and how to go the distance, are all things everyone needs to know. So many stressed-out business owners fail because they don't have those understandings.

Those who are learning will inherit the earth, while those who have learned will be very well equipped for a world that no longer exists.

How to Go from the Bottom of the Ladder Straight to the Top

If I had not worked in the office at Dale Carnegie Training and with other personal development companies, I would never have had the skills, the strategies, or the entrepreneurial mindset to wake up rich. Even with a great partner, there are things specific to my industry that I just wouldn't have been able to do in launching my business. By learning as an apprentice—humbly working alongside the master—I was able to learn all those skills and drive forward to *instant wealth*.

Many hugely successful people have not been afraid to go to work for somebody else. In the film business, David Geffen and Barry Diller are just two of the many leaders who began their careers that way. Unfortunately, other people say, "Well, I'm too good for that. I don't need to learn anything from anyone else, no matter how successful they are. I'm just going to go out and launch my own thing." I know I have taken several jobs in the past simply for the skill sets that I would learn, because I knew those skills would help me fulfill my dreams. I live by the philosophy that you should never work for what you make; instead, you should work for who you become.

At Dale Carnegie Training, I completed every class the company offered multiple times. After I took those classes, I started assisting in them. One class was about how to give high-impact presentations, and it included a video critique of each person in the class. I asked if I could be the videographer and videotape every presentation. Being on the front row inside the experience really helped me in my own presentations.

Ask yourself, "What's the most important thing for a business owner to have?" I think it's core knowledge and the experience of working your way up. Many very successful people make their children learn the business from the ground up. Tony Robbins's son Jairek, whom I consider a friend, is working his way up through Tony's organization right now. Tony wants Jairek to learn every skill from the ground up.

The Best Place to Enhance Your Knowledge and Skills

Billionaire Mark Cuban—owner of the Dallas Mavericks, chairman of HDNet and HDTV Cable Networks, Internet entrepreneur and investor—got his learning on the job. His first job was as a salesperson for a PC software retailer. Less than a year later, Cuban was finalizing a large software purchase with a customer but was unable to open the store on time. He subsequently got fired. He took what he learned from that company and decided to start his own venture, calling it Micro Solutions. He used some of his previous company's customers to get the ball rolling and ended up selling Micro Solutions to CompuServe for $6 million. It was the on-the-job training he received at his first job that prepared him for the creation of his own company.

Here's another example. My friend Keith Cunningham began his career in cable TV. Keith's job was to raise money for his employers. Over the years, he watched and learned from people who knew how to find investors, and eventually learned how to raise hundreds of millions of dollars. Then he took those skills into a completely different field—real estate. This was in Texas in the late 1980s. Keith built a real estate empire worth hundreds of millions of dollars. Later, when the bottom fell out of the Texas real estate market, he lost the money. It took some time for him to amass a fortune again, but because he had learned how to work the phones, he had the ability to recover.

Money may come and go, but skills remain.

How to Be a Financial Empire in Your Spare Time— Even If You Have a Full-Time Job

My friend Loral Langemeier, a teacher of cash creation, uses the term *straddle move* to describe the concept of doing two things at once. Someone will say, "I want to go out and live my entrepreneurial dreams, but I've got to put food on the table. How can I do that?" This is when you apply a straddle move. You have to create the cash flow to keep yourself alive, but you can simultaneously find a way to bridge the gap between where you are and where you want to go with your entrepreneurial dream. A straddle move is the equivalent of going into a job in which you're not working for what you make but you're working for who you become. It's making a choice to go in and learn a specific skill set while also receiving a salary.

For example, a friend wanted to launch a motivational television network, but he knew nothing about TV. I said, "Jon, you need to take a job doing anything inside that industry. If you have the skill set to get a high-paying job within an organization, then go for it. But if you don't, you might have to start from the bottom and work your way up. Do that even if you have to take a low-level job to learn about that new business and that new industry that you want to get into."

Jon took that advice and got a job with a television company as a production assistant. He learned many valuable skills in that job, including how to network effectively. He even decided not to pursue his original goal, and used his new networking skills to make a sharp-angled turn in his career. He now helps wealthy people make large acquisitions, such as yachts. He has become a kind of executive concierge. He's happier than ever before, and he realizes that he wouldn't be where he is today if it weren't for a straddle move to get him out of what he was doing and into something he enjoys more and that is much more aligned with his heart's purpose.

When I worked for Dale Carnegie Training, I made only $12,000 a year and I spent 90 percent of my time at that job. However, I was very fortunate to get a paycheck for education that I use daily. Even though I had very little time of my own, I got some supplemental money from coaching. I worked eight or nine hours a day at Dale Carnegie, came home, went for a jog, and had 14 more hours to continue to build my entrepreneurial dreams. I built my coaching practice while simultaneously working for Dale Carnegie.

I didn't skimp on my work at Dale Carnegie. They deserved every minute of my time during the workday, and they deserved an incredible job. I did my very best for them. I was determined to underpromise and overdeliver. I'm sure that eventually I could have built a pretty big business with them, if I had stayed on. But that wasn't my dream; my dream was to go out on my own.

If you choose to make a straddle move and go to work for someone, who you choose is very important. If possible, target top players in your selected field. Learn from the best. It's been said that practice makes perfect. Practice does not make perfect. Perfect practice makes permanent. When you're training with the best, then you're practicing at a greater level of perfection. When you can put in your 10,000 hours while practicing at the highest level of perfection, you can rule the world!

Take a moment to list the top five people in your field with whom you could do an apprenticeship. If you're very acclimated in your business, maybe it doesn't apply to you, but if you are starting out, this exercise is invaluable.

1. _____
   _____

2. _____
   _____

3. _____
   _____

4. _____
   _____

5. _____
   _____

When you think like the super-wealthy think, you'll take the actions that wealthy people take. I call this **Cognitive Reimprinting**. When you take the actions that wealthy people take, you'll produce the results that wealthy people produce. There is no way around that. You just need to model people who are successful in your business or career. Of course, you'll bring your unique talents and skills to what you do, but you can be inspired and motivated and educated by those people—if you just open yourself up to the possibilities.

A great way to begin is to start reading the biographies of the people you want to study. Also, subscribe to The Biography Channel on TV and watch the stories of successful people shown there.

Our **Billionaire Boot Camp** event teaches this process in more detail, allowing participants to understand on a much deeper level and enabling them to accelerate the results.

The Best Place to Get a Free Education in Real World Money Secrets

Beyond educating yourself and finding mentors, you must also be committed to learning from the marketplace. Sam Walton firmly believed this was a key to his success. He said: "I spend more time in my competitors' store than I spend in my own" and "I've never had an original idea in my life." You can learn a lot by looking around at what other successful people are doing.

I've learned so much from the marketplace about creating *Instant Wealth*. I saw, for example, how important it can be to give people a low barrier to entry—a taste of what it is they are going to experience from your product or service. Many top players in our field were doing exactly that and I knew I had to jump on the bandwagon. My business partner and I decided to take the risk of offering, for a very limited time, a full scholarship to our **Breakthrough to Success** three-day seminar, which at the time cost $895. Offering scholarships to this program would be an expensive, but great way to introduce new people to our programs. We knew from experience that once a client experienced the transformation in our seminars, that person would have her eyes opened to the tremendous value we deliver. Once most people attended our program, they would inevitably want to continue training with us. The key was getting that person to step up to the plate of transformation in the first place.

Some of my advisers were worried that we would be devaluing our program. They said, "We have competitors in the field that are charging up to ten thousand dollars for the level of value we're delivering. How can we just give it away?!" They suggested just lowering the price by $100 instead of offering a scholarship. But I felt that lowering the price is what would devalue the program. In contrast, we decided to maintain the price—"which is what the seminar was worth"— and simply offer people the opportunity, for a limited time, to a scholarship.

It spread like wildfire! Everybody wanted to share with all their friends the power and the impact that the program had for them in their lives. I was not surprised. From a business perspective, we were doing amazingly well. From the perspective of making a difference, we were transforming lives on a much grander scale. When you come to our **Breakthrough to Success** program, we help you pinpoint everything—at the conscious level and the unconscious level—that's preventing you from getting the results that you want in your life. We help you to break through those conscious and unconscious barriers, with the most cutting-edge, next-generation sciences, processes, and techniques that are currently available. You gain massive propulsion forward. It is a transformational three-day experience that will rock your world. It is unlike anything you've ever experienced. People fly in from all over the world to take this program—business people, CEOs, entrepreneurs, network marketers, artists, people who want to move up the corporate ranks. What they have in common is that they're all people who really want to make their dreams happen.

When we started offering scholarships to friends of graduates based on our awareness of what was happening in the marketplace, our attendance soon increased from 50 people in a seminar and $2 million a year in revenue to up to 4,000 people in a seminar and $22 million in a single year. Our whole business landscape changed by giving more people the opportunity to experience us. After their introduction, they would realize that it was the best investment they ever made and many of them would continue on our Wealth Building Seminar series.

As we expanded, I felt so blessed to be making such a positive impact in the lives of so many people.

Every Virgin company that Richard Branson has launched was directed by the marketplace. Virgin's approach is, "We can provide better value for money, and we'll add our Virgin cheeky sense of humor to it." So, where there's Coca-Cola, it becomes Virgin Cola. Where there's AT&T Mobile, it becomes Virgin Mobile. The company that launched Jet Blue was simply modeling itself after Southwest Airlines. Building on something that's preexisting has always been a smart way of doing business.

The most successful entrepreneurial new businesses are often not the first to market. The first typically face all the difficulties of establishing identity, finding their customers, and proving themselves. Success frequently comes to the companies that follow in the footsteps—and then cleverly outdo their competition. You can do that, too: stop searching for a new idea, if that's what's holding you back from becoming a massive earning machine. Look around instead at what's already successful, and find a way to do that just a little bit better. Oprah Winfrey modeled her show on those of others who were successful before her. She has said she was scared when she first got into radio broadcasting and then later live television, because she had no clue about what to do. So she sat the way Barbara Walters sat. She asked questions like Barbara Walters asked. She said she literally became Barbara Walters, and she got the job by doing that. She modeled herself after Barbara Walters. Barbara Walters was a mentor without even knowing she was being a mentor! Look at what's already out there and build on it. Build on what's already being done.

How to Guarantee Your Success

Things change fast in business. At **Christopher Howard Training**, we make maps of what we plan to do within a three-month time. The maps are a combination of task lists and goal statements. It is a great way to manage the business, because everybody can clearly see what the targets and goals are, and the managers can look at the maps and see who has hit their goals and who hasn't. If someone doesn't make the targets, the manager can ask, "What can I do to support you more in hitting those goals?" or, "What do you need to change in the way you're setting your goals?" It is a great accountability system, because one of the biggest challenges in business is making sure people have the same expectations.

While we've been using that technique in our business, the reality is that our field is changing so quickly that you can lay out your plan, but the next day you realize, "Oh, no, now I've got to do this instead." In this marketplace, with the world changing more rapidly than ever before, sometimes even three months is just too far out to plan. You've got to constantly be in a learning mode, and continually finding new ways to do business as things change.

Arnold Schwarzenegger has said, "The secret of my success is finding a mentor, and passing him up. Find another one, pass him up. Find another one, pass him up." By "pass him up," he means learning as much as he can from each person and then going to the next level.

That may sound cold and calculating, but the skills and strategies that you need tomorrow will be different from the ones that you need today. That's why I ask myself every year, "What are the six skills and strategies that I need this year to guarantee my success?"

Ask yourself the question: "What six skills do I need to be exquisite at this year—which, if I were exquisite at them, would guarantee my success?" Then set out to master those skills.

I've always sought out opportunities for learning, and you should too. I took my first transcendental meditation class when I was just nine years old; I got involved in martial arts at the age of 11, and I've practiced them all my life; I took my first clinical hypnosis class when I was 12 years old. When I worked in the hotel resort industry right out of high school, I was very grateful to have a job in which I could connect with people from all over the world. I learned to speak French fluently during that time, and I also learned how to speak with a microphone on stage. I promised myself during the entire six years that I worked in beautiful resorts around the world that I would improve myself and become better at my job every single day.

But don't stop with your own success. The way to keep the gift of education is to give it away. You really learn and know what's necessary to succeed when you can help develop those same qualities in other people. Find ways to help others after you have become successful. Oprah Winfrey has given more than 50 million dollars of her own money to educate children, women, and families. She opened a youth center in her Mississippi hometown. She founded Oprah's Angel Network, through which members of her TV audience get fully funded scholarships.

Yet Oprah has said that her donations are still not enough. "I don't think you ever stop giving. I think it's an ongoing process. And it's not just about being able to write a check. It's being able to touch somebody's life. It's being able to make people see the light in themselves."

You're either the best at what you do or you don't do it for very long.

—Jack Welch,
former CEO of General Electric

How to Be a Leader and Communicator Others Turn to for Inspiration

In my line of work, communication is definitely the most important skill, but I believe all success is really about communication. Martin Luther King Jr. had the ability to rally the nation. Gandhi was also a master communicator, reaching people not only with his words but also by the example he set.

On a smaller scale, communication includes your ability to put a deal together. Most hugely successful people are superb salespeople. They're able to pitch a deal and get people to join in. Scott Mednick told me, "I went out with people who were pitching deals. I listened to them and I got good at pitching. Then, I just got out there and had the courage to start doing the same thing. I screwed up a lot of times, but gradually I got really, really good."

Learning the art of communication and effective selling aren't the only important skills many successful visionaries focus on. I set new goals for myself every year, and, this year, my goal was to become an even more connected leader. This goal is not about salesmanship or communication. It has to do with being fully present. When I was on Richard Branson's island, I noticed how fully Richard connects with people. He looks you in the eyes when he's talking with you. He owns hundreds of companies, yet he was completely at ease when we were together. He was totally living in the moment, not distracted by anything else. That's personal magnetism.

Magnetism and charisma are hugely important if you want to have large groups of people moving toward a common objective. Our company employs 40 coaches, six trainers, and we have hundreds of volunteer staff worldwide, all devoted to putting the tools for transformation in the hands of everybody on the planet. To keep in touch with all of them, I do something that I learned from Tom Kiblen, who was my boss at Dale Carnegie. I send out personal handwritten cards on a regular basis as a way to connect with the wonderful people on our team. I feel so blessed and fortunate to have these extraordinary people in my life. It is essential to show the people around you that you care, and it is vital to express your appreciation. You can never overestimate the impact of personal attention and really connecting with the people on your teams.

To close this chapter, here's one more very important managerial principle. To be a good leader, especially if your time is stretched thin, controlling your schedule is paramount. I asked myself, "What courses can I plug myself into? What saturation environments can I find?" Attending a course or being in a saturation environment can compress years of trial and error into a very short time.

Consistent education is a must, and the faster the better.

CHAPTER

How to Never Again Fail: Best Way Ever
Discovered to Come Out a Winner Every Time

Rorion Gracie came to the United States with just $2,000 and a fierce dedication to a dream. He would later be known as the creator of the world's fastest-growing sport—a sport that, back in the 1960s, didn't even exist. This is the classic rags to riches story, but with a twist. . . .

Rorion grew up in Brazil with a famous family name—but it was not his name that protected him from the tough streets of Brazil. It was his mastery of the family's highly developed style of Jiu Jitsu. The streets of Rio de Janeiro were like the Wild West; not to mention that in a family of 21 children (mostly boys), there was always someone bigger and tougher challenging him.

The Gracie family was legendary in Brazil for the fighting art created by Rorion's father, Grandmaster Helio Gracie. Helio had developed an adaptation of samurai Ju Jitsu geared for modern day street application, and specifically designed as a system of self-defense for people who were smaller than their attackers. Rorion became the perfect expression of his father's fighting philosophies.

Between Rorion Gracie's charismatic demeanor and movie star good looks (*Playboy* magazine once called him "the toughest man in the United States" and also likened him to a "Brazilian Tom Selleck"), he had always seemed destined for Hollywood rather than the streets of Brazil. And while many people pushed him toward Hollywood and the film industry, Rorion's true passion was teaching "the truth" about self-defense and saving lives.

How a Virtually Unknown Brazilian Created the Most Successful Franchise in Pay-Per-View History

Rorion visited the United States for a short time in 1969, and then later moved there to fulfill his dream: to dispel the gospel taught by most martial arts schools, a philosophy that could develop a false sense of confidence in people and put them in harm's way.

The art of Gracie Jiu Jitsu had proven itself time and again in challenge matches against the toughest martial artists in the world, including professional boxers, kick boxers, Olympic-level wrestlers, and the toughest street fighters.

A man of action, Rorion was not deterred by the challenges encountered during his first visit to the United States, during which both his money and return ticket home were stolen. He had to panhandle, sleep under benches, and flip burgers, but his attitude was always "I am willing to do anything, whatever it takes for the sake of my dream." His decision to follow his passion remained guided by his unwavering drive to succeed.

Rorion saved enough money to get back to Brazil, where he decided to put himself through law school. In 1978, he moved to the United States, where he began spreading the teachings of Gracie Jiu Jitsu. He started by offering a free lesson to everyone he met on the street. At that time, martial arts were just coming into their own, gaining popularity with Bruce Lee and James Bond movies. The Gracie style was not flashy; no high kicks, swinging punches, or jumping. The Gracie technique was created from the streets, where you often end up on the ground.

With other techniques, men and women were given a potentially dangerous false sense of confidence that they could defend themselves from attackers with a kick or a karate chop. That's the myth that Rorion was committed to ending. As he points out, "Most of the fights people find themselves in end on the ground"; his form of Jiu Jitsu was created specifically with that in mind, and fueled by his grander purpose to save people's lives, "teaching them to fight, so they wouldn't have to."

Rorion started looking for places where he could teach his technique. To his surprise, there was not much interest. His unwavering commitment drove him to keep knocking on doors and asking martial arts studio owners if he could teach. He often had martial artists challenge him to fights. Just like in Brazil, he would happily oblige. Some of the challengers were among the biggest names in the world of martial arts, but the outcome was always the same: The martial artists tried to devastate Rorion with fancy kicks and punches that Rorion would adeptly avoid before taking them to the ground and gently putting them to sleep with his trademark choke.

Rorion taught Gracie Jiu Jitsu from his garage with the offer that participants who brought another person would get a free class. This grassroots effort caused a real buzz. Finally, after much searching, he was able to find a time slot at the YMCA and, in 1989, finally opened his own facility to teach. It was a small building, a little bigger than his garage. Opening the Gracie Academy was the first step, but Rorion knew in his heart that to realize his dream, he would have to take a huge risk to bring his vision to the entire world.

In the classrooms of the Gracie Academy, Rorian gathered the financial resources necessary to create a showcase tournament. He handed out more than 80 business plans to his students, explaining that the tournament would be a single elimination pay-per-view event. He invited the best martial artists on the planet to fight each other in an "anything goes" match to find out which was the superior form of martial arts—a sort of ultimate fighting championship. These fights would be held in an octagonal cage. There were no gloves, no rules, no weight classes, and no time limits. Rorion believed that this most accurately represented the situation in a real fight. The Ultimate Fighting Championship, or UFC for short, quickly became what *Forbes* later described as "the most successful franchise in pay-per-view history."

How to Achieve Your Grandest Dreams

On November 12, 1993, in Denver, Colorado, the entire world of martial arts was shocked when Gracie Jiu Jitsu triumphed! Rorion chose his smaller, skinnier, younger brother Royce to fight four much larger men in the same night. The diminutive Brazilian stepped into the cage that night, and beat a professional boxer who had a record of 33 wins and 18 losses. The fight lasted only seconds and not even a single punch was landed. As the evening progressed, Royce would quickly dismantle all of the other fighters through tapouts and chokeouts just as easily as his first match. According to Rorion, "Gracie style cleaned their clocks." His one-man campaign to wake the world up to the ineffectiveness of what was being taught in most schools of martial arts had succeeded.

After the first several productions of the Ultimate Fighting Championship, Rorion saw that the regulators were going to turn it more into a sport, with rules, time limits, and gloves, thus changing the entire game. Weight classes took away from Rorion's whole idea of the UFC being a platform to show that with the right technique, smaller fighters could beat larger opponents. The addition of gloves turned it into a sport that had much less to do with real fighting.

Even with these changes, Rorion felt he had achieved a huge success in waking the world up to one thing: that Gracie Jiu Jitsu was absolutely essential for real self-defense. It was inevitable for the UFC to go down the path of becoming more of a sport than an actual proving ground but, by then, Rorion had already made his point. Today it's impossible to train or compete in the Ultimate Fighting Championship unless you're cross-training in Gracie Jiu Jitsu. As a result of the unyielding drive of Rorion Gracie to launch something never before seen in the United States, the UFC brand is today estimated to be worth over a billion dollars, including the pay-per-view events, clothing, video games, and workout equipment.

Sometimes big dreams require big risks.

What Rich People Know About Wealth Everybody Else Does Not

Today, the Gracie name is the most famous name in martial arts since Bruce Lee. The Gracie Jiu Jitsu technique is used by every major federal law enforcement agency and military organization in the United States. Rorion continues to spread the teachings of Gracie Jiu Jitsu with the Gracie Online University, where you can actually train in Gracie Jiu Jitsu from anywhere in the world. Rorion keeps expanding his original vision through his sons, Ryron and Rener Gracie, who continue to carry on the Gracie legacy. Rorion's unwavering courage and his pursuit of his heart's purpose make Gracie a perfect inspirational example of *Instant Wealth* and **The New Entrepreneurial Mind.**

While my school of martial arts is the Gracie Jiu Jitsu Academy in Torrance, California, I've recently had the good fortune to travel to Brazil so I could train with one of Rorion Gracie's brothers, Rickson Gracie. Rickson is a living legend and the champion of the Gracie family, having had over 400 undefeated fights! After grappling, or rolling, with Rickson for a few hours, we stepped outside and I told him, "You know I feel that the lessons that I have gotten from your family and from martial arts have been more important to my wealth building than anything else that I've learned from any seminar I've ever attended, or anything else that I've done, for that matter."

"Why do you say that?" he asked.

"Have you seen the movie *300*?"

"Yes." he said, and added, "That was a great movie."

I said, "I absolutely loved it! Remember the scene in which the father was grappling with his son, teaching him to be a warrior? That's how I feel every time I train with you, or Rorion, or his sons. I feel like I'm becoming a warrior, a man. You teach me so much about how to live. You teach me how to have confidence and be strong. You teach me how to be humble and relaxed. More than anything, I think it's the character building, because all of success in life comes down to who you really are. Gracie Jiu Jitsu has helped me to strive to be the best person that I can possibly be. There are so many lessons and metaphors that are alive within the time that we fight and every physical lesson that you teach me relates directly to how I can live my life far more powerfully. Having the mindset of a champion doesn't just relate to Jiu Jitsu. It's essential to **The New Entrepreneurial Mind,** and I believe it's the determining factor between all success and failure in life."

"I feel the same way," said Rickson, as he placed his hand on my shoulder and smiled.

I told Rickson, "Whenever I think of a person who is committed to forging their entrepreneurial dreams, I think of you—of your fight against David Levicki." He smiled and I continued, "In that fight, what impressed me most was, here was this guy who was at least twice your size, towering over you, a professional kick boxer, and you looked so small compared to him and yet you were confidently stalking him around the ring. You looked emotionless, like Yul Brynner in *West World*."

Rickson laughed, "My hair was completely shaved then."

"But what impressed me most was that image of you, the underdog, facing a huge challenge and taking it on methodically and almost with robotic confidence. You just went after this huge person and totally dominated the fight. As an entrepreneur, I know that we are fighting what we perceive as being life-or-death battles every day. Many of us live in a constant fight-or-flight mode. Here's my question to you: When you are in one of the most stressful positions anyone could possibly imagine, where a guy twice your size wants to destroy you, how are you able to remain composed?" "Well, I'm actually very much at peace when I fight. I'm very relaxed."

I exclaimed, "You're at *peace!* In a stressful situation like that?! How's that possible?"

Rickson smiled, "You have to develop the **Invincible Mind**. You have to become invincible. And it's all in here," he said as he tapped on my head.

What if you were able to embrace the mindset of a champion, how would that change the way you show up in life? It's this mindset that determines the winners from everyone else in life. And I am now inviting you to step into the winner's circle. Would you like to join all of the highest achievers in the world, to step up and really *win*, spiritually, emotionally, and financially? It's time to grow your wealth exponentially and it all begins in the mind.

The 10 Traits of 1,000 of the World's Wealthiest People

Do you want to wake up to riches, as Rorion Gracie was able to do when he launched the UFC? Of course you do. That's why you're reading this book, taking seminars, and doing everything you can to improve your skills and abilities. You want to have a richer life, and you want to help create a better life for others in the world. To help you do that, to help you become a *winner* in every sense of the word, I've described how you need to embrace **The New Entrepreneurial Mind,** which is open to constant learning, self-education, help from mentors, and modeling super-successful, super-wealthy people. Yet being open is not enough. **The New Entrepreneurial Mind** has as part of its foundation the mindset of a champion. That mindset requires certain traits that will help you be successful in your business and your life:

- You need to have the desire to win
- You need fierce dedication to your goals
- You need to be driven
- You need to be both persistent and resilient
- You need to have courage
- You need to be competitive—and understand the difference between healthy and unhealthy competition
- You need to be daring
- You need to have a determined conviction to succeed
- And you need to be willing to make mistakes and learn

These are traits I've seen in over 1,000 hugely super-wealthy and successful visionaries that we've studied at **Christopher Howard Training**: These traits are virtually always present, and these are the traits I focus on in this chapter. I was fortunate to have many of these traits instilled in me through my experience with various world champion athletes and martial arts teachers.

As I shared with Rickson, I have learned just as much about how to live a rich life from my evolution in martial arts as I have from any seminar or from any business mentor. The mindset of the world champion athlete is a vital component of **The New Entrepreneurial Mind.** Successful people exhibit these characteristics not only in the realm of business, but also often in sports, and even in their philanthropic and charitable work.

For example, Ted Turner built CNN with his intensely competitive nature and desire to win. But he is also an avid racer of sailboats.

The same quality that makes an Olympic athlete a gold medalist makes an incredible entrepreneur. Michael Jordan channels it in sports; Bill Gates channels it in business. Warren Buffett has said that Bill Gates would have been massively successful in any field or any business he might have chosen. You need to develop that same desire and drive if you want to achieve your own entrepreneurial dreams.

The Unvarnished Truth About What It Really Takes to Succeed

As an entrepreneur, I love to succeed, to grow, to expand. I have that same attitude in my practice of martial arts. I show up day after day. Some days, I have a great training day, and sometimes I have a harder training day, in which I feel like my performance was terrible. But I keep showing up with Bushido, or **Warrior Spirit**. Your performance on any given day matters far less than your commitment to keep showing up every day, day in and day out.

People often ask me, "What does it take to succeed?" I believe success requires three things: heart, spirit, and the willingness to find the right guides or mentors each step of the way. When I say heart and spirit, I mean channeling your passion, channeling it in the right direction, but also having a kind of warrior spirit.

My introduction to the concept of **Warrior Spirit** came from my first martial arts instructor, whom I mentioned in an earlier chapter. His name was Owen Watson, or the O'Bo San, as his students referred to him. The O'Bo San had been a famous competitor during the 1970s. He taught me a lot about competition and martial arts, but the most important lesson I learned from him happened when I was only 12 years old.

I was a competitive martial artist at the time and I would almost always leave a competition with a trophy. At one tournament I took a hard blow to the solar plexus that completely knocked the wind out of me. I was still fighting but I could barely keep my hands up. The O'Bo San was refereeing a match on the other side of the auditorium but he glanced over at me from across the gym for a moment and saw that I was barely holding my hands up for protection, my eyes were down, and I was being forced backward by my opponent.

He shouted out to me from across the auditorium, with a booming voice, "Stop running away!!! Get your spirit out of the gutter! Keep your spirit high! Bushido!!!!"

The O'Bo San knew that the moment that you lift your eyes— "getting your spirit out of the gutter"—you can choose to bring a whole new attitude to what you are doing, you can set a new target for your emotional state and you can choose to step up with Bushido, or the warrior spirit. The moment I heard his voice, I shifted my attitude immediately. I took a deep breath and brought in my warrior spirit and at that point I poured every shred of my energy forward and I shuffled in with a barrage of punches that quickly ended the match in my favor. I had been hit real hard, and it had almost completely drained the spirit right out of me. But with the right inspiration, I was able to find the **Warrior Spirit** within to move beyond my fears and win in spite of them.

Be aware of the spirit and attitude that you bring to everything you do. When you've that **Warrior Spirit**, the mindset that failure is not an option, you keep moving forward no matter what. That's what it really takes to be an incredible entrepreneur, because you need to have the willingness to fall down four times—and get up five. No matter what the circumstances of the moment.

There are many examples of how the O'Bo San taught me the warrior spirit. During our martial arts classes, when I was still 14 or 15 years old, he used to have us sit in what's called a horse-stance, which is a very low stance like you're sitting in a chair, but the chair is removed, and we'd be sitting in this position for an hour or maybe even two, with sweat pouring down our faces and our legs wobbling, shaky, and weak. And he would swing a samurai sword above our heads, so if you moved, it would take your head right off. That experience helped me to develop a spirit where you have to push on, regardless of anything that's happening.

Another experience of the **Warrior Spirit** in my early martial arts practice occurred when I was working with nunchuku, a weapon popularized by Bruce Lee, made of two sticks attached by a single chain. I remember practicing my katas (simulated fights in prearranged movements and techniques) with the nunchuku when suddenly there was a terrible cracking sound as one of the thick sticks slammed hard onto the bone of my shin. The pain was excruciating. I knew that I couldn't show the pain in my face, because I would have to do pushups or I would get in trouble. As a warrior, there was no room to let potential opponents know that you were hurt. So I just kept doing my kata. I glanced down and I could see in the mirror where the blood was pouring down my shin and soaking my gi pants. But I just kept going, not because I was so tough, but because I had no choice other than to suck it up. While it may sound harsh, I consider myself to have been very fortunate to have these experiences at such an early age because that spirit transferred into my adult life and into all of my affairs.

Cry in training, so that you laugh in battle.

That kind of heart and spirit is so essential to winning, whatever you do. Over the years that I've been coaching people, I've run into so many people who beat themselves up when they have a setback. But I also see other people who never give up; they go out and start over. You need to keep getting back up with the warrior spirit if you want to realize your entrepreneurial dreams and live a richer life.

I believe my competitive drive has helped me to be in the truly blessed position that I'm in today with the entrepreneurial results we now thankfully enjoy at our company. From the time I started doing martial arts at 11 years old, I remember wanting to perfect every movement, whether I was doing the katas or whether I was sparring. I always wanted to be the best I could possibly be.

I think one reason for that was because I wasn't a natural at sports at school, and my parents were divorced when I was five. I didn't have a father around to teach me how to play sports at an early age, but I could excel at self-directed learning—so the martial arts suited me perfectly. In the arts, I could also find a mentor who could coach me and guide me. In my case, the O'Bo San became that mentor. In addition to helping me find my spirit, he also said one thing that has always stuck with me, "If you want to have precision and you want to be the best, then you have to work a little bit harder than all the rest." I really took that to heart. It shaped the way I approached everything in life throughout my entire life. I never felt like I was a natural at anything, but I realized that if I was willing to work harder than anybody else, then I could really improve myself and be the best.

When I was 14 or 15, I jogged five miles to the dojo (martial arts training hall) every morning before school, no matter what the weather was. In Lake Tahoe, it was often in the snow. I had my own set of keys to get in, and I practiced relentlessly so I could be better. My hard work would show up when I sparred with other people, and my hard work would show up in class.

If you want to have precision and you want to be the best, then you have to work a little harder than all the rest. Let's look at a couple of people who did just that, but in very different ways. . . .

Michael Bloomberg achieved his personal best and realized his entrepreneurial dreams after being fired from Salomon Brothers investment bank in 1981. He had the indomitable spirit to get back up and launch even larger when he went out on his own. He founded Bloomberg Financial Markets, a company that originally sold financial information terminals to Wall Street financial firms, but has expanded enormously over the years to include a news service, radio, TV, Internet, and book publishing operations. The company currently employs more than 10,000 people in more than 130 countries around the world. And Bloomberg himself has a net worth of $16 billion, according to the Forbes 400 list of 2008, which also identified him as the eighth-richest U.S. citizen and the wealthiest New Yorker. After all of this and the many challenges that came with it, he faced even bigger challenges when he committed himself to stepping even more into the global spotlight by jumping into politics. He chose to expand into a field where facing intense and constant criticism is the name of the game. Michael Bloomberg ran for and was elected mayor of New York City in 2001.

Bloomberg's fierce dedication to his dreams has put him in a position of extreme privilege. He has been rewarded with the opportunity to give back enormously. Michael has donated at least $300 million to his alma mater, Johns Hopkins University. But that's not the only way Bloomberg gives back: He contributes approximately $140 million every year (through anonymous gifts) toward education, public health, the arts, and social services in New York. He has contributed to the World Trade Center Memorial Foundation, the Campaign for Tobacco-Free Kids, the Centers for Disease Control and Prevention, the World Lung Foundation, and the World Health Organization, as well as many other charitable organizations. Clearly, Bloomberg's courage, drive, persistence, and resilience during the course of his career have paid off not only for him, but for so many other people he has helped.

From the age of six, Joanne Rowling knew she wanted to be a published writer. This was the dream she wanted to wake up to. She loved telling stories to her sister, and they would often act out the parts. She wrote a story called "Rabbit" and read it to her family. When her mother told her that it was wonderful, all she could think was, "Are we going to get it published?" At age 11, she told a school friend about her serious ambition to be a writer. The friend said she believed Joanne would be a success.

Fourteen years later, while on a train from Manchester to London, Joanne was inspired to write the story of Harry Potter. Joanne (better known now as J. K. Rowling) continued on the four-hour train ride while the story came to her. Although she was too shy to ask anyone for a pen, she believed that the inability to be distracted by writing the ideas down immediately allowed her to let the characters and story to develop in her mind. For the next several months, she continued to write without telling anyone what she was working on. Six months later, her mother passed away.

Joanne regretted never telling her mother about her project. She decided to leave the British Isles and teach English in Portugal while she continued to write the story of Harry Potter. While in Portugal, she got married and had a child. After separating from her husband, she returned to Edinburgh to be closer to her sister and to restart her life. She was now a single mother, living on welfare, looking to provide for her child, but she was driven with a determined conviction to follow her dream to publish her story. She would devote every moment to her baby girl and she would write at a nearby café while the baby slept beside her. She would write anywhere from 10 minutes to 10 hours in her unyielding determination to finish the story. She said, "I was very low, and I had to achieve something. Without the challenge, I would have gone stark, raving mad."

As a result of her resilience and persistence, six years after that inspirational train ride, she finished her book and sent the first three chapters out to find a publisher. Several of her manuscripts were mailed back almost immediately. Nonetheless, she was unwavering in the ferocious pursuit of her dream. Finally, she found a publisher will-ing to take a chance on her. Almost a year later, her book was sold for

$4,000, and the following year she was informed that after an American publisher auction, her book was sold again for more than $100,000. She realized that her dream had come true, and with the money she now made, she could buy a house for her family. She continued to write the Harry Potter series for 17 years. She went from being on welfare to being one of the 12 richest women in Britain. J. K. Rowling dared to dream and her commitment eventually put her in a position in which she could share her wealth with others. In doing so, her experience of life has become even richer, emotionally textured, and truly wealthy. She now spends her time doing philanthropic work for One Parent Families, Multiple Sclerosis Society of Great Britain, Comic Relief, and Children's High Level Group, among others.

How Asking Yourself this Simple Question Gives You the Courage to Keep Moving Towards Your Dreams

One of the techniques that gave the courage to keep moving forward, in spite of the challenges or the fears that come up, has been to look at worst-case scenarios. When I was having challenges in my career and my life, when I was really struggling. I thought, "What's the worst that could possibly happen if everything were to fall out from underneath me?" In my case, I could move to Belize and live very inexpensively and perhaps run an online business; in other words, I could live a much simpler life. Once I accepted that worst-case scenario and then focused on my greatest ambitions, I could relax and let go of the fear-based need to control everything.

If you face worry or fear or stress, I strongly recommend you consider your own worst-case scenario and make peace with it and accept it. Because once you do, it's easier to move forward and say to yourself, "I can do that, if need be—it's okay. And while my worst-case scenario is not what I expect, I can accept finding joy and happiness within it." Facing your fears and the worst that can happen is incredibly freeing: If you're prepared for the worst, then any success you do achieve is that much sweeter!

Now it's time for a quick exercise. We all want to do the best that we possibly can, but when we get negatively attached to our outcomes and we feel that we have to control everything, it sets us up for fixations, fear, worry, stress, and even addictions.

Recently I had a great conversation with my friend Wayne Dyer. Wayne has written more than 40 books. We spoke about the concept of desire versus attachment. We agreed that desire fuels all great things, but attachment is and can be the problem that creates struggle, stress, worry, and concern. Inherent in accepting the worst-case scenario, and really accepting it, we automatically release all tension, worry, stress, concern, and control. What most people don't realize is that the moment they release all attachment to their outcomes, they become far more empowered to make them happen. They become magnetic for people, resources, and opportunities instead of chasing these things away out of desperation.

So right now, please take five minutes to describe your worst-case scenario from a business perspective. Paint it out and also paint out how you could positively turn it into something you could find satisfaction with. What's realistically the worst case? This is not about creating drama, it's about finding a realistic comfortable worst-case plan. And then once you've painted out the worst case, *accept* it completely. Embrace it. And then build upon it and create far more. But always work with the acceptance of finding the joy and happiness in the worst. The moment we accept things, we can stop struggling, and start consciously creating.

In the space that follows, describe the worst-case scenarios for your business and your life and how you could positively deal with them and find joy in them while accepting them completely. Remember—no drama, just a matter-of-fact worst-case scenario that you could live with. Acceptance is the key to happiness. Now for the next step. Take five minutes and write out the best-case scenario for your business and your life. This is your target and what you aim for with certainty.

Now that you realize you can find happiness even in the worst, build on it with an unwavering vision of the best. Move forward confidently with the joy of being on an inspired path!

What to Do If You're Scared of Failing

Michael Bloomberg believed in his talents, skills, and abilities enough that when he was fired from a high-profile job, his courage and conviction allowed him to transform what many people would have perceived as an unhappy setback into an opportunity to test his entrepreneurial mind. And he clearly did so with great success: the Bloomberg companies brought in $5.5 billion in annual sales in 2008 alone. He didn't let any adversity stand in the way of his success.

But I know so many others who either just give up or don't work hard enough at showcasing their talents or skills. For example, I have a good friend who is an incredibly talented musician. But she doesn't want to fail. She won't put herself out there, because she's so afraid of not being perfect. Instead, she's waiting for perfection, so she continues to train and get lessons, but she never gets out there and does what it takes to really succeed, which is to get momentum by moving forward. That takes courage and a warrior spirit—getting the momentum, moving forward, whether or not you're going to fail, whether or not you're going to fall down.

And you *will* fall down. Every successful person in every field has fallen down along the path to success. When Jeff Bezos launched Amazon.com, he said that one of the things that allowed him to move forward was the realization that there was a 70 percent chance that he would fail. He said he could wipe out all his fears of failure when he simply realized and accepted that failure was likely.

His reasoning was that when you realize it's most likely you will fail, that there's a 70 percent chance of failure, then all you have to do is improve on those odds. You look to minimize the areas where there is the greatest risk of failure along the way until you've gained so much momentum that you become a behemoth that has so much motion, you can't be stopped.

Bezos has spoken about something else that I really appreciated. It was about finding the courage to act, whether or not other people believe that you're going to succeed. When he was launching Amazon.com, a lot of people said, "There's no way this can work."

At that time, in the early 1990s, Bezos was working for a hedge fund, and his boss had asked him to look for new business opportunities on the then-fledgling Internet. Bezos discovered that web usage was growing at an annual rate of 2,300 percent and that the U.S. government was just starting to allow buying and selling through the Internet, so he started to look for possible mail-order businesses that would work well and could be successful on the Web. He narrowed his choices to a few, but he settled on books and proposed it to his boss, who wasn't convinced that Jeff's idea would be profitable.

But Jeff was undeterred. He told his boss he wanted to leave the company and pursue this idea as his own entrepreneurial venture. His boss took a walk with Jeff, and they had a long conversation. His boss said, "That sounds like a really great idea for somebody who doesn't already have a job. But you have a great job. Why don't you think about it for twenty-four hours and call me back?" Jeff went home after work that day and discussed his plans with his wife, who really supported him. So he decided to go for it, in spite of what his boss had said to him. He quit his high-paying job and launched Amazon.com. Within five years, Jeff was on the cover of *Time* magazine as the Person of the Year and his company, Amazon.com, was worth about $10 billion.

What helped Jeff Bezos find the courage to step up, to make the decision to move forward in the face of what nobody else believed possible was picturing himself at the age of 80 looking back at his life. He thought, "Would there be any regrets if I didn't do this?" And the answer was "yes": he felt he would have many regrets. So he needed to find the courage to wake up to the riches of his entrepreneurial dream.

Courage is not the absence of fear. Courage is the realization that there's something more important than the fear.

—Christopher Howard

CHAPTER

How to Overcome Your Fears and Get Rich Beyond Your Wildest Dreams

Many entrepreneurs face situations in which others don't believe they can be successful. Popular opinion is often not supportive. But those who are committed to **Instant Wealth** and waking up rich know they can't listen to the maddening crowd; they listen to their inner voice instead. They just step up, stand their ground, and pursue their entrepreneurial dreams. They maintain their conviction and dedication, which are essential to **The New Entrepreneurial Mind**.

Obviously, the bigger you become, the more criticism you will attract. When people say, "You can't do that!" simply reply, "Watch me!"

There will always be dissenters along the way, no matter how much good you are doing for the world. There have been people who actually put down Mother Teresa! Actors and actresses get written about in the tabloids and other media all the time. They know they need to ignore what they read.

As your brand grows, awareness of who you are also increases. So you'll find that many people will love you—but for every person who loves you, there will also be people who don't. No matter how much good you're doing for the world—just like Martin Luther King Jr., who received many death threats a day—the more you do, the more you're going to face criticism. I've faced it, and I decided to just stay away from it. So, if you are committed to extraordinary success, get committed to developing a tough skin. You'll need it.

Developing a thick skin is vital.

The Single Most Important Element that Affects Your Wealth and Success

In April of 2009, I brought the **Billionaire Adventure Club,** which is my "elite inner circle" seminar group, to Rio de Janeiro, Brazil, with me.

We brought experts in finance and other aspects of business to expand the members' social network and expand their world financially. We do trips to exotic places once a year, but this was a particularly special trip for me, because I was getting married while there. We had a small private ceremony, with my wife, Lauren, and me and Rickson Gracie as my best man and Rickson's fiancé, Cassia, as Lauren's maid of honor.

Every morning during the trip, while the participants were learning how to raise money for any business dream they'd ever had, I would grapple, or roll, with Rickson for two or three hours.

At the beginning of the week, Rickson told me a story.

I had a student who was a former commander for the U.S. Navy SEALs. He told me how troops would have to go through what was called Hell Week, before they could actually graduate and make it to the highest designation. During Hell Week, the SEALs would be worked physically and mentally throughout the day: running laps until they dropped, swimming until they could no longer do it, pushups in the mud with full back packs, and then finally at the end of the day they were allowed to go to sleep. Fifteen minutes into sleep, the sirens would sound and they would be ripped from their beds and forced to run down to the ocean where they would be up to their chests in water. They would have to run in place lifting their knees all the way up to their chests while simultaneously pumping their rifles up and down in the air. After a couple of hours they would be allowed to run back to their bunks and go back to sleep. Ten minutes later, the sirens would go off once again and they would repeat the whole process.

One of the final tests involved swimming a 200-meter lap pool, with a flag at the end. They would have to grab the flag to succeed. The challenge was that they had to swim the entire length under water, and if they came up at any point they would be disqualified. Most Olympic athletes can do about 60 meters under water. But during the test for the SEALs, the real idea wasn't to test whether they made it to the flag or not, it was to weed out the people who would give up. If they came up for air, they were automatically eliminated. The organizers wanted to see who had what it took to simply keep going until they actually passed out underwater. Those were the ones who passed the test.

During this training, Rickson told me that he was going to make it my hell week. He said, "Chris, I know you travel all over the world and train with many instructors in martial arts. It makes no sense for me to teach you a winning technique. You can learn techniques anywhere. I need to teach you how to think like a winner. You must be resilient. You must develop a no-fail attitude. You have to have the psychology of a champion. My goal is to make you invincible."

Rickson continued, "When I was a kid, I was very claustrophobic, so I had one of my brothers roll me up in a thick carpet where I couldn't move an inch, and I could barely breathe. There was just the tiniest hole to breathe through. At first, I would freak out completely, but as I became accustomed to it, I could do it for longer and longer periods, and then I learned to be completely calm and at peace in that situation. I was then able to translate that level of calm and peace to my fights, when I was under tremendous pressure, yet it was imperative that I remain calm, cool, and collected."

All I could think of was how important every word that he said would be for my business and my entrepreneurial ambitions. These were without a doubt the most important things I needed to hear. There were many times when I was faced with challenges that caused enormous stress and caused me to spin in ineffectiveness. I was committed to embracing this invincible mind that he spoke of. This is the same mindset that, when adopted, will guarantee your success. Your mindset is everything.

Rickson was concerned that, as I traveled the world and worked with different martial arts trainers, they would all handle me with kid gloves, because of my fame. He said that that was unacceptable because it would be like being a five-star general who had never actually been tested in battle. So for the entire week, Rickson rolled with me and threw me around like a rag doll. He put me in some of the most uncomfortable positions you could possibly imagine. He would look to create a panic state in me, and my goal was to stay cool, calm, and collected, at peace. I had to remain totally resilient even if there was no way out or even if I was about to pass out. This hell week in Brazil was one of the most valuable experiences I had ever had, and, like all of my lessons with the Gracies, it translated directly into my business and my life.

What to Do When You're on the Verge of Giving Up

Many times in my business career I didn't feel like I could possibly go on. Those are the times when panic sets in, intelligence goes down, and fatal errors are made. Under any kind of pressure, even if it feels that the world is about to end, the key is to bring your invincible mind to the situation and remain calm, cool, and collected.

Never give up, and never say die. Keep your intelligence about you and find your way out of the situation at hand. Find your comfort. Remain at peace. Remain relaxed. If you remain in discomfort, that discomfort will simply continue to ratchet up until it's unmanageable. It will just continue to get worse and worse.

Instead, focus on remaining relaxed. Breathing and staying present to what is right in front of you will allow you to remain mentally alert and to plug in to the flow state—which is where you must be so you can respond in extraordinary ways. You must be present and resilient, no matter what the external circumstances. This is the warrior spirit.

There are many ways to deal with high pressure. The first thing to do is to find your comfort in the situation. Interrupt the pattern of stress. Here are a few ideas if you are feeling the stress of high-pressure circumstances:

- Go for a half-hour run on the spot—bring your exercise clothes with you to work if need be
- Do deep breathing exercises—inhale and then exhale at a one-to-two ratio for 10 minutes—shut off all phones and distractions
- Meditate for 20 minutes—close your eyes, shut off all distractions, and just focus on your breath, as you let your thoughts drift away and be replaced by the focus on your breath

I also believe that having the desire to win, the desire to attain every goal you've ever had, and the desire to attain your entrepreneurial dreams, all require commitment to a larger dream. And while it may be important to accept the worst, paradoxically, you must really believe that failure is not an option, because on the path toward your entrepreneurial dreams, people will always come along and say, "You can't make it." This can never shake you.

When I was growing my business, I remember a time when things weren't looking that bright from a financial perspective. My business partner called me and said, "I think this could be it; I don't see any more options to grow." Some people would have given up then, but I told him, "We haven't come as far as we have just to quit. Quitting is not an option. Failure is not an option. We may have to get creative, or take a different path, or do business in a different way, or find new partners, or find new joint ventures, or think outside the box. But there's no way that we can quit; that is not an option."

Entrepreneurs are faced with difficult situations, problems, and challenges each and every day, and the attitude to embrace is a winner's attitude. Steve Case, a co-founder and former chairman and CEO of AOL, said essentially the same thing: He said that when he was confronted with challenges, he simply doubled his commitment toward the end result.

Failure is not an option.

A Billionaire's Secret for Never Giving In

Steve Case, who built AOL, has taken **The New Entrepreneurial Mind** that contributed to his success as a business entrepreneur and is now applying it to his philanthropic work, as it is the exact same mindset that works best to solve almost any problem and forge any dream. Case says that one of the things that he is most focused on now, with the Case Foundation, is the notion of social entrepreneurship.

The question, Case says, is how do you get more change, more out-of-the-box thinking, and more focus on scaling in the charitable sector? He says one of the key challenges is helping these organizations get access to capital in a more sustainable way. In the business world, if you have a little idea, you get seed financing from a venture capitalist. Case says that only "sort of" happens in philanthropy. There's no equivalent of going public. So we're trying to figure out a way to fill that vacuum and really encourage not just business entrepreneurs but social entrepreneurs, Case says.

Clearly, Steve Case has embraced **The New Entrepreneurial Mind** and he believes that failure is not an option in the not-for-profit world, either. He's working hard to overcome the scalability problem, so that new nonprofits can grow and succeed and help people in new ways.

How to Make Charitable Work and Giving Back Grow Your Wealth

Steve Case aimed high, with his goal of building AOL from nothing and then merging it with Time Warner. When asked what the American Dream means to him, he has inspiring words for anyone who is pursuing an entrepreneurial dream:

I think it's really about hope and optimism and possibility. Anything is possible if you put your mind to it, and you really work hard, and you bring the right perspective to it. You shouldn't focus on why you can't do something, which is what most people do. You should focus on why perhaps you can, and be one of the exceptions.

I find it interesting that in America, even though most people are more optimistic and most people around the world do view America as the city on the hill and more entrepreneurial and more risk taking and less traditional, still in America, most people don't take risks, and most people are pretty traditional. It's actually a relatively small number of people that really are those risk takers, and a relatively small number of people that end up really having an impact on the world, and it doesn't take a lot of people. It just takes a few people who really care and stick with it, and I think that's what America is about. It starts with somebody having a dream and sticking with that through thick and thin.

Clearly, Case believes that persistence and resilience pays off! When successful entrepreneurs use that same drive, that competitiveness, and desire to win, and when they bring that same energy to philanthropy, that's the way to change the world. This is why **The New Entrepreneurial Mind** is so well suited to not only deliver value through the creation of your greatest dreams, but also well suited to solve the greatest issues on the planet today. Many charitable organizations or individuals who have huge hearts and are very caring and want to make a difference in the world usually don't, unfortunately, have the same drive and the zeal that an entrepreneur has. This is a unique quality that an entrepreneur brings to philanthropic endeavors that can make a huge difference in our world. It's not only the ability to watch the bottom line and to channel their business mindset into the philanthropy that the entrepreneur brings, but also the competitiveness, desire, and the drive to win.

That kind of drive and ambition allows an idea to spread very quickly. A lot of people say, "We should pursue philanthropic or altruistic goals only from the mindset of wanting to make a difference." And they make people wrong whom they think might be philanthropic minded for self-serving reasons. But the ego or the drive to win and to compete can be channeled into making a huge impact on the world and if that is done, I'd say it's a good thing.

Some people, for example, made comments that what Bill Clinton was doing with the William J. Clinton Foundation, was self-serving—that the foundation was more about him than it was about making a positive difference. Admittedly, Clinton does have an ego (as do you and I), but he has successfully channeled that desire for self-expression in a powerful direction. Whatever his subconscious motivation may have begun as, as he creates positive change in the world, does the impetus of the motivation really matter? It's also important to realize that this is the path of the evolution of thought. Much philanthropic good is done from a Values Level Five, or achievement-oriented mindset. The longer an individual pursues this path, the more of an opportunity he has to truly shift into Values Level Seven, or sustainability thinking. In my book, Bill Clinton has a heart of gold and is coming from a place of wanting to make a genuine difference in the world.

Martin Luther King Jr. did not originally want to be an activist. He had to be talked into it. All he wanted at the time was to be a preacher, which was the career path that had the most prestige for a young African-American man at that time. Over time, though, his feelings evolved toward the truly revolutionary direction that changed the face of the nation. He moved from Values Level Five to Values Level Six and Seven. Martin Luther King Jr.'s invincible spirit lives on even to this day through the legacy of his incredible dream.

Regardless of how or why you start out as an entrepreneur, you can connect with other motivations as your feelings evolve. To think negatively about people who do philanthropic work from a Values Level Five source of motivation misses the most important part of the picture. I don't care what the original motivation is. The first question is, what is the result? What does the work of an entrepreneur accomplish? Does it leave the world a better place? The second thing to realize is that a shift in behavior can also lead to an evolutionary shift in values.

Bill Gates has operated from a Values Level Five perspective throughout his life, but he and his wife started the Bill and Melinda Gates Foundation because they are keen philanthropists. The foundation has committed more than $3.2 billion to global health, $2 billion to improve learning opportunities to low-income families, $477 million to community projects, and more than $488 million to special projects and annual giving campaigns. Find your passion, achieve your goals, and you, too, may find that you race up the evolution of thought and go on to make a profound difference in the world.

The Most Valuable Education You Will Ever Get in Life

The New Entrepreneurial Mind includes having an invincible spirit. That spirit of Instant Wealth is always present and alive in every moment, regardless of external circumstances.

One of the big mistakes I made in my career also turned out to be a blessing in disguise. I was contracting for Dale Carnegie Training, teaching on my own, and also starting a business with a partner. Another company offered me a job for more money than I had ever earned before. But the principals of this company wanted me to work inside the office. I didn't want to do that. I was a speaker, so I wanted to be out in the field. I wanted to train. I began to negotiate with them so I could train full time and be out on the road. Although they agreed to this, they also told me I couldn't finish up the training work I had already agreed to do with my partner. I responded, "From an integrity standpoint, I have to finish up my obligations with my partner, and I won't leave him without making sure he's in good shape when I make this transition." The owner of the company looked at me and told me in no uncertain terms—in a manner I can't repeat in these pages—that I would regret this decision.

The opportunity to work for that particular company was important to me. It was one of the world's largest companies of its kind. But I was shocked at the way they were communicating with me. I should have listened to my intuition, which told me that it would be a mistake to work with them. But my desire to move forward, to learn what I could, and to work at a higher level motivated me to take that job anyway. They ended up allowing me to finish my contract and hiring me simultaneously. I did learn a great deal while I worked there; in fact, it was an incredible learning experience, but the way they communicated with me at the start stayed with me the entire time I worked with them. The working environment became more and more toxic as a result of that negative energy.

In fact, it was such a dysfunctional place that I finally realized I had to get out. I could not allow the circumstances of the moment to break my spirit. I had to keep my spirit high and keep my eyes on the future. That's when I decided to follow my entrepreneurial dreams and start my own company. I probably would have stayed in the other job forever if the working environment had been healthier. So in the end, I'm grateful for everything that happened. The overall experience was the catalyst for my starting my own company. Moreover, that experience taught me how important it is to trust my intuition in regard to the people. As Warren Buffett says, "Always work with people that you like, trust, and admire." I really embrace that advice more and more as I move forward in my career, and I continue to remind myself that I need to surround myself with the right people. You need to do the same thing: find the right people who can help you achieve your entrepreneurial dreams—without compromising your integrity.

> ### "Always work with people that you like, trust, and admire."
> ### —Warren Buffett

Just because something works for someone else doesn't mean it will work for you—remain invincible as you test options to succeed.

In addition to learning from your own mistakes, you may also find that adopting ideas that other entrepreneurs used successfully might not work for you. So you need to remain invincible and simply learn from those mistakes as well.

For example, Richard Branson has been a terrific role model for me. I learned as much as possible about how he ran his businesses, so that I could find ways to expand my own companies. Modeling others and adopting the strategies of other successful entrepreneurs is a great way to achieve your own success in your business. And it's a key component of the new entrepreneurial mindset of being a champion.

Just as Branson had run some of the Virgin companies out of residential homes, I decided to run my first company out of my home. This worked really well for a while, until I had so many employees coming in and out that the neighbors complained and the zoning people came in and said I had to leave the area—and justifiably so. It was disheartening at the time and I was stressed about "where I would go, and how I would bounce back." This method might have worked for Virgin in the United Kingdom, but I realized I couldn't use this strategy as I moved forward, but I had to keep my spirit high!

Other strategies Virgin used also didn't work for me. For example, Virgin is now in the business of branded venture capital. In other words, the company gives a piece of a branded Virgin business to someone who is authorized to run it. This shows how much Richard Branson encourages entrepreneurial zeal in those he trusts. He leaves those people alone for the most part and lets them run the business within the guidelines of the Virgin brand. They have had many successes and some failures among these businesses. I thought that I would extend my own brand in the same way. Since I was already speaking to audiences around the world, I thought I could take my brand and lend it to other products.

We did that with a couple of businesses, which we branded under the name "Christopher Howard." But as I was spending 90 percent of my time on the road teaching, we found it was really difficult to manage the people who were running the different off-shoot businesses that varied too much from what we knew worked for us. The managers had their own ideas of the way things should be done. There were conflicts regarding the basic visionary dream. They weren't managing the businesses profitably, so they were coming back to me and asking for more money. The businesses became a black hole for both funds and energy. At the same time, we had so many areas that we were making really work in our core business that it made more sense to expand what was already working.

That was so much easier for us than the strategy of branded companies that weren't being run well by their managers and took energy that could be better used elsewhere. Emotions ran high in each of these situations, and that is typically when intelligence goes down. So the key is to maintain the inner peace and resolve. I can't say that I was perfect, but I certainly learned more and more about the importance of this concept through these events.

One of the great benefits of studying hugely successful people is seeing how often they failed along the way. It's always useful to look at the timeline between when somebody started, when they actually hit millionaire status, and ultimately billionaire status. That really puts things into perspective. Richard Branson launched his first business when he was 16, but he wasn't a millionaire until 9 or 10 years later. You can say to yourself, "Okay, that gives me some perspective in regard to pacing myself: I don't have to be successful in the first year of doing business."

Their example serves as your pace car. You can ask yourself, where should I be at this point in the process? There are people who have launched their businesses and their dreams at all different ages. Some people might look at Branson's story and think, "Gee, he was wildly successful because he achieved $1 million by the age of 26." On the other hand, you might think, "Even Branson needed 10 years to become a millionaire."

Why It Only Takes 3 Steps to Becoming a World Class Performance

Now that you know something about the indomitable spirit that is necessary for *Instant Wealth*, let's take a look at how you can begin to embody the resources you need to succeed.

You can do this through another exercise. Take a moment to get clear, and then ask yourself this question: Where in your life are you not operating with the mindset of a champion? Where do you not have the warrior spirit in your life? Where can you really kick up what you are doing to a brand new level?

This exercise demands brutal honesty. You are going to identify everything in your life that isn't being done with the mindset of a champion and the spirit of a warrior. It doesn't necessarily just have to pertain to your entrepreneurial ambitions. We are holistic beings and every aspect of our lives touches on all of the other elements.

Are you not adopting that warrior spirit in the context of your relationships? Are you carrying work issues home and taking them out harshly on the people you love? If so, how is that affecting your life? Is that affecting the richness of your life in a negative way? Does that also wrap back around and affect your career in some way? Are you giving up too easily in certain situations? Are you not really being resilient? If you have a challenge, do you let it knock you down? Are you not really going for it? Are you not really living at your entrepreneurial edge? Are you pushing beyond and through your fears? Are you not playing at 100 percent? Consider everything that was discussed in this chapter.

Remember, the mindset of a champion means:
- You need to have the desire to win.
- You need fierce dedication to your goals.
- You need to be driven.
- You need to be both persistent and resilient.
- You need to have courage.
- You need to be competitive—and understand the difference between healthy and unhealthy competition.
- You need to be daring.
- You need to have a determined conviction to succeed.
- And you need to be willing to make mistakes and learn.

Where are you currently missing the mark? Be totally honest with yourself! Use the following space to write your thoughts.

An extension of this exercise can be extremely powerful for integrating new traits, attitudes, and mindsets. It also works very well for developing skills and capabilities in areas such as athletic performance, which we explore in some of our advanced trainings.

Circle two or three of the areas you identified in your notes, areas in your life where you're missing the mark in regard to the mindset of a champion. Just circle them so you know what they are. Read through the following steps and then complete the exercise.

Three-Step Visualization for Performance Enhancement

First, close your eyes and imagine an expert, a person who is thoroughly an expert in those areas in which you've been falling short. For myself, if I feel I'm too stressed out, or struggling too much, I imagine Richard Branson or Royce Gracie, the original champion of the Ultimate Fighting Championships. Royce is one of the most relaxed and playful people you could ever meet. Clearly visualize your chosen expert adeptly going through the situations in which you choose to succeed.

Second, superimpose your body on the screen of your mind over the body of the expert. See yourself go through challenging situations with the same emotional resources as the expert and succeeding just as they would succeed, with the same level of relaxation, poise, peace, resilience, and persistence.

Third, imagine yourself stepping back into your own body in the same situation. You're seeing things through your own eyes and hearing the sounds around you. But as you're experiencing this, imagine once again going through those activities perfectly, now bringing with you the resources of the ideal person who can do it so easily. That person has now become you.

This three-step visualization process can serve you amazingly well for bringing out the resources you need to make your life work the way you want it to. In short, it's an incredible technique for bringing out the best in yourself—which is what **The New Entrepreneurial Mind** excels at.

The Missing Ingredient—Nobody Ever Taught You in School—On How to Build Your Own Fortune from Scratch

It's the job of an entrepreneur to continually be in that mode of figuring out how to grow the business. That often means raising capital. It's great if your business can be self-funding each step of the way. But there are many times when you're going to have to raise capital on the path of entrepreneurship.

There's one quality that's shared by virtually all of the super-wealthy, super-successful entrepreneurs I've studied. They all know how to turn obstacles into opportunities. They're flexible and extremely resourceful—especially when they have to raise capital. They know how to use their entrepreneurial intelligence to come up with the resources they need to succeed. We look in this chapter at how some of the most successful entrepreneurs do exactly that. You'll learn from the best and get the money you need to grow your business.

Before we go any further, think about this:

- What's the next deal you want to make in your business?
- What's the next project you're working on?
- What's the next alliance that you are targeting to grow your business?

If you're stumped by this, think about what Oprah Winfrey has done. She went from radio to television and then extended her brand into other media, including her magazine. How can you do the same thing? How can you grow your business to the next level, gradually and naturally? What might be a natural next step up the ladder from what you're already doing right now?

Remember: **The New Entrepreneurial Mind** is obsessed with expansion, constant growth, and always looking for the next opportunity. Great wealth is created through concentration rather than diversification of focus.

- What's distracting you from your main purpose, your key goals? Find it and eliminate it! You need to concentrate, not diversify!
- What are you not focusing on that you should be focusing on? Figure that out, and then refocus your energies on that single point.
- Where are you most successful in your business? Then focus like a laser on whatever that is, and build out from there.

How You Tap into Your Inner Creativity and Use It to Make Yourself Rich

I've seen a lot of creativity in the entrepreneurs I've studied over the years. Jeff Bezos of Amazon.com was always getting into things as a child. He took apart his crib with a screwdriver. He constantly set up booby traps throughout the house: He set alarms to go off when anyone walked into a room. His parents were worried that he might dump a bucket of nails on their heads when they walked through a door. He had this very creative mind, even as a kid, that transformed into *Instant Wealth* later in life.

What areas are you creative in? How can you bring creativity to your business, to help you achieve your goals in ways you may not have thought possible?

What's the artistry in your business? There's artistry in every business; you simply need to focus on yours, and then expand that focus so you can be even more successful.

Both Google founders, Sergey Brin and Larry Page, went to Montessori schools, which take a very creative, independent approach to learning. Both credit their Montessori educations as a major factor in their success. They were taught to be self-starters and to think for themselves. And of course, it was their creativity that led to the creation of Google.

Although many people already know the story of how Google was founded, it bears repeating here, to illustrate the creativity of its founders. While they were both at Stanford pursuing their PhDs, Larry Page noticed that if a research paper was cited in other studies, it had greater credibility. The more studies in which the paper was cited, the more credibility it was perceived to have. Meanwhile, Sergey Brin was exploring how to mine data from the Internet. They decided to put their two interests together, and came up with the so-called rank relevance algorithm. That simply meant that a search engine result would be ranked on the basis of how many web sites cited it. This was the underlying idea that led to the creation of Google.

As we all know, that genius idea paid off. In March 2009, Brin (then age 35) and Page (then age 36) shared the distinction of being the world's richest billionaires under age 40: each had $12 billion, even after the market downturn. It was all because of the creative approach they took toward Internet search.

That creativity shows up even in their workplace in Mountain View, California. The environment has green Astroturf, massage chairs, and big Swiss balls to sit on. Sergey Brin sometimes roller-skates to work, and employees play roller hockey on breaks. It's a very loose, stimulating environment that fosters creative energy.

Larry and Sergey have captured that same creative approach to work at Google and brought their own creativity to it. Because they have created a creative work environment, creativity infuses the work they do at Google today as well. The entire company has been created with that spirit.

What creativity can you bring into your work environment? Think about what might motivate you and your team better, so that you can be even more resourceful and successful in growing your business.

The beauty of making more money is that you can also give more money to whatever organization, individual, or charity you choose. Larry Page and Sergey Brin have already pledged $1 billion of Google's profits to the company's philanthropic division, which will funnel money both to nonprofit charities and companies that deal with global poverty, environmental issues, and renewable energy. This ties in to the founders' belief in the Kabbalistic concept of repairing the world.

Since the two are only in their 30s and have achieved their personal wealth only recently, they are cautiously committing to charitable contributions: after all, they have many years ahead of them to make these decisions; even Warren Buffett didn't make his largest donations until he was almost 80 years old.

As Sergey Brin says, "I take the philosophical view that, aside from some modest stuff now, I am waiting to do the bulk of my philanthropy later, maybe in a few years, when I feel I'm more educated. I don't think it's something I have had time to become an expert at." He and his parents, Michael and Eugenia Brin, do support a few charities. "There are people who helped me and my family out. I do feel responsible to those organizations," he says. One of them is HIAS, the Hebrew Immigrant Aid Society, which helped the Brins come to the United States from Russia in 1979, when Sergey was six. Eugenia Brin serves on its board and heads its project to create a digital record of Jewish immigrant archives.

That's a beautiful circle of giving: HIAS helped the Brins immigrate to the United States, Sergey got a terrific education here that fostered his innate creativity and led to the founding of Google, and Google's success allowed the Brins to give back to the organization that helped them in the first place.

Richard Branson's Secret to Growing a Business on a Shoestring Budget

While the Google founders channeled their creativity to creating the product their company provides, Richard Branson's creativity is expressed in the various ways he's attracted publicity to his company: He uses publicity in lieu of other resources. For example, in its early days, Virgin Atlantic Airways didn't have money for marketing, so the company took a creative approach. Richard crossed the Atlantic in his boat, the Virgin Atlantic Challenger, looking to break the speed record, which generated a lot of publicity—which then helped his company grow and be successful against all the more established airlines. Richard believes that the publicity was worth many times the advertising dollars he could have spent (if he had had the money to spend!). He got much more publicity from that trip across the Atlantic Ocean than he would have gotten by using traditional marketing or advertising.

He has used one attention-getting stunt after another to get more free publicity for other Virgin companies, which has helped them grow and succeed. He dressed up in a bridal gown to launch Virgin Bridal. He drove a tank through the streets of New York and crushed a pyramid of Coca-Cola cans to introduce Virgin Cola. And he flew in a hot-air balloon around the world, again looking to break the world records for speed. All those antics were designed to get a lot of publicity, and they did.

What can you do to generate publicity for your business, instead of spending valuable advertising or marketing money that you may or may not have?

There have been times in my own career when I had to get incredibly creative while growing my business. At one point, I had a cash crunch because money that we had expected to come in didn't come in, after all. At the same time, we had an enormous business opportunity on the horizon that we expected would come to fruition in six or seven months. But to make it until then, we had to get creative to keep our cash flow flowing.

We had to shift our business slightly to partner with someone else. We had to fill in some of the services that we didn't currently provide for our clients. We knew one group of people who focused specifically on branding, which is a service we weren't offering, so we partnered with that group, which created some cash flow. Another person, Kevin Nations, specifically focused on sales—and although we teach how to be an incredible communicator, we don't have anyone who specifically teaches how to sell more effectively. So we partnered with Kevin. That also provided greater service to our clients, and at the same time created a flood of cash flow for us. Those new partner relationships allowed us to traverse our six-month gap, and to reach the point at which greater financial success was waiting.

Who can you partner with so you can offer some product or service that you don't have but your customers might want? Wake up to the riches you could develop in a business relationship with a potential partner.

The Simple Secret to Turn Every Obstacle into an Opportunity

A classic marketing book called *Positioning*, by Al Ries and Jack Trout, describes the battle for the consumer's mind. Ries and Trout say that once an entity owns the number one spot, it's very hard to knock it out of that place. So you need to get creative to challenge that number one position.

For example, instead of trying to get Coca-Cola out of the number one spot, 7-Up positioned itself not as a rival, but as an alternative: "the un-cola." Red Bull also took a very creative approach in its marketing: instead of trying to compete as a cola or even as an energy drink (many of which were emerging at the time), Red Bull put itself in the beer category and designed the product with a sleeker can. Then the company linked the product to extreme sports, and the Red Bull logo was seen on people who were skydiving and Windsurfing. Red Bull knew the publicity value it would generate by linking itself to people doing extreme things. That's an extremely creative approach to getting the brand out there.

Every successful entrepreneur has had to turn obstacles into opportunities for *Instant Wealth*. It's not whether you have obstacles that matter; it's what you do with them that make the difference. For example, once Sergey Brin and Larry Page had created their model for developing a more effective search engine, they wanted to sell it for $1 million. They shopped it around, but they couldn't find anyone willing to buy it. Out of desperation, they decided to go ahead and build it themselves, because they still believed they could sell it and make money from it, but they didn't really want to run it themselves. They found one of the original people from Sun Microsystems, who was willing to put in $100,000, and they called him their first angel investor. That was what launched Google, which today, of course, is a $150 billion company. Sergey and Larry became billionaires because they were unable to sell their product for $1 million—a clear case of an obstacle becoming an opportunity.

What are the obstacles you're facing in your business? Can you think of alternative ways of looking at these problems that might reveal a new solution?

During my own career, I've also had huge obstacles that threatened to put an end to my entrepreneurial ambitions. Yet when I woke up to the solution, it turned out to be the very reason I was catapulted to a whole new level of success. During a downturn in the economy, fewer people were attending seminar programs—even though a recession is a time when people need seminars the most!

It's during hard times that you see true winners emerge. That's the energy we wanted to connect with. We asked ourselves, "How can we do our job more effectively? How can we reach out to more people? How can we deliver even better value for the money? And how can we get people to see that now is the time when they need to invest in their own dreams to get to where they want to go?"

We became more focused on our marketing efforts and even more focused on delivering greater value for the money to our clients. As a result, when other people in our industry saw their sales dropping, our sales actually increased. And we began to expand in a very, very powerful way, while a lot of other people in our industry were folding. When you can survive and thrive in the leanest of times, you're really positioned to thrive in the best of times. That's part of **The New Entrepreneurial Mind,** the mind of a champion to move forward.

Think about how you can grow your business even in a down economy: Is there something you can make, offer, or provide to your clients that will help them be more efficient, effective, productive, or satisfied? Even in the worst of times, there are basic goods and services that people need, and if you can provide them, your business can survive and possibly even grow.

The Quickest, Easiest, and Best Way to Get a Never-Ending Supply of Creative Solutions to Your Problems

Whenever you find yourself making excuses for setbacks or delays, you need to ask yourself better questions and you'll get better answers. That's what you'll do in the exercise that follows.

You're going to take any goal that you have and you're going to write that goal in the form of a question. For example, if your goal is to come up with $50,000, you'd write that goal in the form of a question, "How can I come up with $50,000 to launch the business?"

But there's more. You also want to be very conscious of the assumptions within the question itself. Rather than saying, "How can I come up with $50,000 to launch the business?," you can phrase the question like this: "How can I come up with $50,000 to launch this business easily and quickly?" Emphasize the words *easily* and *quickly*.

Those presuppositions or assumptions are very important, because you're going to get very different answers when you phrase the question that way. Remember, you can do this for any goal that you have and any place that you feel stuck. Remember: it's never a question of resources. It's always a question of resourcefulness.

Once you've written your goal in the form of a question, it's time for what we call **Green Light Thinking.** It's a playful type of thinking in which anything that comes to mind goes on to the paper, even if it seems crazy.

Now, the key is to come up with 20 answers to your question. The first answers will seem to flow very easily. The last ones will seem like you're squeezing water from a stone—but there must be 20 answers in **Green Light Thinking.** Once you've done that, you're going to circle the best one, take immediate action, and enjoy the results.

Now, write your goal in the form of a question. Be cautious in regard to the assumptions within that question. Then use **Green Light Thinking.** Come up with 20 answers. Circle the best one and then take immediate action!

Question:

_____

_____

1. _____

2. _____

3. _____
4. _____
5. _____
6. _____
7. _____
8. _____
9. _____
10. _____
11. _____
12. _____
13. _____
14. _____
15. _____
16. _____
17. _____
18. _____
19. _____
20. _____

The Major Obstacle Stopping You from Realizing Your Dreams

Bob Proctor, famed host of *The Secret*, and I were talking recently with Mark Victor Hansen and Dr. Reverend Michael Beckwith. We were discussing the reasons somebody would be most likely to succeed, and we all agreed that you need to think big, dare to dream, and have the drive to go after your goals.

Bob said one of the major obstacles to realizing one's dreams is getting too caught up in having to figure out in advance exactly how it's going to happen. Unfortunately, most people get too involved in planning every step of the way. Jeff Bezos has said the same thing in interviews. He said that even though you write a business plan, everyone knows it never stands the test of actual use. The purpose of the plan is simply to give you some direction, because figuring out where you're going is a great exercise. But once you start dealing with reality, things change too fast, and the plan is never the template for how you should get to where you go. Things move too quickly, so you have to be flexible.

For example, if you were to decide to climb an ice wall, you make the commitment to get to the top. But figuring out in advance how you're going to get to the top is very unproductive because of the constantly changing conditions as you climb. You just have to be resourceful along the way.

In my own case, I not only made the commitment to my entrepreneurial dream, but I burned all my bridges: I gave away all my clients from my previous career. In essence, I gave away all of my income flow—so my only option was to move forward and be resourceful. I'm not suggesting that's the right approach for everyone, so don't go out and quit your day job just yet! But this was the right decision for me. I needed a fresh start, I needed to focus all my time, effort, and attention on being more resourceful so that I could expand my entrepreneurial mind and realize my entrepreneurial dreams.

One of the best ways to be resourceful is to ask better questions. Instead of, "Why can't I do this?" you should be asking questions like these:

- How can I do this?
- How can I do this easily?
- How can I bring in the resources I need?
- Where can I get them from?

What the Founder of Amazon.com Wants to Teach You About Building a Billion Dollar Company

When Jeff Bezos launched Amazon.com, he had no resources for that dream. He talked to his parents and told them, "Listen, there's a seventy percent chance that you're going to lose everything, because most start-ups don't succeed." He said at the time, he knew he was giving himself 20 percent more of a chance than he actually had, because only 10 percent of start-ups actually go anyplace. And even though he warned his parents that he had a 70 percent chance of losing everything, they agreed to invest $300,000, which was their entire life savings, into the company that became Amazon.

Fortunately, their $300,000 in life savings has now made them 6 percent owners of Amazon. But when they made their original investment, they weren't investing in Amazon; they were investing in Jeff. When he was raising money for Amazon, it was still two years before the Internet boom and the arrival of huge numbers of venture capitalists and angels, and it was very, very hard to get capital.

At first, Jeff set up the computer stations in his two-bedroom home, and he had the computers set up in the garage. He had 300 of his friends test the system by placing orders online when he first got the system up. There were no bugs, so he was able to fill those orders. He told that test group of 300 to tell their friends about Amazon and, within a month, he had orders in 50 states and 46 different countries.

The company was making $20,000 a week, $80,000 a month by September of the first couple of months in business. But they needed a second round of financing to raise $1 million so they could expand. Nobody was going to throw down $1 million, because again, the hordes of venture capitalists had not yet arrived. So Jeff had to get really creative. He talked to 60 people, and 20 of them threw in $50,000 apiece, which gave him the $1 million he needed to expand. Most entrepreneurs would agree that when you need $1 million, it's easier to get $50,000 from 20 people than $1 million from a single investor, especially if you can show them you've been doing business of $20,000 a week, or $80,000 a month, in just the first two months.

I felt the need at one time to raise some money for my business. It was a fairly modest amount, about $100,000, but I didn't know how I was going to get it. Then my business partner asked me a great question. He said, "What exactly would you do with the money if you had it?"

I couldn't immediately answer that. What *would* I do with it? So he said, "Get clear on that first, and then start thinking about raising the money."

So for about a week, I focused on this one question: "What would I do if I had the money? And I began to think: Well, okay, I might invest it here in this portion of the business, or I might look to grow this other aspect, or I might create this product, or I might do X, Y, and Z." I gradually got an idea of the types of things that I'd do with the money if I had it.

Then I began to have more conversations with my partner. He began as the consummate mismatcher. He was always looking for the things that won't work. That's important for an investor, because people are pitching you on anything and everything all the time. You have to be very shrewd about where to put your funds. I started running ideas by my partner, and he'd say, "No, that's not going to make any money, and that wouldn't work . . . and that wouldn't work . . . and why would somebody want to invest in that?"

I gradually began to get wiser in the way of figuring out how I would use the resources if I had them until I had a finely tuned plan. I grew confident that when I brought the resources in, the risk would be low and the return could be very high. It became easy to say, "Hey, I'm looking for $100,000 and this is how we're going to use that money. Here's why we know we will get a return on it."

Right now, I want you to think of an amount of money that you could use to expand your business or enlarge your dreams. If you've never raised money before, then maybe it will be $20,000. If you have raised money before and you've got some growth in your business, then maybe it's $50,000, or maybe it's $1,000,000 or maybe it's $50,000,000. I just want you to come up a figure that would let you take a giant leap forward rather than creep along at a snail's pace.

Once you've got that number in mind, ask yourself: "What would I do if I had that money? Exactly how would I use that money?"

Use the spaces below to write your thoughts:
Your target amount:

Exactly how will you use that money?

Now that you've written out the ways that you'd use that money, here's your next task. I want you to now write down a list of the smartest, most intelligent, most shrewd business minds you know. People you can actually reach out to personally and test your ideas with. I want you to come up with at least five or six different people whom you can talk to about this.

You don't want to go to your uncle Joe, who is broke. You will want to go to the richest person you know, and if you don't know anybody who's really rich, think of somebody you know who knows somebody who knows somebody.

This is one of the best ways to begin a mentoring relationship. Just say, "I'm looking to bring in some money. These are the ways that I'm thinking of using it. My ideas are really raw, but I'd love to get some feedback."

> Write in the following space the names of five or six people you could approach. Maybe you don't even know them yet, but somebody you know might know them, and could help you make the connection.

Now that you've written those names, here's your next assignment. Over the course of the next week, seek those people out. Start today! Take immediate action so you can test the effectiveness of your plans for the money you're requesting.

If you ask the right questions or you're humble enough, then these conversations should help you be able to formulate a return structure for your investors that warrants the risk that they would be taking for putting money into your business. Once you've got the ideas fleshed out and you're looking for, say, $50,000, you could then begin the next phase. Go back to the same business people and say: "Based upon these facts, what kind of return do you think an investor would need before considering putting forward the money? What kind of deal structure makes sense for this?"

How to Raise Funds for Your Business Idea

A friend once asked me to sit in on a class he was giving. The editor of *Entrepreneur* magazine was there, and the person who launched Vans tennis shoes was there. They were talking about creating a business plan and finding capital to launch an entrepreneurial dream. When I heard the conversations that were held in the class, I was inspired. I thought to myself, "You know what? That's exactly what I'm going to do."

I had never launched a business before. I knew nothing about business. I had a background only in personal training and I had worked in management in hotel resorts. Nevertheless, I began to write a business plan for what would become **Christopher Howard Training.** I started asking people questions. I became ferociously curious. I asked everyone I knew, "How would you do this? Where would you get the money? Where would you get the funds? What would you do if you were going to start this business?"

It can certainly be challenging to get the initial money when you're starting a business from scratch. Most entrepreneurs get their first start-up capital from friends and family. I found some really ingenious ways for getting as many people as possible fired up about my ideas. I called just about everyone I knew and inspired them about the potential returns from my business. That's how I was able to pull $30,000 together.

Once I had educated myself and I had proven myself by working for other companies, I had created a track record of success. The better your track record, the easier it is to raise funds.

When it came time for my next round of fund raising, I made a hit list of every single person I knew and I started calling. I was very uncomfortable asking people for money. It was very hard for me to ask other people to invest their money into my business. But I simply dialed for dollars, which is often the job of an entrepreneur. I asked everyone on my list, "Hey, do you want to be a part of this opportunity? Here's how I think I can make it a win for you."

As an entrepreneur, you have to be able to find the courage to do whatever is necessary to continually grow your dreams. Yet, I've noticed that this courage is often missing, and I believe that's one reason so many start-up businesses fail. Those entrepreneurs don't have the mental flexibility and the courage to do whatever they need to do. Some people sit around and make one call a day, but if you have 70 calls to make, you should make them all in one sitting. Then you can follow up on them as you move forward.

I did end up bringing in the money for that round of financing. Later on, I had to raise close to a million dollars for the business. By that time, though, I had a track record, so it wasn't as difficult.

A Billionaire's Secret on How to Get Rich Starting from Scratch

My buddy Bill Bartman started his company because he had run into a great obstacle. He was deeply in debt because of the failure of a previous business. He hadn't paid his bills in months, and his creditors were bugging him. That's a situation a lot of entrepreneurs get into, quite frankly. At first, he was distraught. Then he decided the guys calling him were jerks and that they would never see any of his money.

He also began wondering, "What would happen if they were nice? They'd probably manage to get a little bit of money out of me." Then he thought, "What if I were to buy some of that bad debt from people and try to collect it myself? What if when I call them to collect it, I act like a nice guy?" If he did, he reasoned, people would be more apt to give him the money.

He went to the bank. He didn't have one piece of collateral, but he managed to get a loan for $13,000. Then he bought $13,000 of bad debt, for pennies on the dollar. He started calling people and being nice to them. Just as he had suspected, he succeeded just by being nice. He started collecting on those debts. Eventually, he went back to the bank and got a larger loan. He used that loan to go buy more debt, started calling more people—and started making even more money.

He just kept ratcheting everything up, starting with that small $13,000 loan, and his company, Commercial Financial Services, grew into a huge success. *Inc.* magazine did a story on him called, "The Billionaire Nobody Knows." And he did it all by starting with that one small loan. My point is that one option is to start small and then get as resourceful as you need to, to build up your track record of success.

Why You Can Turn Setbacks into Growth that Sustains You for Life

I read a story once about a young man who launched a business and wanted to impress his father. When he made $100,000 during his first year in business, he called his dad and said, "Hey, Dad, guess what? I made $100,000 this year."

His father said, "You know, son, that's good."

A couple of years later, the young man made a quarter of a million dollars. He called his dad and said, "You know, Dad, I made a quarter of a million dollars this year!"

And his dad said, "That's good, son."

The following year, the young man made a million dollars. He called his dad and said, "Hi, Dad, I made a million dollars in a single year!"

And his dad said, "You know what? That's good."

Then, a couple of years after that, the young man called his dad and said, "Hey, Dad, this year, I had to borrow a million dollars just to stay in business."

His father said, "Son, now you're a man."

What I've tried to convey in this chapter are a few key points: You need to expand your mind to think more creatively. You need to ask questions and find people who can help you grow your business. You need to turn obstacles into opportunities, because every time you overcome those obstacles, who you are, as a person, also expands; you're able to take on greater and greater challenges. And as you become more successful, you can help even more people so they too can wake up rich.

11

How to Train Money to Obey Your Every Command

Money is simply a measurement of the value we bring to the marketplace and to the world. Wayne Huizenga, who founded Blockbuster Video, put this very clearly: "Money is a convenient means of keeping score." The more value you create in your market, the more money you make; the more money you make, the more you can give to others.

To increase your wealth, keep asking yourself: "How can I create more value for people?"

Almost everyone wants more income, and many people succeed in getting it. People launch their own business because they think they are going to make more money. But there's no amount of income that you can't outspend. Some CEOs and business owners are living paycheck to paycheck just like their assistants. So it's not increasing your income that's important. It's increasing your net worth so that it changes your world. That's what I mean by wealth, and that's the real goal.

To reach that objective, we need two pieces of information:

1. Where are you now financially?
2. Where do you want to be in the future?

Below is a simple financial statement. Write in today's date, and then fill out the statement to the best of your ability. Be honest, so that you have an accurate assessment of where you really are. Remember that assets are what you *own*, and liabilities are what you *owe*. When you've listed both these categories, subtract the liabilities from the assets to come up with your current net worth. Of course, if you have a negative net worth, you'll subtract your assets from your liabilities. That's a wake-up call—but there's a lot you can do about it, starting right now.

Below assets and liabilities are your income and expenses. Evaluate these on a monthly basis. Include salary, dividend payments, commissions, bonuses, and anything else that enters your bank account. Some of that may be passive income, for which you don't do any hands-on work. Once you have these figures, you will know your total monthly income.

Your monthly expenses include credit card payments, tax payments, car loans, car insurance, food, groceries, utilities, new clothing—anything that requires money during a 30-day period. Once again, you'll subtract the expenses from the income to come up with what's left over at the end of the month. But once again, many people are living above their means. If that's the case, it's a good thing you are being brutally honest with yourself. Go for it.

Once you've finished your current financial statement, the next step is doing one for three years in the future. This is very empowering, because many people set goals to increase their income but not to increase their net worth. At the top of this second statement, write the date three years from today. Then complete the form exactly the way you intend it to look at that point in the future.

CURRENT PERSONAL FINANCIAL STATEMENT

Date:

ASSETS	**LIABILITIES**
Cash on Hand:	Home Mortgage:
Other Cash:	Real Estate Mortgage:
Real Estate:	Car Loans:
Motor Vehicles:	Credit Cards:
Stocks:	Store Credit:
Life Insurance:	Bank Loan:
Businesses:	Unpaid Taxes and Interest:
Other Assets:	Businesses:
	Other Liabilities:
Total Assets:	Total Liabilities:

**TOTAL OF ALL ASSETS
LESS TOTAL OF ALL LIABILITIES**

NET WORTH

Income:

Salary:

Bonus:

Commissions:

Passive Income = ———————

(Cash Flow from Interest + Dividends + Real Estate + Businesses)

Dividends

Rental Income:

Businesses:

Total Income: ———————

Other Income:

Expenses:

Taxes:

Home Mortgage:

School Loan Payment:

Car Payment:

Credit Card Payment:

Store Credit Payment:

Other Expenses:

Child Expenses:

Bank Loan Payment:

Monthly Cash Flow: ———————

(Total income minus total expenses)

FINANCIAL STATEMENT 3 YEARS FROM NOW
Date:

ASSETS	**LIABILITIES**
Cash on Hand:	Home Mortgage:
Other Cash:	Real Estate Mortgage:
Real Estate:	Car Loans:
Motor Vehicles:	Credit Cards:
Stocks:	Store Credit:
Life Insurance:	Bank Loan:
Businesses:	Unpaid Taxes and Interest:
Other Assets:	Businesses:
	Other Liabilities:
Total Assets:	Total Liabilities:

**TOTAL OF ALL ASSETS
LESS TOTAL OF ALL LIABILITIES**

NET WORTH
Income:

Salary: Passive Income = ———————

Bonus:

Commissions: (Cash Flow from Interest + Dividends +
                                 Real Estate + Businesses)

Dividends

Rental Income:

Businesses: Total Income: ———————

Other Income:

Expenses:
Taxes:
Home Mortgage:
School Loan Payment:
Car Payment:
Credit Card Payment:
Store Credit Payment:
Other Expenses:
Child Expenses:
Bank Loan Payment:

Monthly Cash Flow: ———————

(Total income minus total expenses)

Now you have clear financial goals. It's time to address the big question . . .

How to Increase Your Wealth Without Working Longer Hours

The answer always involves finding a means of *leveraging*. For example, if you're a massage therapist, you can launch a massage therapy school and then franchise that school. You can also make products, such as audiotapes. You can write a book to teach your skill to an even larger market. There's always a way to increase the value that you create.

I started out doing coaching one-on-one. Then I started coaching groups, which gave me greater leverage. I could affect more people's lives, and create more value for people. Of course, the amount of money that I made also increased. But there was a limit to that as well. I thought, "Even though I've created greater leverage that's delivering better value, how can I leverage even further, to the next level?"

So I began coaching trainers, and now I have three or four different programs that are always happening somewhere in the world, even when I'm not on site. And this way, I'm able to extend more value.

Constantly ask these questions: "How can we increase the value we offer customers? How can we increase our volume?"

There are so many other possibilities we're exploring now. For example, we're looking toward more internet delivery of content through a subscription site so people can access our content from anywhere in the world. Will we be rewarded financially? Of course, and we should be, and you should be rewarded for your work, too. We all have a mission and a purpose on the planet: You should do what you're born to do, and you should be rewarded very well. We're rewarded along the way on our path to transformation, but the true focus is on transformation itself.

How to Turn Your Ideas into Money

Since there are only 24 hours in a day, there's a limit to how much time you can sell, no matter what your price. You need to make money by expanding your business in other ways. You need to sell your ideas, not just your time.

Lots of people have great ideas, but few people know how to actually turn them into money. But all great entrepreneurs do have that ability, which is an essential element of *Instant Wealth*.

Why is this so hard for the average person? One of the main reasons is an unconscious inner resistance to the possibility of success.

Here's a case in point. In Sydney, Australia, a woman named Anita was in one of my seminars. She was a very spiritual and kind-hearted person, but she never was able to manage her finances well or to make enough money. In this seminar, she told me right away, "Chris, I have to make more money. I desperately need to have a breakthrough financially. I just don't think I deserve it."

From a spiritual perspective, everybody is deserving. From a worldly perspective, there's the law of reaping and sowing: If you're not sowing the seeds, you don't deserve the harvest. Yet Anita had never thought that way before. By the end of the seminar, she realized that what she was really passionate about was *helping people*, and she decided that the new path for her was to open up nursing homes. Now what she needs to do is learn how to pursue the money that can come from the great idea that's motivated by her passion. What she has is something she can take with her on that really long hill, with the really wet snow, and create that snowball effect that Warren Buffett talks about. She has all the motivation and energy to make that happen. It's inherent in who she is.

However, Anita has a blind spot when it comes to creating income. To help with that, she made a commitment during the seminar to get a really tough business coach. She enrolled in our **Billionaire Boot Camp** training specifically for this purpose. I suggested that she also get some business mentors, because she had been looking at everything from a spiritual perspective. She was a really good person, but she needed to radically shift her approach to make her new business successful.

The Biggest Mistake Poor People Make that Keeps Them Stuck

We see this in philanthropy and nonprofits all the time: people who have never learned how to make their ideas financially sustainable so they can really work.

I've devoted years to studying the accelerated human transformation process that will produce superior results. I was 24 years old when I began in this field, and I've been researching the science of success ever since. I realized early on that to grow my business's profitability and my own long-term wealth, I needed to create products. So I began to launch businesses and to create products that would extend the reach and longevity of those businesses. In fact, this book is one of those products. This has helped me weather challenging times, because the risk factors are very high if all your financial assets are in just one business.

I haven't always been this farsighted. When I was younger, I focused all my energies into running and growing my business. I didn't really take good care of my financial future. I thought I would never retire, that I would always be working. *Don't make that mistake*, because even if you don't retire, that doesn't mean that you don't need to take care of yourself financially so that you *can* stop working at any time. You need to know how to turn your ideas into revenue-generating products that will bring in money for many years to come.

An Unusual Way Warren Buffett Uses Small Change to Build His Wealth

One of my favorite stories about Warren Buffett shows the deep respect he has for the value of money. Years ago, Warren was walking with Katharine Graham, publisher of the *Washington Post*, when she said, "I have to make a phone call. Do you have 20 cents?" Buffett reached into his pocket, pulled out a coin, and replied, "I've only got a quarter; let me go get change."

Katharine was incredulous. She said, "What are you talking about, Warren? It's only a quarter. It's only a nickel more. Give me the quarter!"

But Warren refused, "Yes, it's only a quarter more, but do you know what that five cents is worth, at thirty percent compounding interest over time? That's huge! So I'm going to go get change."

I love that story because it speaks to the way Buffett really respects the value of money. In my **Billionaire Boot Camp** training, I tell this story to help drive home that concept. Some people hear that anecdote and say, "Well, that's just stingy," or, "That's just miserly." But it's not. When you get the high returns on your investments that Buffett gets on his, then you evaluate every nickel from that perspective.

Many super-rich and super-successful entrepreneurs—people who are self-made—have that same respect for the value of money. That doesn't necessarily mean they all live lavishly. But they do avoid waste. If every person on the planet were to look at everything simply from the perspective of the compounding return their money could earn, it might change how everyone spends their money, and there might be a lot less waste.

I often ask in my seminars, "How many of you feel as if there's no waste in your business or your life?" Nobody ever raises a hand. Everyone knows that there are places where they could trim back. Yet many people who come to our seminars resist that whole concept of avoiding waste. They hear that story about saving the nickel, and they think it's just ridiculous. They think, "I wouldn't want to live like that," rather than making the shift and saying, "No, that's the *intelligent* way to live. What's not intelligent is the way I have been living, with the waste that I have in my life."

The Real Reason Rich People Often Live Modestly

Warren Buffett still lives in the same house that he bought in 1958 for $31,500. He lives a very frugal life. This is just his authentic lifestyle. He doesn't need a lot of material possessions to feel great. Many super-wealthy people are like that. It ties into respect for the value of money.

A film editor I worked with years ago told me he was once on a movie set at the DreamWorks movie studio when Jeff Katzenberg drove up in an old truck. The editor couldn't believe it. He was extremely offended to see a billionaire driving around in an old car. But I found it interesting that the editor—who was broke—found it offensive that a rich person was driving around in an old truck. While he was telling me this, I was thinking, "Well, no wonder you're broke."

When Sergey Brin from Google made all his billions, his lifestyle didn't change a whole lot. He did buy a new house on the peninsula south of San Francisco. And he and his partner, Larry Page, did buy a plane, because they had meetings all over the country. Yet he still shops at Costco, and he even introduced his parents to shopping there. He's trying to teach himself not to be so frugal, but he still holds to the frugality he was raised with.

I've learned to be more frugal in my own life because my mentors showed me how watching the bottom line could help my business. When I first launched **Christopher Howard Training** and **The Christopher Howard Companies**, my business partner, Bob Shearin, and I went out to buy some furniture for the office. Bob was already very wealthy; he had built and sold a $70 million wholesale clothing business. So when we went shopping, I wanted to buy a plush chair, with a head rest, that I could lean back in and be really comfortable when making phone calls and doing business. But Bob took me to Office Depot and bought the cheapest chair the store had. He taught me, right from the very beginning, why it's smart to be frugal, especially when you are building a business on a shoestring budget.

As an entrepreneur, you need to know that you have all the resources at your disposal to create any dream that you have ever had. There is $13 trillion_ of _Instant Wealth_ circulating the planet every single day, waiting for someone to take care of it. It may as well be you! Having said that, you must understand that resources _are unlimited,_ but you should nevertheless act as if resources _were limited._ So many people who drive themselves out of business do so because they can't manage their resources. That's what business is really all about: maximizing margins, and maximizing net returns to your investors.

Being able to think from a frugal and unwasteful perspective, while having a state of wealth consciousness, is the key to success.

Unfortunately, this is the viewpoint that most charities and non-profits are missing, which is why Warren Buffett hesitated for so long to give his money to philanthropic organizations. He felt they were unworthy, not in the causes they supported, but in regard to their ability to handle money. So he waited until he found a good custodian for his wealth—which he found in Bill Gates. Buffett said Gates would be a billionaire even if all he ever did was run a hot dog stand in New York, because he has the entrepreneurial mindset that enabled his business to prosper tremendously.

What May Be the Best Money Question You Can Ever Ask in Your Business

When I learned how Warren Buffett evaluates every purchase and every expenditure of money, I started thinking about my own business expenditures. Before I spent anything, I'd ask myself, "Could this money be spent more wisely on something else?" I realized that *every purchase you make inside a business, including salaries for every employee, is an investment in your business.* So I learned to start thinking as an investor in my own companies. When you evaluate everything in your business that way, you become much more aware of the bottom line.

Think about every dollar and every penny you spend as an investment in your business, and then decide if that investment is worthwhile.

Sometimes this caused me to spend *more*, especially on my education. The value of investing in education is priceless. On the other hand, for other activities, I wouldn't spend at all. This type of thinking has completely transformed my business. You can transform *your* business, too, by thinking carefully about what you're spending money on and making sure it's not wasteful, but worthwhile. It's an absolutely essential element of *Instant Wealth*.

An Easy Way to Minimize Risk in Business

Many people have approached me over the years with opportunities to partner with them. Naturally, I ask about their experience, their track record, and their previous work with companies like mine. More often than not, I find that they haven't really done anything. That's a huge red flag for any kind of partnering arrangement in whatever you do.

Minimize your risk by making sure that there's a track record of success in the companies and the people whom you partner with.

I believe you should partner only with the best of the best. I'm also aware that some of my competitors don't think that way. I know well-known speakers and trainers who have accepted large sums to give seminars in new venues. They really wasted their time, because the people they partnered with were very unprofessional. Those speakers actually lost business in the long run.

On the other hand, you can't stay within your circle of confidence without *ever* exploring something new. My business has generally been live events with many people in large seminars. But as the world changes, and as media change, there are new ways of delivering content and communicating. You can't deny the reality of the changing marketplace, but you need to have a strategy for evaluating new opportunities. Ask yourself: "On a scale of zero to ten, what's the likelihood of an opportunity paying off big? And what are the risks?"

When Jeff Bezos started Amazon.com, he knew there was a 70 percent chance that he would fail. But knowing that actually took away the pressure, because all he needed to do was improve on those odds. Risk factors are different for start-up companies. When you're already established and looking to expand into different markets, the criteria begin to evolve. Successful entrepreneurs are not necessarily people who take the greatest risks. In fact, they often try hardest to minimize their risk. Someone once asked a billionaire hotel casino owner, "Isn't it risky to own a casino?" He replied, "It's a lot riskier to gamble in one."

Warren Buffett summed this up very well: "You don't have to swing at every pitch. Deciding whether to pass on a project requires an internal check. If it's something that you really want, it's your heart's desire, then you're going to have the fuel to make it successful. Otherwise, you won't. An entrepreneurial endeavor takes so much energy and effort. Pursuing every opportunity is just not going to work. Moreover, great fortunes are not made through a diversification of efforts. They can be *maintained* through diversification, but they're *made* through with concentrated energy."

What You Must Do If You Want to Successfully Grow Your Business With Less Risk

How can you know when to wait and when to move? When you're starting your own business, you have to *make sure the business you have chosen is the true expression of your soul's purpose.* To be successful, you have to get that initial momentum. Once you find that passion and you're just starting your new business, you shouldn't even be looking to branch out. That next step will come later, *after* you've become successful in your initial endeavor.

For example, you may find people telling you about the need to get involved in a new Internet application or networking site. You may even get some tempting financial propositions for that kind of involvement. At that point, you need to be very skeptical. What sounds like a good use of your time is more likely to be just a drain on your resources. You have to ask about the cost to your time, and possibly money as well.

On the other hand, I *know* that if we expand into Asia, we're going to make many millions of dollars. India, especially, is an emerging market, with a growing middle class. We've been looking very carefully at which promoters to work with there. So how do I minimize my risk in deciding how to choose one? First, I want to work with people who have a strong track record. I do what I do well, and if I know they do what *they* do well, there's virtually no risk.

In everything you do, think about specific targets that you want to hit financially. An easy way to clarify this is by thinking of four stepping-stones to monetary success: financial stability, financial security, financial freedom, and financial opulence.

How to Attain Financial Stability

Financial *stability* means you have two to three months' of living expenses in a savings account and enough money to cover your basic insurance. This should be separate from the money you need to run your business day to day—because as you're growing the business, you still know that your personal financial needs are taken care of.

Your financial stability goal will be attained when you can cover your financial needs for three months and have purchased insurance.

In my seminars, I ask everyone to calculate their basic living expenses. Some people call that "the nut." This doesn't include the luxuries you would like to have in your life; instead, it's just what you need to keep you alive. What would that be for three months, and how much would it include if you purchased insurance? Then you'll know that you've hit that financial stability goal.

How to Attain Financial Security

The second goal is financial *security*. We define this as "enough capital invested at a return of 8 percent to cover your basic living expenses on an ongoing basis." That includes mortgage or rent, utilities, car, food, loans, and basic insurance.

Remember, financial stability was only enough money to cover two to three months of your basic living expenses. So, if you took financial stability money for three months, and you multiplied by four, you'll see what you need for a full 12 months. That's the annual income you would need to cover your basic needs.

Let's say you need to make $50,000 a year to cover your basic living needs. What is the sum you would need to invest at 8 percent that would yield $50,000? You've achieved financial freedom when you have enough capital invested at 8 percent to cover your current lifestyle without having to work again.

How to Attain Financial Freedom

The third goal is financial freedom. To determine what that amount of money would be for you, say to yourself: "My financial freedom goal will be attained when I've accumulated enough capital invested at 8 percent to provide an annual income of _____."

We refer to 8 percent because that is a very doable rate of return on most investments. Warren Buffett says, "Investors who don't know what they are doing, or uneducated investors who are fairly passive investors, who are not going to be taking an active role in investing, would be far better off investing in an index fund than giving money to a managed fund, because the index funds have outperformed the managed funds over the years." The index funds have historically returned above 10 percent. Given that, 8 percent should be a reasonable number.

How to Attain Financial Opulence

Financial opulence means you have enough capital invested at 8 percent to live the life of your dreams without ever having to work again. To calculate this number, think about it this way: "My financial opulence goal will be obtained when I've accumulated enough capital invested at 8 percent to provide an annual income of _____."

Of course, it all depends on what you want! Some people will say, "*It's a quarter of a million dollars.*" Some people could say, "*It's $100,000—that would give me enough to go retire and live in Bali.*" Others need $1 million or $2 million. You need to figure out what *your* targets are. Once you have them in mind, you can start taking whatever you're making from your business—either through income or through dividend payments—and investing that money in the right way.

Doing this doesn't mean you have to retire some day. It means that you will have the choice to do whatever you want. When the fear of going broke disappears, life is a lot more fun. You can be a lot more playful as you're out there building your dreams. You can also give more back to others who are in need, and in any way you choose.

The Seven-Day Money Challenge that Brings Riches into Your Life

Let's close this chapter with an exercise. For the next seven days, just before you go to sleep, take seven minutes for subconscious reprogramming again as discussed in Chapter 6. Here are the steps once again:

1. Sit in a quiet place.
2. Close your eyes and pretend you can't open them.
3. Try to open them and find that you can't.

Remember to set aside your critical faculty. Suspend disbelief. As you do this over the next seven nights, I want you to program your mind in a very specific way. Once you've removed the critical faculty by pretending that you can't open your eyes, give yourself direct suggestions and use end result imagery again.

1. How will your life improve once you've mastered your finances?
2. What will you do?
3. Where are some of the places you'll go?
4. What are some of the things you'll experience or create?

Don't forget that the magic number is three. You're going to give yourself each of the direct suggestions three times, and in three different ways. Do this for seven minutes before you go to bed for the next seven days. Then wake up to *Instant Wealth!*

12

CHAPTER

The Shocking Things Most People Believe and Do—that Keep Them Poor

You've now begun to master the financial aspects of building and growing your business. This is a key aspect of *Instant Wealth*. It's also something that many would-be entrepreneurs are afraid to look at closely. In the previous chapter, you took the first, all-important steps! Now we're going to take a wider view. We're going to see how you can set up your life for the long haul—and enjoy the journey all the way.

For so many people, having a career is a lifelong struggle. They make the creation of their dreams into old-fashioned *work*. But you can't go the distance if you're struggling that way. People who try are stressed and eventually overwhelmed. Moreover, a life of struggling won't help you bring the exciting opportunities and positive people into your life. In fact, the opposite is true: struggling repels people, resources, and opportunities.

But when you're living in that zone where you're really enjoying the journey, in a positive state of mind, and playfully and joyfully going out and creating your success, then you will find yourself attracting people, resources, and opportunities, just like a magnet attracts iron filings.

The ability to channel energy consistently in a certain direction requires the passion that I've described throughout this book. If you have a grander purpose to your life, if you're thinking about your legacy, and if you are aligned with your passion, you will be more motivated to succeed in your career or your entrepreneurial venture. But it's how you live the journey that makes the journey worthwhile, not just the destination.

The Biggest Reason Most People Are Not Wealthy

Really infusing your chosen lifestyle into the expansion of your entrepreneurial dreams is essential to getting to wherever you want to go. Then every moment of every day becomes a moment spent in the embrace of God, and it becomes a celebration while you're moving forward. What could be more important than that?

The first principle to really embrace for making the journey an extraordinary self-propelling adventure is a state of *wealth consciousness*. The biggest reason why more people aren't wealthy is because they think that wealth is something outside of themselves. They're still sleeping. They think it's a dollar number that they have to attain. They say, "One day, when I have one million dollars, or ten million dollars, or one billion dollars—that's when I'll be wealthy." *Those people need to wake up rich!*

Real wealth is an emotional state. It's not something that comes with the achievement of a financial goal. Once you hit the first goal, you're just going to set up another one. That's the nature of goal setting. There's always another goal in front of us. So you can't say, "One day, I'll be successful, happy, wealthy, or feel like I've made it, once I hit this goal." Instead, chances are you'll achieve your goal and then say, "Okay, well, what's the next goal out in front of me?"

In my own life, before I learned any real business skills or acumen, the first financial issues that I had to overcome were actually spiritual issues that I had around money. I had an inner conflict about money: I didn't know if it was morally right to make a lot of money, and I worried that I should have a greater intention in life than making money. I wondered if my life should be about making a difference, instead of about making money. I didn't realize at the time that I could do both at once, that they were intimately intertwined types of conflicts and stop people dead in their tracks.

You don't have to choose between making money and doing good.

I remember attending Agape spiritual center in Los Angeles, a nondenominational church I attended whenever I could, and listening to Dr. Reverend Michael Beckwith. He gave a rousing sermon, explaining it was God's will for us all to live with wealth and abundance. He's one of the most spectacular spiritual guides on the planet, and he has really made a profound impact on my life.

Once I accepted that I really deserved great wealth and that all my financial and spiritual goals of making a difference were aligned, the door for the next phase opened, which was learning the entrepreneurial skills that eventually led me to financial success. Of course, not everybody walks the same path that I did, but to this day, my spiritual connection is a large part of my continued ability to attract people, resources, and exciting opportunities.

How to Feel Rich Now (Even If Your Bank Balance Is Low)

People ask me all the time, "How can I live in the state of wealth consciousness?" My answer is, "Live in an attitude of gratitude." It's an attitude with which you focus on those things you do have in your life, and you feel grateful for them on a regular basis.

Are you living in a place of gratitude? The first five minutes of your day set the tone for the rest of the day. I encourage people, when you first wake up, to ask yourself:

What specifically am I grateful for?
and
Why am I so grateful for that?

Let yourself feel gratitude for what you have. When you're starting your day, think about five things in your life that you're really grateful for. That sets up a great state of wealth consciousness for the day because what we appreciate, appreciates, and what we focus on, expands. It's a continual reminder to experience all the wealth you already have in your life.

Maharishi Mahesh Yogi wanted to open a healing center, and one of his disciples asked him, "Where are you going to get the money? You don't have any money." Maharishi replied, "We will get it from wherever it is at the moment." Every great entrepreneur knows that for any dream you have, you bring the resources in from wherever they are. But most people are boxed into lack and limitation, focusing on what they don't have, so they never open their minds to the fact that there are resources everywhere.

If you live in that attitude of gratitude for what you have, you can allow the wealth you already have to expand as you continue to identify new goals and continue to work toward them. From this place, you can start attracting those goals like a magnet attracts iron filings. But if you attach the feeling of wealth to the attainment of goals, you will never achieve that feeling. The only way to be wealthy now is to *wake up* to what you have already.

The Little Known Secret of Happiness Nobody Has Told You Before

I've known a lot of rich people who weren't living rich lives. They may have had a lot of money, but they weren't happy; they weren't fulfilled. A good friend of mine says, "No matter how much money I make, I just never seem to be happy." That's because he's attaching happiness to future financial goals rather than being happy and going out and making money today.

The reason why someone like my friend never feels satisfied, no matter how much money he makes, is that he has linked his happiness to something that he will never achieve. Learning to manage your emotional state is what enables you to be successful in the largest sense of the word. So does detaching your emotional state from future outcomes. The secret to living a rich life is not attached to your bank statements, now or in the future. Authentic wealth is something you achieve right now, through the choices you make about your attitude toward what you already have in your life.

The first step is simply waking up to this reality. It's *waking up rich*. You have to become aware that happiness is not something outside of you or something that you achieve over time. Wealth consciousness is also not something that happens over time. Success is a feeling you can have now. It's not something you arrive at as a result of attaining your goals. You can feel successful, wealthy, and fulfilled right now.

Happiness is an inside job.

How can you do that? Some people say, "I'm not successful, Chris, because I don't have the money." And they look at somebody else and say, "Look at Richard Branson; look at Oprah Winfrey; they have so much more money than I do. Or, look at my neighbors next door. They have so much more money than I do. How come I'm not successful?"

But if you look at the lives of people who believe they're not successful, you'll usually find that they are doing well in some areas of their lives. It might not be their career or their business, and it might not be their finances. It might not even be their health. It may be their family or their connection with their husband or wife or children that's really successful, and that makes them happy. If you consider all aspects of your life, not just money, you should be able to find success somewhere in daily experience. For that, whatever it is, you should be grateful every day.

Think of happiness the same way you think of success. Now, do the same thing with happiness. Surely, there are certain things that you're happy about in your life right now. Find them! Again, most people are focused on what they don't have rather than what they do have. But if you focus on what you do have, that can expand, and then you can achieve the goals you've set for yourself. You can feel happy, feel successful, and feel wealthy right here, right now. Life changes when you do that. It's hugely important to make life a celebration. It's the foundation of waking up rich.

How to Build Wealth and Have Fun at the Same Time

All of this pertains to your lifestyle, as you're moving forward. For people who are hugely successful financially, everything is truly about the journey and about how to make their success sustainable. If it weren't about the journey, they couldn't stick with it for very long.

Most people wish they were wealthier, wish they were healthier, and wish they had great relationships. But if just wishing were enough, everybody would be wealthy. When you view your work as a joyful process and a playful process, then you'll have the energy to see it through. You'll always be in the zone of Instant Wealth-Making the most of every moment, enjoying every second. Even when successful entrepreneurs transform their journey into philanthropic or charitable work, enjoying it along the way is what is important. Not everybody does. A lot of people make their career or their business or their work into a struggle, and it becomes strife-filled and stressful. As a result, they can make it only part way toward their goals. They often have addictions and or other problems. I've seen that again and again.

Every now and then go away, have a little relaxation, for when you come back to your work, your judgment will be surer, since to remain constantly at work will cause you to lose power of judgment.

—Leonardo Da Vinci

Sam Walton used to infuse fun into his meetings with Wal-Mart employees. He had a fun attitude, and when he came in to a store, there would be a celebration. He dressed up in silly costumes, and he had fun with the employees. He wanted to inspire people and bring that attitude of lightheartedness into everything that they did, because he knew that when you're growing an organization, the atmosphere that your employees are working in makes a difference as to whether or not your business is successful.

If you're angry and stressed out and feeling overwhelmed, that negative energy is going to filter down to your team. They're going to have the same feelings, and you're going to have a terrible work environment. If you're the CEO or the head of an organization or company, it's your job to live the values of the organization and set an example for the people you work with.

Richard Branson, of course, is the epitome of fun. He wore a wedding dress to launch Virgin Bridal. When he launched Virgin Ballooning, Richard and a friend were in a hot-air balloon that looked like a spacecraft. One of them was dressed up as E.T., and the other was a different type of space alien. It was just a gag, but some people thought it was a real UFO. The police were even called in to investigate.

I've always appreciated Richard's playfulness. When I visited with him on the island he had just bought, I challenged him to a sailboat race. When my girlfriend and I beat him, he threw her in the ocean. It was playful, and we were having a great time. We also played poker with him every night. I saw his fun spirit all the time, and I appreciated the competitive, but lighthearted atmosphere. That is exactly what makes him so charismatic and magnetic—to his employees, to friends, and to his brand.

When I first started teaching seminars and developing my training company, I attended hundreds of seminars; when I'm not teaching them, I'm taking them. I saw what I liked and what I didn't like in other people's programs. I also noticed, in most seminars or training programs, that some listeners were engaged, but many weren't.

During the six years I worked in the hotel resort industry, I was on stage every night—doing shows, entertaining our guests from all over the world, and engaging them so that they could have a great time. The whole environment was one of fun, playfulness, and entertainment. When I decided to launch my speaking and training business, I took everything I had learned from my past experiences and not only used that in my seminars, I taught my team to do the same. We created a branded entertaining education and transformation experience for people that powerfully helped them to produce for superior results in their businesses and their lives.

Once we did that, our programs took off like wildfire. People were engaged and captivated and they really learned the information we were teaching. The students absorbed it both consciously as well as subconsciously, which enabled them to make some profound shifts physically, emotionally, spiritually, and financially, catapulting themselves to powerfully move forward. As they began to tell all of their friends, families, business associates, and others, people began to flood in to go through this out-of-this-world transformational experience. Attendance at our programs jumped from about 30 to 50 people at a time to as many as 4,000 people in a single seminar. To a large extent, this was a direct result of creating such a playful and thoroughly engaging rock concert–type of learning environment.

It's not that I want money. It's the fun of making money and watching it grow.

—Warren Buffett

How to Love What You Do

Bill Gates's first employees typically worked 18-hour days, yet they shared a spirit of enjoyment in building Microsoft. It's not only the spirit of the entrepreneurs themselves that is important, but how they infuse that spirit into the cultural DNA of their company. The entrepreneur's example is a powerful nonverbal suggestion: The way you behave and conduct yourself at work indicates how you want and expect your employees to behave and conduct themselves in carrying out their responsibilities. Oprah often talks about working because she enjoys work. She says, "I don't know what I'd do with myself if I wasn't working."

I personally enjoy what I'm doing so much that I often lose track of time. When I teach our **Breakthrough to Success** or **Wealth Propulsion Intensive** programs around the world, I often work 15-hour days. And although I also have other trainers who teach portions of the program now, I'm there for much of them. I'm often up on stage for three days straight, connecting with the audience—and when I'm doing that, nothing else in the world exists. There is nothing happening outside, I'm totally engaged with the room, and I'm totally focused on making an impact and helping people blast through performance issues and really make dreams come true. Before I go on stage, I pray for the ability to connect with everybody in the audience in exactly the way they need to be touched, so they can go out and transform their lives and create the success they deserve.

The Closely Guarded Secret of the World's Most Successful Entrepreneurs

The most successful entrepreneurs in the world make their work a lifestyle. That's how they're able to infuse so much energy into what they do. It's not merely a job. True, there are people who see their work as a kind of necessary evil, as something they do from nine to five, a task from which retirement will set them free. But that's absolutely *not* the viewpoint of an entrepreneurial mind.

The most successful entrepreneurs have merged their work with their lifestyle, and that's how they're able to pour so much consistent energy into what they do and what they've achieved. The super-wealthy entrepreneurs decide on the lifestyle they are committed to having and use it to make them money.

Not every entrepreneur has a sense of physical adventure, but for many it's a part of their lifestyle. Oprah says, "I'm really hooked on skiing, and it's the first sport I'm pretty good at. But I'm not looking to be a champion. Just adequate." Richard Branson tried racing across the Atlantic in a speedboat, twice. The first time was in 1985, and the boat sank. On his second attempt, in 1986, in the Virgin Atlantic Challenger, he broke the record. While Richard loved the adventure of this, the amount of publicity he got far outweighed any marketing dollars he could have spent. It was worth its weight in gold.

Ted Turner was an avid sailor. His love of sailing created tremendous wealth from the publicity he too garnered as he dominated sailboat racing in the 1970s, and he won the America's Cup in 1977 with his boat *Courageous*. In 1979, he entered a boat called *Tenacious* in the Fastnet Race—from Plymouth, England, around the coast of Ireland, and back again. There were 302 boats in that race. A storm broke out in the middle of it, capsizing most of the boats, and of the 302 boats that had started the race, only 92 finished it—and Turner finished first. He was very much into the competition aspect of it, but even more important is his great sense of adventure and the kind of lifestyle he was leading—working hard, playing hard, while growing wealth—which is often the way of the most successful entrepreneurs.

Google continues to grow rapidly and a major reason is the unique and edgy lifestyle brand that is created by the company's founders. Lifestyle is the flavor of your existence, and the company is the expression of the soul of the founder. This puts your unique stamp on the company and it actually allows you to get richer and richer just living your truth, celebrating life, and living life to the fullest.

Oprah initially got her fun and adventure from acting and being involved in films. She started speaking from the pulpit at the age of only three, in various churches and traveling around. Everybody said she was a little actress, and that's all she wanted to be. In fact, she created her empire for the purpose of being an actress along the way, and she did appear in the movie *The Color Purple*.

She also became very interested in philanthropy and giving back, making a difference and helping people take responsibility for their lives: She expresses her soul through her philanthropy. Her sense of adventure comes through that as well—for example, when she launched the Leadership Academy in South Africa, that's an adventure. She also built the women's dorm at Community and Individual Development Association City Campus, the first free university in South Africa.

In other words, you don't have to have the same sense of adventure that Richard Branson engages in with ballooning and flying around the world, or that Ted Turner has with sailing. You just have to have the opportunity to add emotional texture to the journey by picking any lifestyle you desire and feeling great about it. You need to have passion for what you do, along with the resources that make it sustainable. It's really a matter of "living within your means," and people who are hugely successful know how to do that. If you have extraordinary financial resources, yachts and vast estates are still within your means, regardless of how unlikely that might seem to the rest of the world. But if your resources diminish for a period of time—and this happens to everybody—you'll want to cut back until things turn around. **The New Entrepreneurial Mind** means knowing how to get just as much enjoyment from eating marshmallows around a campfire as flying around in a private jet.

Some entrepreneurs like to live ostentatiously and others very frugally. "I don't measure my life by the money I've made. Other people might, but I certainly don't." Warren Buffett is purely involved with business and his collection of companies. He does have fun in that he works only with people he likes, trusts, and admires. He surrounds himself with people who are his friends; and he infuses a light-hearted, playful, and fun nature to this work—his artistry.

I don't measure my life by the money I've made.

Personally, I've been most inspired by Richard Branson's exploits and the spirit of adventure he brought into his business and his life. And I've noticed many more successful business people who have brought this spirit of adventure into all of what they do. It was because of that spirit that I created our **Billionaire Adventure Club,** to teach other people the same things I was learning—that if you can infuse that spirit of adventure into your business and your life, then it can make very, very profound changes and help you achieve your entrepreneurial dreams, and help others, too.

Through the **Billionaire Adventure Club,** we take groups of people to travel around the world, helping our participants infuse that spirit of adventure in their life, while simultaneously increasing their wealth by increasing their social network. After all, your network is your net worth, so if you can increase your social network, your wealth can expand exponentially.

The **Billionaire Adventure Club** was also established to help teach people that their wealth can have a greater purpose, that they can make a difference in the world. As Oprah says, "I don't think you ever stop giving. I really don't. I think it's an ongoing process and it's not just about being able to write a check. It's about being able to touch somebody's life." We have charity interests all over the world that we're involved with. But the real purpose behind the **Billionaire Adventure Club** was to teach people how to think this way, how to live, how to make their life an extraordinary adventure while increasing their wealth and making a difference on the planet so that we could help infuse this new entrepreneurial mind into the next generation of entrepreneurs.

Moreover, this club and our trips have expanded my own life and my own business beyond belief. Doing this has been as much a transformational journey for me as it has been for the members of the club. While in Peru, we climbed the cliffs in Machu Picchu. In South Africa, we stayed at a game reserve, and every morning and every night, we went on a safari, and I spent the night at Richard Branson's private reserve.

After South Africa, we visited Cambodia and rode the tuk-tuks, which are the streetcars that take you zipping around the cities. Our next trip was to Mongolia, where we went horseback riding and I entered a wrestling competition with the local champions. We went to the Maldives and stayed in the huts over the water, where we saw baby sharks swimming around in the crystal blue iridescent water. Our most recent journey was to Brazil, where I married my beautiful wife, Lauren, and Rickson Gracie was my best man. We went to the jungles of Belize, where we stayed in tree houses and went on caving adventures. We have ventured to places most people would never even dream of, hidden corners of the world that had really awakened that spirit of adventure and infused it into my life.

To go on these yearly scheduled trips with the club members has added an entirely new emotional texture to my life. The spirit of adventure has been really fantastic, while it's become an integral part of my creating my entrepreneurial dreams. It has also become an integral part of the lives of the members of the club. Finally, in each place we went, we worked to make a difference in the lives of the people who live there.

An Unusual Way Rich People Have a Great Lifestyle and Build Wealth Simultaneously

Many entrepreneurs who are successful at the billionaire level choose the lifestyle they want, and then allow their dreams to build their wealth. Richard Branson's purchase of The Manor was a lifestyle choice: He wanted to have a recording studio out in the country. It was also a smart business move. He was able to live in a beautiful country home, and have rock stars come to him to record their music there as well.

Similarly, buying Necker Island for the equivalent of $300,000 was also a business decision. He spends three months out of the year on the island, and when he's not there, he rents it out for $53,000 a day! That's what people who are playing at a huge level can do. Branson also bought the adjacent Mosquito Island next door, which is a famous spot for celebrities, for $46 million. Commenting on the price, he said, "It's hard to negotiate a deal when you have money. When you don't have any money, it's much easier."

Let your lifestyle fund your dreams.

As mentioned in Chapter 7, Google co-founders Sergey Brin and Larry Page finally bought a plane. Sergey lives a fairly modest lifestyle, but he and his partner bought the plane because they had to travel so much for business. The purchase of that plane has allowed them to make more money, because they can go and do more. It's the same situation as when Warren Buffett bought the plane that he initially called "Indefensible." He said, "Okay, my lifestyle increased, and now I've got a private jet, but it's because the jet is allowing me to make money."

Ted Turner and Mark Cuban both purchased sports teams: Turner bought the Atlanta Braves and Atlanta Hawks, and Cuban purchased the Dallas Mavericks in 2000. Owning those sports teams is something they love, something they're passionate about, but it's also something that makes them money. Cuban also co-owns a company called 2929 Entertainment, which includes a film production company, HDNet and HDNet Fights. He's passionate about sports. That's also a lifestyle choice for him, and it's something that turns an incredible profit.

How to Create Enormous Clarity About What You Want in Life and the Person You Want to Be

Now you're going to create a *vision board* for the lifestyle of your dreams! You'll need a large page piece of construction paper or poster board. Then I want you to begin collecting print images that represent the lifestyle that you want to live.

When I did this exercise, I created a complete "vision house." I had pictures cut out from various magazines of my lifestyle and it was much to the dismay of my landlord. It covered all of my walls, my doors, and everything inside. Instead of covering your walls with pictures, you are going to cover this piece of cardboard paper with a collage of imagery that represents the lifestyle of your dreams. This could include places you want to go, things you want to do, have, and create. Be artistic with this.

Have fun with this! When you look at your completed vision board, it will be a collage that really represents who you are, at your soul level. Everything you want to be, do, have, and create there in imagery. You can keep it someplace inside your house as a visual reminder for everything that you're committed to having in your life. Do this exercise, begin it today, complete it within the next week and gain a tremendous amount of clarity around everything that you want to be, do, have, and create in your life.

What High Performing Entrepreneurs Know About Success You Don't

High-performing entrepreneurs have mindfulness and presence that makes them magnetic. They are very much keyed in to the moment. They have the "power of now;" they're not stressed out about the future. Instead, they're playfully living out their dreams. The power of now is being present in the here and now.

There are two exercises that you can do that can help you to cultivate a leadership presence, so you can be fully in the moment at any time. This is not something that necessarily happens overnight.

It's a practice—something that you continue to remind yourself of and weave in to your lifestyle; you make the commitment to live in this way. When you do, this will not only make you more magnetic and charismatic as a leader, but it will make the journey all the more enjoyable.

The first exercise is for a waking state of mindful meditation. You want to practice this on a fairly regular basis. A few times a week would be great. The best way to practice this type of meditation is to find yourself standing outside, someplace outdoors. You could do it on the balcony of your home, or you could do it out in a wooded or secluded area. You want to have it where there aren't a lot of stimuli that might distract you.

Stand with your arms at your sides, letting your eyes gaze at nothing in particular. Just relax. If possible, do this exercise outside in nature, in a secluded area. Don't think! Just be aware of what is coming in through your senses. Let your mind to move from sense to sense, focusing on different aspects of what's happening.

If you find yourself becoming distracted, get out of your thinking and come back to your senses. That's what this meditation is about. Stay with this exercise for 10 minutes, and try to do it three times a week. It takes some practice to quiet your mind. I am by no means perfect at this myself, but it is something I'm glad to have brought into my life. Being fully present in the moment is definitely a skill you'll want to cultivate.

Lose your mind and come to your senses.

—Fritz Perle

A second exercise that I highly recommend is a simple mindful meditation that you can do once a day, five to seven days a week. Pick whatever time works for you.

Sit in a secluded place with no distractions. Turn off the telephone, shut the doors, close your eyes, and just go inside yourself. As you breathe in and out, just focus on your breathing. Feel each breath as it comes in and out.

Do this for 10 minutes. The idea with all forms of meditation is to eventually bring the meditative state into your daily life. In meditation and in entrepreneurship, it's how you show up in the moment that really matters. Are you playful? Are you relaxed? Are you enjoying the process? Are you having an adventure? If so, you will not wake up rich, because you already are.

13

The Mysterious (and Little Known) Law of Wealth Known Only by the World's Richest People—Now Revealed to You

You can have the most beautiful dream in the world, but it takes people to build it.

—Walt Disney

Take our twenty best people away and I tell you that Microsoft would become an unimportant company.

—Bill Gates

To realize your entrepreneurial dreams and attain the goal of *Instant Wealth*, be aware that you *can't do it alone.* You can't wake up to *Instant Wealth* if everybody else is still asleep. Even if you want to run your own business as a one-person shop, **leveraging** your resources is critical—and not only your financial resources. You'll need to attract 10, 20, 30, and then 100 and 1,000 *people* or more to turn your dreams into reality. Your ability to get groups of people moving in a common direction is critical to your success and the wealth you desire. This is what can propel you forward infinitely faster than ever before.

> *The enlightened business leader is the person who can assist people to self-actualize through the accomplishment of the noble objective or noble dream.*

> **—Roy Cammarano, author of**
> ***Entrepreneurial Transitions***

This last quote really expresses what leadership is all about: enrolling people in new possibilities and bringing out their best. Jack Welch describes the ideal leader as "somebody who can develop a vision of what he or she wants their business unit, their activity, to do and be. Somebody who can articulate to the entire group what the business is, and then gain acceptance of the vision."

A couple of years ago I took my **Billionaire Adventure Club** group to Peru. We went into a community isolated in the hills where education had never been provided beyond the primary school level. We worked together with the adults in the community to build a high school. At one point, there were about 60 of us working on making and laying the bricks, creating the rooftop, and so on. My question to you is this: Do you think we were able to build that school any faster with 60 of us working together rather than if it had been just one person working alone? Of course we did. This is called **leverage.** And with **leverage** you can accelerate your dreams a thousandfold.

> ***Coming together is a beginning; keeping together is progress; working together is success.***

> **—Henry Ford**

Richard Branson's Secret to Hiring and Keeping the Best Employees

Richard Branson has between 200 and 400 different companies at any given time. When I asked how he handles managing so many businesses, he replied, "I foster an entrepreneurial spirit within my organizations. I give a percentage of ownership to the individuals who are running those companies, so they run them as if they were their own. They have guidelines in terms of the branding of the company. But really, they run the company as if it's their organization. They take ownership." This allows Virgin to effectively grow the brand at light speed.

I teach at events all around the world, and we can't pull off an event without the support of an outstanding on-site crew. Everyone needs to feel the sense of responsibility and ownership that makes an organization successful. That's why I enroll my crew members in all of our transformational seminars. Within the team, I foster a spirit of ownership and personal responsibility. Everyone works much harder because of that attitude. And our mission of transformation spreads far more effectively and far more expansively.

That's also Jeff Bezos's philosophy at Amazon. It was very easy in the early days, because the company started with just a few people working out of his garage. Everyone had to be able to handle every aspect of the business. They were all enrolled in the big picture. If your employees think of their work as divorced from the big picture, they're not going to feel important and they're less likely to care whether they do a good job. But if you can help them see their part in the larger reality, they'll be much more committed to your organization's success.

Here's an example of how this works. There's a beautiful hotel in Singapore called the Pan Pacific. A personal concierge meets your car when you arrive. If you ask where something is, they walk you all the way there—even to the other side of the hotel. When I stayed there with my wife, we were always noticing how incredible the service was. Each employee took personal responsibility for every customer's experience.

Richard Branson wants his whole team to feel like "the host of the party." Richard Branson will pick key players and say, "Okay, you own ten percent of the company. You're the CEO." He wants to convey that sense of ownership. Warren Buffett wants his employees to be owners too, but he handles this differently. Buffett says, "I don't believe in giving away ownership. If they're going to share in the upside return, they should also share in the downside risk. If people want to purchase stock, I highly encourage that—and they can do it with the bonuses that I give them on a yearly basis. I'd love to have them as partners, but I want them to share that downside risk."

A Powerful Way to Inspire All of Your Team to Build Your Dream

It's not only ownership in the company that motivates employees, of course. Sometimes, it's sharing ownership in the leader's vision. When Martin Luther King Jr. said, "I have a dream," he was speaking to people who were disenfranchised and needing to feel inspired. King's dream was powerful, and he inspired and attracted others to share in his dream. He was magnetic, and he moved people to work toward realizing a dream of equality and civil rights. You need to do the same, even if your dream isn't as lofty as Martin Luther King Jr.'s. Whatever your dream is, you need to enroll people to help you achieve it, and to do that, you need to persuade people to believe in your dream as much as you do.

Steve Case has said that, in the early days of building America Online, all his employees shared the belief that their company would be successful. They had ownership in that dream. When everybody around them was saying it wasn't going to happen, that they had bet on the wrong horse, Case fired them up and painted the dream and enrolled them in the vision. Case was famous for walking around the organization saying, "We're on a march to get a million subscribers." This was before anybody believed that was even possible. But he kept saying, "We're going to get a million! We're on a march to a million subscribers!" That was his motto.

You need to have a clear goal in front of you and all the people you're working with, so that you—and everyone else—can really see what you're striving toward.

What is *your* dream?

Is your team aligned and enrolled in your vision? Do they feel a sense of ownership?

What can you say to inspire those around you to share in a common goal?

Once you've answered these questions, you need to *ask for commitment*. You need to say, "Are you with me in my vision?" My own vision is to put the tools of empowerment that we teach at **Christopher Howard Training** in the hands of everybody on the planet. At some point, I have to ask for people's commitment to that vision: "We're moving forward. We're going to cross that river. Are you going to cross it, too?"

I truly believe that enrolling all of the people you work with in an inspiring future is how you get leverage to accelerate things and create success beyond your wildest dreams. Your ability to do that is far more effective as a unifying force than any amount of *money* that people make. Money can be a good motivator—but when people feel like they're part of something that's bigger than themselves, they'll do a lot more to achieve their goals.

My goal is to keep my employees with me for life. Toward that end, I want to show them how, by being with us, they'll have the most growth and the greatest fulfillment of any business or any career. I need to enroll them in that possibility. So I give my employees lots of opportunities in our organization. As those opportunities expand and connect with their interests, they know they're contributing to our shared dream.

I'm also aware that sometimes a team member's own dreams will lead in another direction. Joey Martin was my head of research and training for a year or two. She contributed greatly to the start of the company, and she helped us build up our seminar programs. But when she said, "I want to launch my own business," I wished her all the best. My attitude was, go do it! Duane Alley stepped into her role and we continued to expand even more rapidly, always grateful for the contribution of the team members who helped to take the vision so far.

How to Build a Championship Team

My attitude as an employee was always to be like a samurai warrior for the organization, to do everything I possibly could to help it grow while I worked there. When I worked for Dale Carnegie Training, I poured my heart and soul into it—but I was getting so much value out, too. I wasn't working for what I earned; I was working for who I could become, and I learned so much as a result. If and when you leave, there should be a sense of gratitude from both sides.

If you're currently working for someone else, make sure you're also learning skills that can help you achieve your own personal goals.

To rally your troops in that way, make sure everyone feels like they are on a mission to be successful: *they'll* be successful, and *you'll* be successful. That's the way to *Instant Wealth!*

Again, it's the leader's job to rally everyone around the dream. Richard Branson does that beautifully. His dream has always been to provide better value and affordability for his customers. He started the Virgin Atlantic airline to offer consumers a cheaper and better way to travel. When he launched Virgin Cola, he wanted to provide an alternative to the established soda companies. His companies always go after a competitor that isn't giving value for money. He always positions his companies as the consumer's champion. Then he makes sure that his team feels aligned with that mission.

Use your entrepreneurial mind and your magnetism to rally and enroll *your* troops.

Oprah Winfrey has done the same thing in building Harpo Entertainment and her other projects. Oprah's mission is very clear: To have people take responsibility for their own lives. Everything she does has that simple purpose, which translates into an inspiring vision for her team. This becomes something her people want to be a part of. In fact, when we think of a woman who has the power to communicate a vision, Oprah is the first person who comes to mind. Everybody wants to be a part of Oprah's dream because of the values that she lives every day. You need to provide the same kind of inspiration for your team, Make sure everyone shares your vision, and you'll be on your way to *Instant Wealth!*

I've been amazed over the years by my own team. We've gone through tough and lean times and when the workloads were through the roof—but all along, our mission has been to put the tools we teach into the hands of everybody on the planet. That mission is what inspires us and keeps us moving forward.

I like to cite the story of the man walking down the street who sees some bricklayers. They're doing their work in a very sloppy, haphazard way, and the man asks them, "What are you doing?" And they say, "We're laying bricks."

He walks a little bit farther, and he sees some other people laying bricks, but they're working more carefully, making sure that the bricks are laid right and the cement is laid cleanly. He says, "What are you guys doing?" And this group says, "We're building a wall."

The man continues walking and sees a third group of bricklayers. They're working extremely meticulously, and they're consulting with one another about how to do it, and they're paying close attention to see that every brick is being laid perfectly. So he asks this group, "What are you doing?" And the response is, "We're building a cathedral."

That story beautifully reveals the power of purpose and teamwork. It's the type of viewpoint you should strive for in your own business: *Don't just lay bricks; build a cathedral!*

In hiring, look for three qualities: integrity, intelligence, and energy. But the most important is integrity—because if they don't have that, the intelligence and energy are going to kill you.

—Warren Buffett

A Proven Way to Ensure You Hire the Right Employees

Before you can get people working synergistically, you obviously need to know you have the right people. In fact, when Jeff Bezos was launching Amazon.com, he said, "The most important thing is the hiring."

It's *still* hard to get a job at Amazon.com. Even when the company desperately needed people, the hiring process lasted a long time.

In the early days, Jeff did all the hiring himself. He wanted to hire people like himself, people who were all about service, were risk takers, and who had a passion for the business. Once he got the core team, he stepped out of the hiring process because he knew the core team would hire the kind of people that he wanted. Then Jeff Bezos devoted himself to becoming the living, breathing embodiment of his company's values.

In the same way, Warren Buffett lives the values of Berkshire Hathaway. In the early days of the company, when the price of a single share rose to more than $100,000, many people asked, "Why don't you lower the share price? Why don't you do a stock split?" After all, Microsoft became very profitable this way: The company split its stock, the market became flooded with new stock at half the former price, and people bought shares. The market had grown so accustomed to the share price being double that of the new shares, that pretty soon, from a psychological perspective, the value of the new shares doubled to the old price per share, and nobody noticed the difference. So the value of Microsoft doubled practically with every stock split, and they did stock splits consistently over the years.

But Warren Buffett said, "No way. Keeping the price high is the only way that I can control who comes in and who I play with." He has said many times that he likes to do business only with people he likes, trusts, and admires—people who share his investment philosophies. Just as other people were careful in their hiring process, he was careful about whom he allowed to invest. Most stock buyers want to know, "Is it high today? Is it low today?" They want to trade, but Warren Buffett wanted people with the same approach as his own, which is to buy and hold.

He ended up creating a B share category, for two reasons. Many grandparents wanted to give gifts of Berkshire stock, but they couldn't pay $100,000 per share. Also, others were creating funds that mirrored Buffett's philosophies, and those shares were a lot cheaper. So, he eventually ended up doing a stock split. But he resisted it for a long time, just to make sure he had the right people investing in his company.

Buffett doesn't hire new people to run the businesses he acquires. Instead, he buys companies with good management already in place. Then he simply lets the existing management team continue to run those businesses. He says to his managers, "Write me a one-page letter explaining exactly what I should do if one day you get hit by a bus, and tell me the sequence I should do it in. As long as you guys are turning a profit (and I'll be able to judge that by your year-end reports) and as long as you talk about your mistakes freely and openly (because the good stuff won't take us down, but the mistakes will), I'll stay out of your hair."

How to Be an Inspirational Leader Others Trust

As a leader in the classroom, my job is also to move people to an inspired, decisive, and determined state of being—so they will become committed to go out and change their lives.

I always ask people, "What's your dream?" A housewife may raise her hand and say, "I don't know what my dream is. I have children; I have obligations." When I ask her what has she always wanted to do, she's afraid to even say what her dreams are. She doesn't feel like she can do anything else with her life, so she lives in a state of fear and resignation.

My job is to get her into a state of inspiration and a state of believing in herself, a state of certainty that not only can she make her dreams happen, but also that she can empower her children to also unleash their full potential. If I can get her inspired, then she might take different actions, and she might actually go make her dreams happen. She might make her home, her community, or even the world, a better place.

Nelson Mandela was in prison for 27 years, but he made decisions that other prisoners did not. He decided no one would ever take away his dignity. So he walked with dignity and lived in a state of commitment to make a different world. And as a result of the emotional state he lived in, he did make a difference in the world. He became a magnetic force. People recognized that he could be a powerful figure. He helped change the face of South Africa.

You don't have to be Nelson Mandela to create that type of change. If you see an employee who is thinking he's not going to go anywhere in his career, or his business, or in achieving any personal dream, perhaps you can inspire that person and help that person become committed and motivated to act. If you can change that person's emotional state—then you're bringing out the best in that person. You're enrolling them in a compelling future.

The emotional state of a leader is crucial. If a leader is stressed out or overwhelmed, the entire culture of the organization will be in the same state. It's essential for you to be in a good emotional state and to bring your employees into that same positive frame of mind. That's the only way you can all focus on the bigger picture of achieving the goal you've set for yourselves.

Why You Must Never Use Money to Motivate You

Strange but true: People will do much more for recognition than they'll do for money. My boss at Dale Carnegie, Tom Kiblen, taught me that by example. He used to send me *Successories*, motivational postcards with simple messages like, "Christopher, you're doing a great job. Keep up the good work!" Even though it was just a few words, getting those cards in the mail at my home really meant a lot to me.

Appreciate everything your associates do for the business. Nothing else can quite substitute for a few well-chosen, well-timed, sincere words of praise. They're absolutely free and worth a fortune.

—Sam Walton

About six times a year, I send postcards to my employees and to everyone I work with. I did this just last week, and it took me almost two days, but the value is immense. I believe it makes all the difference in the world in the matter of how effectively my team and I work together. People call me up afterward and say, "Thank you, I was so inspired by that." That's the job of a leader.

A friend of mine owns the largest picture framing company in the world. His company sells picture frames to Target and other retailers in Australia and the United States. He believes so strongly in motivating and energizing his employees that he calls all of his employees on their birthdays—every single one of them. That's a lot of employees to call, but he writes the birthdays into his calendar, and he makes time for it. He reaches out to them with a personal touch, and they love it and appreciate it. That's an example of creating personal magnetism from a leadership perspective.

Richard Branson obviously has so much to do, yet I know he gives out his personal e-mail address to people, and I know he responds to messages. How does he do that? I don't know, but I do know that making himself accessible is really important to him. At Dale Carnegie, Tom Kiblen's door was always open. Whenever I walked in his office, he was always so enthusiastic and always made me feel that he was excited to see me. He pointed out mistakes when it was necessary to do so, but more importantly, he believed in giving massive approbation for everything anyone did that was right. I never had a better boss than Tom. He was a real champion for other people, and that quality is also critical for good leaders: being able to look at others and see all that they can be, seeing someone's potential.

Dale Carnegie said that you should *"Give someone a grand reputation to live up to."* I think that's part of what makes a leader charismatic. You are enrolling them in a grander vision of themselves. That leader sees a person's capacity to be the best. Your job is to bring out the best in the people around you. It's that simple.

My martial arts teacher Rorion Gracie is also a great leader. The greatest leaders I've had have been champions for me. They looked at me and saw something that maybe I didn't even see in myself, and they helped to develop that. One of my early martial arts instructors wrote me a letter that said, "I see more in you. I see what you're capable of. I see your potential, and perhaps you don't see it yet, but I see it." That stayed in my heart for a long, long time. Knowing someone believed in me helped me to believe in myself.

Oprah Winfrey was giving recitations in church when she was just three years old, and one day she heard the ladies in the back talking to her grandmother, saying, "That child's gifted."

Oprah remembers, "After a while, I started to believe it."

How the Rich Use Intuition to Make the Best Business Decisions

Women talk about intuition more than men do, but all great business leaders are very intuitive. Oprah Winfrey says, "The universe is always trying to get your attention. Sometimes, it starts out as a whisper. Then it gets to be a storm. First, a pebble hits you on the head. And before you know it, you've had the house fall down."

More than anything else, the one thing that has allowed me to achieve both material and spiritual success is the ability to listen to my instincts. I call it my inner voice, but it doesn't matter what you call it: nature, intuition, or a higher power. It's the ability to understand the difference between what your heart is saying and what your head is saying. I now always go with the heart. Even when my head is saying, *"Oh, but this is the rational thing, this is really not what you should do,"* I always go with what I'm feeling.

Great business leaders follow their feeling. Warren Buffett walked into a furniture store owned by a woman named Rose Blumkin. He didn't have to look at the books. She basically summed up for him what her business was, and he knew intuitively that the business was a good purchase. Other investors do an enormous amount of due diligence, but Warren Buffett knew intuitively that what Rose Blumkin was telling him was right. He bought her business on the spot.

Of course, Buffett reads 2,000 annual reports a year. He understands business, and has *developed* his intuition. An investment decision by Warren Buffett is going to be better than yours or mine, because he's developed his ability to intuit in that specific context. But listening to that inner voice is something everyone can do. The more you teach yourself to trust your intuition, the more powerful you become as a leader.

I'm guided by a higher calling. It's not so much a voice as it is a feeling. If it doesn't feel right to me, I don't do it.

—Oprah Winfrey

An Enrollment Exercise

With the following list, name 10 people you need to enroll in your vision of the future. Who is it going to be? Your family? Potential investors? Friends? Your employers or your employees? Come up with 10 names.

1. _____
   _____

2. _____
   _____

3. _____
   _____

4. _____
   _____

5. _____
   _____

6. _____
   _____

7. _____
   _____

(continued)

8. _____

_____

9. _____

_____

10. _____

_____

    The second stage of this exercise is an interactive action step. How can you communicate with those 10 people? How can you paint the picture of your vision for each of them? Make a plan for telling people about your vision, and then ask them: "Are you with me?" "Will you help me with this?" Be bold and brave when you ask that question! Do it over the course of the next week. You have 7 days to enroll 10 people in your vision!

14

The Greatest Money Making Secret in History

*I had a hectic schedule traveling the world while
training ten- to twelve-hour days, spending
additional hours preparing for these trainings
and honing my own skills, and I loved every
minute of it. I had become like the pianist that
did not notice the room, his hands, the keys, the
score, but instead became conscious of only being
one with the music and expressing emotion.*

—Dr. Mihaly Csikszentmihalyi, author of
Flow: The Psychology of Optimal Experience

You know that feeling when you become so immersed in what you're
doing that you completely lose track of time? Some people get lost in
a book, some get lost surfing the Internet, and some people get lost in
their work. Whatever it is, *you're in the zone.* Total immersion in what
you're doing is another key to unlocking your entrepreneurial mind
and waking up rich. When this level of mental energy is connected to
your business, you can easily achieve your financial goals for yourself
and others.

But first, you have to recognize that almost-meditative state. Then you need the power to enter it at will . . .

The Secret to Living in a State of Inspiration and Creativity

The idea of a *flow state* or *zone* has been thoroughly explored by the psychologist Mihaly Csikszentmihalyi of the University of Chicago. In an interview, he recalled studying students at the Chicago Art Institute in the 1960s. When they started painting, the students would almost fall into a trance. They were oblivious to everything else around them. After completing their paintings, the students would look at their work and feel good for 5 or 10 minutes about the work they had done. They would then put those paintings aside and seemingly forget about them. What was important was the *next* painting.

"Playing in the zone" means . . .

1. Being completely involved, focused, concentrated—either because of innate curiosity or as the result of training
2. Experiencing a sense of ecstasy—of being outside everyday reality
3. Having great inner clarity—knowing what needs to be done and how well it is going
4. Knowing the activity is doable—that the skills are adequate, and being neither anxious nor bored
5. Feeling a sense of serenity—no worries about self, feeling of growing beyond the boundaries of ego—a feeling afterward of transcending ego in ways not thought possible
6. Experiencing timelessness—thoroughly focused on present, don't notice time passing
7. Being intrinsically motivated—whatever produces *flow* becomes its own reward

Csikszentmihalyi noted that when those conditions were present, people would begin to forget all the things that bothered them in everyday life. "You felt as if you were a part of something greater and you were just moving along with the logic of the activity. It feels effortless and yet it's extremely dependent on concentration and skill. So it's a paradoxical kind of condition where you feel that you are on a nice edge between anxiety on the one hand and boredom on the other." This concept also has exciting applications in the business world. Excite co-founder Joe Kraus says, "I think the flow state is addictive, and the only way I know to get there is through a business start-up."

The zone opens up when your skill level meets the challenges at hand. If your skill is a level 2 and you have a level 10 challenge, there can be anxiety or panic—because your internal tools aren't equal to the task. But if your skills are a level seven, and you've got a level eight challenge, you could experience some *very positive energy*. The challenge is just beyond you and you have to stretch for it. That's how you avoid boredom, that's how you avoid anxiety, and that's how you enter the zone of increased productivity, success, and waking up to wealth!

Living on Your Personal Edge

I met recently with one of the members of our **Billionaire Adventure Club** to do some coaching. He told me, "Chris, I get bored easily. I work as a consultant, and I'm really good at going into an organization and helping increase sales. I'm well paid, but if I'm just making money, my motivation just disappears. I find myself dropping all the way back down to where I'm broke again. I've repeated this pattern over and over and over again, and I don't know why I can't get the motivation to keep moving forward."

He stops working, he loses energy, with the result that he's no longer bringing in money. Then he finds himself troubled financially. So I asked, "Why do you think this is happening? Give me the first answer that comes up."

He mentioned again that this might be happening because he gets bored easily. But he also admitted, "Maybe my goals are so big that I'm *afraid*. I don't really believe I can make them all happen. I have all these lofty plans and ideas, but I get paralyzed by fear—and simultaneously bored. Then I'm stuck."

I suggested that one of the most important things anyone can do in business is to continually live on your personal edge. Then we spoke about his fears and how to deal with them. Most people won't admit they have fear, so all that emotion ends up expressing itself as angry outbursts. They take out their feelings on other people because, for some reason, getting angry is more socially acceptable than being afraid. Most people think it's more powerful to be angry than to be fearful.

We talked about accepting his fears and sitting with his fears, and, especially, realizing that his fears are transient: they will come and go. I also told him that if he doesn't recognize his fears, if he only allows himself to express his fears through angry outbursts, then he will be doomed to continue living a fearful life—and it's very possible that he will never attain the goals he has set for himself as an entrepreneur.

When you can recognize your true feelings and let them go, and realize that they are transient, then you have power over your feelings.

An Easy Way to Be Continually Motivated to Create Your Dreams

If you want to continue to be motivated as you're moving forward in your career, you need to continue to increase your skills. That requires you to increase the challenges you face. You need to try things that scare the daylights out of you, and that stretch the expression of your entrepreneurial soul. If you continue to stretch yourself, you'll continue to grow—in your career, your personal relationships, and in your life in general. And if you can get into a zone where you're stretching yourself, you'll feel enormous pride that you've succeeded after pushing yourself to do more.

However, if the goal you set for yourself is too far out of your range of thinking—if it's really too big or too difficult for you to achieve, at least right now—that can also create inertia. You can be caught up in fear of trying to reach a goal that is too difficult. So you don't do anything, for fear of failing.

So, you don't want to be bored, but you can't be afraid either. You need to find a balance in which you're challenged enough that you don't get bored, but not so much that you're afraid to move forward. Throughout your entrepreneurial life and while you're working to achieve your dreams, you have to find and always keep in mind your personal edge, and live on that edge. That's where true joy and *instant wealth* come from.

The most successful entrepreneurs are addicted to getting into that zone. They'll continually look to raise the challenges facing them and to increase their skill levels to meet real challenges, and there's a thrill that comes with that. So there's both the meditative state of being in that place, but also the thrill of overcoming obstacles that are within your circle of competence.

When Warren Buffett plans to invest in a business, he concentrates on tried-and-true businesses. Gillette, the razor company, is one example. There are three billion people around the world growing hair, and some of them want to shave it off every day or so. Nowhere on the planet are there a couple of kids in a garage developing a new technology that's going to bury Gillette. Warren Buffett says he prefers to make very safe investments in companies he understands. By staying within his circle of competence, by staying in his zone, he can operate in that state of flow from an investment perspective. As Buffett says, "I don't try to jump over seven-foot bars; I look around for one-foot bars I can step over."

How to Use Your Greatest Strengths to Make Money

It may take some time to recognize the zone in which you play best. It took Richard Branson awhile to see that his zone is branded venture capital. Then, he branded more than 200 different companies worldwide. "Lending the Virgin name to other companies is our zone. We can increase an existing company's brand value and take a large portion of their business while they run it as the entrepreneurs, and that's a place where we play well."

Peter Boyd, the CEO of Virgin Mobile in South Africa, told me, "Richard does best when he can be the consumer's champion, when he's coming out and delivering better value for money." This idea is clearly stated on Virgin's web site:

> *We believe in making a difference in our customers' eyes. Virgin stands for value for money, quality, innovation, fun, and a sense of competitive challenge. When we start a new venture, we base it on hard research and analysis. Typically, we review the industry and put ourselves in the customers' shoes to see what could make it better. We ask fundamental questions. Is this an opportunity for restructuring a market and creating competitive advantage? What are the competitors doing? Is the customer confused or badly served? Is this an opportunity for building the Virgin brand? Can we add value? Will it interact with our other businesses? Is there an appropriate trade-off between risk and reward?*

When I was launching and building my own business, we realized that I was at my best when I was on a stage, coaching trainers, or where people could hear my voice. Those were really our core competencies: taking my knowledge, passing it along to other people, and building up the system from there. When we ventured out and we bought another business and put our label on it—thinking we were going to get into branded venture capital like Virgin—we didn't do well. We couldn't control the output of what others were doing, and the situation became too complex for us to manage well. We realized we needed to go back to our core competence rather than other areas that just weren't in our zone.

Where do you get your best results? And how can you expand by focusing on these areas even more? If my company has several markets in which we attract 2,000 or 4,000 people into a room, and others where there are only 400, how can we focus 80 percent of our time on the 20 percent of areas that are producing the most results? This kind of thinking is part of the evolution of the entrepreneurial process. You learn to play more and more in your zone, where you can really hit the ball out of the park every time and be successful in each new aspect of your business.

For that reason, Warren Buffett picks companies that are already up and running, which have a healthy profit margin, and where management is in place. Then he just gives the entrepreneurs a different type of wealth by buying them out, and keeping them in management roles as employees. Instead of earning their money over time, the former owners now have a big lump sum in the bank, and Warren Buffett has a company that is already up and running. That's his in-the-zone strategy for the accumulation of companies.

Richard Branson's strategy is totally different. He is only interested in launching company after company, finding start-ups that are hip and sexy and that meet his investment criteria. He gives each new venture about six months of attention, he brands it, then he disappears and it operates as a totally separate entity. Lending his brand is how he plays best.

Ted Turner plays best by doing mergers and acquisitions in his television empire. That's what he did really, really well, doing deal after deal after deal to add to the breadth and the width of his empire.

Oprah Winfrey plays best by expanding her core brand, which has a single theme: helping people take responsibility for their lives. Creating *O* magazine or building Oxygen Media—all of it is tied into that theme.

Warren Buffett says he's 85 percent like Benjamin Graham and 15 percent like Philip Fisher in his investment strategy—that's his zone. Phil Fisher was the author of *Common Stocks, Uncommon Profits*, and Ben Graham, of course, is the father of value investing.

Warren Buffett's company, Berkshire Hathaway, published an advertisement in *The Wall Street Journal* that was in the form of a want ad for businesses:

Here's what we're looking for:

1. Large purchases (at least $10 million after-tax earnings and preferably more)
2. Demonstrated consistent earning power (future projections) are of little interest to us, nor are "turnaround situations"
3. Businesses that are earning good returns on equity while employing little or no debt
4. Management in place (we can't supply it)
5. Simple business (if there's a lot of technology, we won't understand it)

6. An offering price (we don't want to waste our time or that of
the seller by even talking about a transaction when the price is
unknown).

Warren Buffett is a business analyst and he buys good companies,
regardless of market conditions. He looks for growth and intrinsic
value. And getting this done from Omaha instead of Wall Street is all
part of Buffett being in his zone.

Why Your Greatest Opportunity Is Already Within You

You have to figure out where your unique zone really is. Studying how
that process was handled by the most successful entrepreneurs can
definitely help with that. It's not about imitating others, and it's not
about doing exactly what someone else does. It's about learning from
what someone did, the way Warren Buffett learned from Ben Graham
and Phil Fisher.

I started studying successful entrepreneurs because I was looking
to increase my talents and skills, especially my financial and business
acumen. I learned some skills that I didn't know I needed; I didn't even
know they existed. It was incredibly useful to study how other people
made decisions and found their zone. You can do the same. That's
where you'll find your opportunity to really get into the flow state for
maximum success in *your* business.

How to Change the World

What happens after that, of course, is up to you. But I want to close
this book by emphasizing one very important fact: *In the twentieth-first
century, waking up to wealth means sharing the wealth you wake up to.*

You alone, of course, should decide when you want to do that.
It might be now, while you're building your business. Or it might be
later, after you've achieved some of your own personal goals and you
feel you can take more time to think about how to give back, or you're
at the point at which you've amassed such an amount of wealth that
your power to contribute becomes even far greater.

Some entrepreneurs start giving back when they're very young. Michael Dell wasn't even 35 years old when he and his wife Susan set up the foundation that bears their names. Other entrepreneurs wait until they're much older—like Warren Buffett, who was 79 years old when he announced that he was giving 85 percent of his $44 billion fortune to five foundations. And some entrepreneurs are still allowing their ideas to unfold about how to best make a difference with the wealth that they accumulate. Google co-founders Sergey Brin and Larry Page are in that category, although one possibility is their investing in new ways of producing energy and finding alternative energy sources.

Larry Ellison, co-founder and CEO of software giant Oracle Corporation, has an estimated net worth of $22.5 billion. He has said:

> *I think we should think of altruism—giving—as a strategy for happiness. Forget the morality of it all: "It's the right thing to do." Think of it as something totally in your self-interest. If you can help others, you will feel great. The more you can help, the more intelligently you can help, the bigger lever that you can get on the world to make it better, the better you will feel about yourself. The more joy you will experience. That is the road to bliss. That is the intelligent pursuit of happiness. That is what we should do. That is my argument for giving, not simply that it's the right and moral thing to do. It happens to also be that, but I don't find that as persuasive as that it is the road to happiness.*

You don't make a living by what you get. You make a living by what you give.

—Winston Churchill

More and more people are waking up to this idea of combining entrepreneurship with philanthropy. I hope that you, too, will embrace that principle in your own life to make a difference in the world. Share your **New Entrepreneurial Mind**—both your thoughts and the material rewards of your thoughts. That isn't just charity. It's self-interest in the truest and most accurate sense of the word.

To Keep It, You Have to Give It Away

Instant wealth is a *gift*. The experience of waking up rich is a *gift*. Side by side with the material rewards of your entrepreneurship, it's a huge gift just to realize that you can create any dream that you have ever had—to know that you have the tools and strategies for making that happen.

But here's the paradox. To hold on to this gift, you must give it away. **You *must* share it with other people.** This paradox is at the foundation of many spiritual systems. And again, it's not just charity; it's authentic self-interest. When you *teach* someone, or *mentor* someone, or *coach* someone, you learn as well. When you give something away, you become a larger person. Your wealth increases as the wealth of the world increases. This is true even on the most basic physical level—which Henry Ford understood when he gave his entire workforce a raise so that they'd be able to buy Ford cars.

You may choose to coach and mentor and teach people inside your own organization. Or you may choose to teach the next generation of entrepreneurs to go out and change the world in positive ways. Or you may choose to solve social problems by sharing the financial profits of your work. Best of all, I believe, would be to choose "all of the above."

The lives of so many people are deprived because they've bought into the social hypnosis of playing small—that is, that we're living in a zero sum world in which what one person has must necessarily deprive someone else. Not true! Your key to maintaining wealth, to living a rich life, and to maintaining your own entrepreneurial power is to share *everything*. **Pay it forward. Pass it on.** Help foster these concepts in other people. Spread the gift of *Instant Wealth*.

Share it with everybody you know. Share it with your family, share it with your children, share it with your up line, share it with your down line, share it with your sales team, share it with your co-workers, share it with your loved ones, share it with your extended family. Share it even with the people you like the least, because when you are doing that, you are truly stepping up from an inspired place of transformation. Then you will have a truly global vision of transformation for the planet that goes way beyond just yourself. Share this information with the world. That's your challenge.

When you meet that challenge, your own transformation is assured. In 12-step programs, when somebody is looking to gain freedom from habits that have held them back, just as you are committed to moving beyond the mindsets of the past, **one of the most important steps is sharing your information and your *experience* of transformation with other people. In teaching and sharing your experience, you keep your own transformation alive.** The same principle applies to the information in this book. **You must share it if you want to keep it.** You must give it away so you can sustain your own transformation. So the biggest task before you now is to find people who need the unique gifts that you have to give. Then serve people, and always live on your entrepreneurial edge. Remember, *"If a thing is humanly possible, consider it to be within your reach."* Do this, and you will unleash your potential to become the person you were *really* destined to be—and the impact you make in the world can create not just a ripple effect, but a tidal wave effect that will have a positive impact on generations and generations to come.

■ ■ ■

It has been my great pleasure to serve you!

■ ■ ■

Until we meet again, always remember, love deeply, shine brightly, and make your life an extraordinary adventure!

Kicking Your Dreams into High Gear: The Next Step

Because of Your Dedication and Commitment to *Instant Wealth* I Have a Gift for You!!

You've made it this far. Congratulations!! Now in order to **fast-track your path to your dreams**, I've included this introduction to the next-generation expansionary tools and strategies that can be **the greatest investment in your dreams that you could ever make**. In this sense, this is not the end, but rather a new beginning!

It's time to rocket yourself forward toward your greatest entrepreneurial visions at a faster pace than ever before. Get ready to **create the type of wealth you truly deserve!**

Because my mission first and foremost is to **put these tools in the hands of everyone on the planet**, I am also about to give you an **extraordinary GIFT** to help you gain the real momentum and acceleration you desire now! I will reveal this gift to you as you read on. . . .

But first, it's important for you to really understand who we are at **The Christopher Howard Companies** and **Christopher Howard Training**, so I have asked my team to put together a description of our companies and the educational path we provide to help you on your quest to create your entrepreneurial dreams. Remember I am about to give you a mind-blowing gift!

The Christopher Howard Companies

Who are we?

The Christopher Howard Companies next-generation global enterprises are committed to elevating the quality of life for all people and nations. This world-class organization is a self-propelling force of expansion, purpose, and prosperity, with the intention of transforming billions of dreams into real-world results.

Our philosophy is making the impossible possible by harnessing vision and heart into creation, contribution, and global expansion.

Christopher Howard Training™

Christopher Howard Training is the trusted global leader and renowned authority on transformational education for the attainment of real-world results. Our next-generation tools, best-selling multimedia products, and award-winning programs are essential to business leaders and professionals worldwide.

Christopher Howard Training provides individuals and organizations with next-generation tools and systems of personal and professional achievement. At Christopher Howard Training, we aim to help you turn your boldest goals and dreams into realities and real-world results.

Christopher Howard Seminars and Training Programs

Breakthrough to Success Weekend

Christopher Howard's **Breakthrough to Success Weekend** is the next generation of personal and professional achievement. This three-day weekend program will change your life and the way you do business forever as it launches you on the fast track to personal and professional success! Whether you have already achieved significant success or have just started on your journey of success, this one weekend will transform your thoughts and actions like never before.

The Wealth Propulsion Intensive™

This powerful program is a live transformational experience based on the concepts presented in the book *Instant Wealth: Wake Up Rich!*

Over the course of three days you will gain massive propulsion toward your greatest dreams and learn to create extraordinary wealth in life. You will experience cutting-edge tools for subconscious reprogramming to break through past conditioning and reprogram your mind for total success. You will learn the secrets that can allow you to catapult yourself to a level of achievement that most others only dream of.

Christopher Howard Training's Academy of Wealth

Christopher Howard's **Academy of Wealth** consists of six revolutionary live training programs designed to build the mind-sets, attitudes, and behaviors necessary for you to achieve success and fulfillment in all areas of life. Each of these programs works as a blueprint of wealth and ultimate fulfillment. The six core **Wealth Academy™** training programs include: **Billionaire Bootcamp, Rich Heart—Wealthy Mind, Warrior Spirit Training, Wealth Acceleration Certification Level One, Wealth Acceleration Certification Level Two, Wealth Acceleration Certification Level Three.**

Billionaire Bootcamp
Duration: 7 days

If you would like to revolutionize an industry like Bill Gates, utilize obstacles to your greatest advantage like Richard Branson, empower millions of people like Oprah Winfrey, and master money like Warren Buffett, now you can install in yourself the brilliant mind-sets it took these magicians of the material world a lifetime to learn. Learn how to accomplish this mastery at **Billionaire Bootcamp.**

Rich Heart—Wealthy Mind!
Duration: 3 days

Achieve clarity on your life's purpose and master what you need to make it happen. Learn next-generation **Subconscious**

Reprogramming techniques to install unconscious habits within yourself to turn your boldest dreams into reality and tangible results. Finally, uncover the path to your destiny so that you can commit to it with laser focus.

Warrior Spirit Training
Duration: Multiday

Warrior Spirit Training builds leadership skills for influence and persuasion. Apply the most powerful techniques of **subconscious reprogramming** to the business environment to revolutionize the way you negotiate and achieve your career and life goals. Develop the "X-factor" for success. Stand out from the competition and get the edge you need to move powerfully forward with pinpoint accuracy.

Wealth Acceleration Level One
Duration: 5 days

Take the skills modeled from masters of personal and professional leadership and put them in your hands to achieve mind mastery and the most powerful skills of influence in existence. This series is the ULTIMATE in advanced leadership training. Harness the power of the subconscious mind to enhance personal excellence and lead others to produce exceptional results. While 70 percent of the participants come just for the tools, upon successful completion of this five-day training program you can take the test to receive certifications in **Neurolinguistic Programming (NLP), Neurological Repatterning, Ericksonian Hypnosis**, as well as testing for recognition as a **Chris Howard Certified Results Coach**.

Wealth Acceleration Level Two
Duration: 5 days

This advanced level of personal and professional leadership is the second half of the full body of knowledge for mind mastery and the ability to influence others in powerful ways. Delve into the art of influence and the psychology of achievement at the deepest levels. This program is an essential component for anyone seeking to make rapid and sustainable change in one's life, and it's an absolute must-do for those wanting to do high-level coaching or business performance consulting. While 70 percent of the participants come just for the tools, upon successful completion of this five-day training program you can take the test to receive certifications at the **Master Level of NLP, Advanced Neurological Repatterning, Master Hypnosis**, as well as testing for recognition as a **Chris Howard Certified Master Results Coach**. *Prerequisite for certification is Wealth Acceleration Level One.*

Wealth Acceleration Level Three
Duration: 7 days

Learn 40 proven behaviors of the most outstanding speakers on the planet, and install these behaviors at the subconscious level so that you integrate them into your presentations without conscious thought! Your enhanced mastery of language, interpersonal skills, and effectiveness to create instant responsiveness and to powerfully influence the masses will enable you to expand your personal and professional sphere of influence, and take your success and dreams beyond your wildest expectations.

■ ■ ■

Christopher Howard Coaching and Mentoring
Duration: Ongoing

Receive one-on-one **Wealth Acceleration Coaching** from your very own **Christopher Howard Training** certified **Master Results Coach**.

This will give you the accountability you need to create extraordinary results. The coaching and mentoring program is the greatest gift you could give yourself as you ferociously pursue your grandest dreams.

Christopher   Howard   Training   also   presents   the **EXCLUSIVE**...

Billionaire Adventure Club
Your Master Mind Alliance
Duration: 1-week adventures—Year-round mentoring

Billionaire Adventure Club membership allows members access to travel in a small group to unique areas around the world for closed-circle personal mentoring and coaching with **Christopher Howard**, the Christopher Howard Trainers, and Chris's own entrepreneurial mentors and guides. You'll journey to exotic locations like Brazil, Peru, South Africa, Cambodia, or Mongolia. Perhaps you'll have lunch with Chris and Scott Mednick from Legendary Pictures on the Great Wall of China, or go caving in the jungles of Belize with financiers who can help to finance your next entrepreneurial venture. On every adventure, you will expand your own **Mastermind Alliance** by becoming acquainted with people who are legends in finance or other skill sets that can catapult you to greater levels of success. The **Billionaire Adventure Club** is the entrepreneurial adventure of a lifetime!

And **NOW**, for **YOUR EXTRAORDINARY GIFT:**

Imagine if you could create a life filled with WEALTH on every level, spiritually, emotionally, physically, and financially . . . incredible entrepreneurial success, a wildly passionate life, vibrant health, and lasting happiness. What if you could achieve every goal you ever set in your life . . . more easily, faster, and more enjoyably than you ever thought possible? Imagine feeling unshakable confidence in yourself and your ability to create the results you desire. Imagine if it were truly possible to transform your life, then design it just the way you've always envisioned it!

What would that mean to you?

If you're anything like me, your dreams are what you live for, and because of your commitment to them you have a willingness to do whatever it takes to polish up every weakness in your game until it becomes your greatest strength! Can you imagine what your life would be like if you were to completely obliterate the thoughts or the fears that have kept you playing small? What if you knew how to expand so far beyond what you previously thought possible that you could increase your net worth exponentially; you could create all the energy you'd ever need to forge any entrepreneurial dream you've ever had; and you had the ability to transform your relationships so much that you could create tremendous leverage and accelerate the accomplishment of your dreams a thousandfold? What if you could accomplish all of this in one weekend?

Even if you've read all the books...listened to all the audio courses...and attended all the seminars...perhaps you're still not getting the results and the level of transformation you want. Maybe you're real-world results haven't caught up with all of the things you've been dreaming of yet.

Well, then get excited, because you are about to embrace a whole new way of living!

The Breakthrough to Success Seminar and The Wealth Propulsion Intensive are NOT just inspirational or motivational programs. They are experiential events where radical transformation takes place over the course of three days so that you literally transform your life on every level.

If you're honest with yourself you KNOW that you have *so much more potential* than you are currently exhibiting. Well, NOW you have the opportunity to finally harness that potential and allow it to propel you forward beyond anything you have ever imagined! **Christopher Howard Training** works in conjunction with our promotional partners to run these programs all over the world throughout the course of the year.

Tickets to **The Breakthrough to Success Seminar** or **The Wealth Propulsion Intensive** normally cost up to $895 each, depending on the country they are run in. However, in order to reward you for your commitment to *Instant Wealth*, and also to help further our mission to put these tools in the hands of everyone on the planet and to create worldwide wealth...

For a limited time only, I am **gifting you two tickets** to one of these programs *in participating countries* **at no charge**. That's right, **two** tickets: for you and one guest absolutely **FREE!**

Simply go right now to www.chrishoward.com/instantwealth to find the closest participating area near you and to activate your **two tickets to either The Breakthrough to Success Seminar OR The Wealth Propulsion Intensive**. This promotion is for a limited time only and can be stopped at any time without forewarning.

These programs are VERY popular and they always sell out. As this offer is limited to the number of seats available, it is first come, first served only and admission is not guaranteed. You must **enroll early** in order to ensure your attendance. So, if you are really committed to claiming the life you deserve, register your attendance **IMMEDIATELY** for an upcoming **Breakthrough to Success** or **Wealth Propulsion Intensive** seminar at www.chrishoward.com/instantwealth.

If you desperately want to revolutionize your life, these mind-blowing weekend programs can be the best investment in yourself you could ever make, as they are the catalyst for a whole new level of accomplishment and fulfillment in life! You will learn how to realize your dreams at faster and greater levels than ever before.

I look forward to meeting you in person at either **The Breakthrough to Success or The Wealth Propulsion Intensive! Remember to register your FREE attendance today at** www.chrishoward.com/instantwealth.

And once again, until we meet in person, I'll leave you with the words that I leave all my newfound friends and family with . . .

Love deeply, shine brightly, and make your life an extraordinary adventure!

Christopher Howard

Bibliography

Allen, Robert G. *Multiple Streams of Income*. 2nd ed. Hoboken, NJ: John Wiley & Sons, 2005.

Allen, Robert G. *Nothing Down: How to Buy Real Estate with Little or No Money Down*. rev. ed. New York: Simon & Schuster, 1984.

Allen, Robert G., and Mark Victor Hansen. *One Minute Millionaire*. Reprint, New York: Three Rivers Press, 2009.

Bach, David. *The Automatic Millionaire*. New York: Broadway, 2005.

Bishop, Matthew, and Michael Green. *Philanthrocapitalism: How Giving Can Save the World*. Reprint, New York: Bloomsbury Press, 2009.

Branson, Richard. *Losing My Virginity*. New York: Three Rivers Press, 1999.

Buffett, Mary. *New Buffettology*. New York: Simon & Schuster, 2002.

Byrne, Rhonda. *The Secret*. New York: Atria Books/Beyond Words, 2006.

Cammarano, Roy F. *Entrepreneurial Transitions: From Entrepreneurial Genius to Visionary Leader*. Santa Ana, CA: Griffin Publishing Group, 1993.

Canfield, Jack, and Mark Victor Hansen. *Chicken Soup for the Soul*. Deerfield Beach, FL: HCI, 2001.

Chu, Chin-Ning. *The Art of War for Women: Sun Tzu's Ancient Strategies and Wisdom for Winning at Work*. New York: Broadway Business, 2007.

Coelho, Paulo. *The Alchemist*. New York: HarperCollins, 2006.

Collier, Peter, and David Horowitz. *The Rockefellers: An American Dynasty.* New York: Holt, Rinehart & Winston, 1976.

Cooper, Ilene. *Up Close: Oprah Winfrey.* New York: Puffin, 2008.

Csikszentmihalyi, Mihaly. *Flow: The Psychology of Optimal Experience.* New York: Harper & Row, 1990.

Cunningham, Lawrence A. *The Essays of Warren Buffett: Lessons for Investors and Managers.* 3rd rev. ed. Hoboken, NJ: John Wiley & Sons, 2002.

Davidson, Andrew, ed. *1,000 CEOs.* London: Dorling Kindersley, 2009.

Dawkins, Richard. *The Selfish Gene.* 3rd ed. New York: Oxford University Press, 2006.

Fisher, Phil. *Common Stocks, Uncommon Profits.* New York: Harper & Brothers, 1958.

Frankl, Viktor E. *Man's Search for Meaning.* Boston: Beacon Press, 2000.

Fridson, Martin S. *How to Be a Billionaire: Proven Strategies from the Titans of Wealth.* New York: John Wiley & Sons, 2001.

Garson, Helen S. *Oprah Winfrey: A Biography.* Westport, CT: Greenwood, 2004.

Gladwell, Malcolm. *Outliers: The Story of Success.* New York: Little, Brown, 2008.

Graham, Benjamin. *The Intelligent Investor.* New York: HarperCollins, 1984.

Graves, Clare W. " Deterioration of Work Standards." *Harvard Business Review* 44, no. 5 (September/October 1966): 117–126.

Gray, John. *Why Mars & Venus Collide.* New York: HarperCollins, 2008.

Hagstrom, Robert G. *The Warren Buffett Way.* 2nd ed. Hoboken, NJ: John Wiley & Sons, 2005.

Hendrickx, Marc, and Connie Kirchberg. *Elvis Presley, Richard Nixon and the American Dream.* McFarland & Co., NC, 1999.

Hill, Napoleon. *Think and Grow Rich.* Reprint, New York: Ballantine Books, 1976.

Kilpatrick, Andrew. *Of Permanent Value: The Story of Warren Buffett.* Alabama: Andy Kilpatrick Publishing Empire, 2002.

Kiyosaki, Robert. *Rich Dad, Poor Dad.* London: Time Warner, 2002.

Lowe, Janet. *Bill Gates Speaks: Insight from the World's Greatest Entrepreneur*. New York: John Wiley & Sons, 2001.

Lowe, Janet. *Google Speaks: Secrets of the World's Greatest Billionaire Entrepreneurs, Sergey Brin and Larry Page*. Hoboken, NJ: John Wiley & Sons, 2009.

Lowe, Janet. *Jack Welch Speaks: Wit and Wisdom from the World's Greatest Business Leader*. 2nd ed. Hoboken, NJ: John Wiley & Sons, 2007.

Lowe, Janet. *Oprah Winfrey Speaks*. New York: John Wiley & Sons, 2001.

Lowe, Janet. *Warren Buffett Speaks: Wit and Wisdom from the World's Greatest Investor*. 2nd ed. Hoboken, NJ: John Wiley & Sons, 2007.

Lowenstein, Roger. *Buffett: The Making of an American Capitalist*. New York: Main Street Books, 1996.

Mandela, Nelson. *A Long Walk to Freedom*. Boston: Little, Brown, 1994.

Millman, Dan. *The Way of the Peaceful Warrior*. rev. ed. Tiburon, CA: H.J. Kramer, 2006.

Rand, Ayn. *Atlas Shrugged*. New York: Plume, 1999.

Rand, Ayn. *The Fountainhead*. New York: Signet, 1961.

Ries, Al, and Jack Trout. *Positioning*. New York: McGraw-Hill Professional, 2nd edition, 2001.

Schroeder, Alice. *The Snowball: Warren Buffett and the Business of Life*. New York: Bantam, 2008.

Shawcross, William. *Murdoch*. New York: Simon & Schuster, 1997.

Slater, Robert. *Jack Welch and the G.E. Way: Management Insights and Leadership Secrets of the Legendary CEO*. New York: McGraw-Hill, 1998.

Sun Tzu. *The Art of War*. Filiquarian, 2007.

Trump, Donald J., and Meredith McIver. *Trump: How to Get Rich*. New York: Random House, 2004.

Trump, Donald J., and Tony Schwarz. *Trump: The Art of the Deal*. New York: Ballantine Books, 2004.

Tuccille, Jerome. *Rupert Murdoch: Creator of a Worldwide Media Empire*. Frederick, MD: Beard Books, 2003.

Wallace, James, and Jim Erikson. *Hard Drive: Bill Gates and the Making of the Microsoft Empire*. New York: Harper Paperbacks, 1993.

Welch, Jack. *Winning*. New York: HarperBusiness, 2005.

Westen, Robin. *Oprah Winfrey: "I Don't Believe in Failure."* Berkeley Heights, NJ: Enslow Publishers, 2005.

Williamson, Marianne. *A Return to Love.* New York: HarperCollins, 1992.

Wolff, Michael. *The Man Who Owns the News: Inside the Secret World of Rupert Murdoch.* New York: Broadway, 2008.

Other Media

A&E *Biography* TV series: "Donald Trump—Master of the Deal"; "Donald Trump—Deal Maker"; "Bill Gates—Sultan of Software"; "Warren Buffett—Oracle of Omaha"; "Richard Branson— The Top of the World."

The Color Purple. Amblin Entertainment and Warner Brothers Entertainment, 1985.

The Island. Dreamworks LLC and Warner Brothers Entertainment, 2005.

Web Sites

www.achievement.org
www.afterquotes.com
www.articlesbase.com
www.beginnersinvest.com
www.bloomberg.com
www.brainyquote.com
www.canadianbusiness.com
www.coolquotescollection.com
www.forbes.org
www.gatesfoundation.org
www.humanity.org
www.newworldencyclopedia.com
www.oprahsangelsnetwork.org
www.quotationsbook.com
www.quotationspage.com
www.quoteworld.org
www.thinkexist.com

Notes

Chapter 1

1. Page 18 NIMH, "The Numbers Count: Mental Illness in America," *Science on Our Minds Fact Sheet Series*, 2006.
2. Page 18-Study published in *Psychiatric Services*, April 2004. Reported in the health news archive Uplift Program: *Pill-Popping Pre-Schoolers, Even Toddlers Get the Blues*, upliftprogram.com/h_depression.html#h80.

Index